Logo
Programming
for the IBM PC

IBM PERSONAL
COMPUTER SERIES

Published by Addison-Wesley Publishers Limited
in co-operation with
IBM United Kingdom International Products Limited
for all users of IBM Personal Computers

Logo
Programming
for the IBM PC

Peter Ross

ADDISON-WESLEY PUBLISHING COMPANY

Wokingham, England · Reading, Massachusetts · Menlo Park, California
Don Mills, Ontario · Amsterdam · Sydney · Singapore · Tokyo
Mexico City · Bogota · Santiago · San Juan

Cover illustration by Jay Myrdal.

Printed in Finland by OTAVA. Member of Finnprint.

OTABIND
PAT PEND

Library of Congress Cataloging in Publication Data
Ross, Peter.
  LOGO programming for the IBM PC.

  (IBM personal computer series)
  Includes index.
    1. IBM Personal Computer—Programming.   2. LOGO (Computer program language)   I. Title.   II. Title: L.O.G.O. programming for the I.B.M. P.C.   III. Series.
QA76.8.I2594R67   1984   001.64′2   84-21714

ISBN 0-201-15028-X

British Library Cataloguing in Publication Data
Ross, Peter
  Logo programming for the IBM PC.—— (IBM personal computer series)
  1. LOGO (Computer program language)
  I. Title   II. Series
  001.64′24   QA76.73.L63

ISBN 0-201-15028-X

ABCDE 898765

For Susan and Rebecca

CONTENTS

Trademark Notice

Acknowledgements

The work of the LOGO group in the Department of Artificial Intelligence at the University of Edinburgh owes much to many people: Ben du Boulay, Colin McArthur, Fran Plane, Tim O'Shea, Peter Ross, Ken Johnson, Ena Inglis as well as the head of the whole enterprise, Jim Howe. Others too numerous to mention have contributed significantly. This book has been influenced greatly by the work of all of these people; although it was written by one of us, all have had a hand in its origins. The Social Science Research Council has supported the LOGO work at Edinburgh for many years — this book would not have existed without their continued support of the group's work.

I would like to thank Geoff Cumming and Jim Howe for reading through the first draft of this book and making lengthy and valuable comments about its contents. My wife Susan O'Brien spent many hours correcting my spelling and style, and encouraged me at every stage — you owe her a lot!

The various quotations used all come from *Sylvie and Bruno* or *Sylvie and Bruno Concluded*, by Lewis Carroll.

1 | **INTRODUCTION**

"Come to me, my little gentleman," said our hostess, lifting Bruno into her lap, "and tell me everything." "I can't" said Bruno. "There wouldn't be time. Besides, I don't know everything."

(Sylvie and Bruno, LEWIS CARROLL)

Aims: This chapter gives some background and historical information about LOGO, and tries to explain why LOGO is different from the majority of programming languages. It also describes the structure of the book. LOGO programming doesn't appear until Chapter 2, but you'd be well advised to start reading this chapter first . . .

1.1 PROGRAMMING AS A TOOL FOR EXPLORING IDEAS

LOGO is a computer programming language.

For some time now, it has been widely held that learning to program a computer gives you skills which are very valuable in worlds other than that of computing. There is clearly some truth in this; although computers work fast, they follow instructions precisely, and programming therefore requires you to be explicit and orderly when expressing what you want the computer to do for you. If you are not, then it does not do what you want, and either you have to re-think your instructions to the computer or you have to modify your goals. The habit of precise thinking that you can learn from this can be very useful in other areas of your life. Unfortunately, it is hard to anticipate how much you can gain by learning to program until you embark on it and find out for yourself. The chief question is, are the benefits worth the effort? Some of the non-technical arguments made in this chapter might help you to decide this (so keep reading).

Computers, whatever their cost or size, consist essentially of the following ingredients:

a) one or more processors (CPUs) which obey instructions,
b) some internal memory,
c) some external memory, such as floppy disks,
d) some links between what is inside the computer and what is outside, such as a keyboard, a screen, perhaps a printer or some 'paddles'.

A computer can therefore be characterised as a quantity of

'empty space' (ingredients (b) and (c)) and some restrictions on what you can do with it (ingredients (a) and (d)). Within the restrictions, only your own imagination limits what you use the empty space for. Normally, some of the empty space is given over to a set of tools, called the operating system, which makes the rest of the computer's facilities much easier to use. For example, one common task much in demand as a small part of larger tasks is that of capturing what is typed on the keyboard at appropriate moments. If you had to spell out every detail of this each time you wrote a program employing it, you might well decide to give up in disgust at the effort required. Having an operating system means that you sacrifice a little of the flexibility of the computer for the sake of being able to make it do such frequently required tasks much more easily.

This trade-off between flexibility and ease of use is also a major factor in the design of programming languages. Any language makes some kinds of tasks slightly easier and others slightly harder to express than in another language; indeed, in some cases the difference is more than slight. Many of the popular programming languages now in use are 'structured'; that is, they allow you — and in fact are designed to encourage you — to chop up the task you want the machine to do, into a series of smaller sub-tasks. You can chop up the sub-tasks too, into finer and finer bits, to the point where each sub- sub-....-task is simple to explain and to program.

This decomposition of something large into smaller and more manageable parts is not peculiar to the world of programming and computers. For example, suppose you decide to repaint your living-room. You do not immediately think "I must find the car keys/get the bus" (unless neurotic about the subject). You are likely to start by thinking "I must get some paint... white, I think..." and then to go on to plan where to get it, and so on. It may be only moments, or it may be days, before you arrive at the first action, namely finding the car keys or finding some money, necessary to the first sub-task of getting some paint. Unfortunately, not many people make the most of this approach — you go to the shops, buy the paint and return home, and then realise you don't have a single adequate paintbrush.

The knack of tackling problems sensibly, by tackling only manageable chunks at a time and in a sensible and effective order, is one of those skills which might be more easily learned or improved through the experience of programming than by other means. In the world of programming, there are not so many of those discordant distractions (such as "I shouldn't be doing this painting, it'll be a mess, and anyway I can't afford either the time or the money"). Also, making mistakes is safe and cheap, and the computer makes it clear that there is something wrong when you have made a mistake

— even if only by failing to react as expected.

There are drawbacks. A computer is immensely less tolerant than you are of leaving things unsaid. Programming languages mostly require you to be very precise about what it is you want the computer to do, and to express it in terms convenient for the machine rather than in some language which would seem adequately precise to you. For example, the following is a small fragment taken from the start of a program written in PASCAL:

```
PROGRAM ANALYSE (INPUT, OUTPUT);
VAR N, TOTAL: INTEGER;
        BUFF: PACKED ARRAY[0 . .511] OF CHAR;
    . . . . . . .
    . . . . . . .etc.
```

To write in PASCAL you must know quite a lot before you start. You need to know what punctuation is required where, what various keywords such as INPUT, VAR and INTEGER mean, when to use round brackets and when to use square brackets, and so on. If you have programmed before, you will certainly know that being careless about such things causes you considerable frustration. There are many other rules that you need to be aware of as well, rules which have no effect on the look of what you write but do concern the content. An example is that, in PASCAL on various microcomputers, quantities specified as INTEGER which you might expect to behave like everyday integers, in fact cannot be bigger than 32767. Naturally, most people who start to learn PASCAL do not think of writing program which involve large integers. If in due course you do, surprising things happen when you run the program. Attempts to deal with integers larger than 65536 will be pointed out as faults (normally in terms drawn from computer jargon, a vast and expanding source of linguistic horrors). However, if some calculation ought to result in an integer between 32768 and 65536 then the result will actually be treated as a negative integer between −32768 and 0. If you do not know about this, it will cost you a lot of effort to find out, because it is not a fault as far as the machine is concerned.

Because normally you need considerable knowledge about the computer itself, knowledge which is not really relevant to your intentions but only to expressing them, you therefore need considerable commitment or interest when you first start to learn to program. Of necessity, you have to start with a fairly simplistic set of beliefs about what is really going on inside the computer, and have to take many things on trust or keep them at arm's length by classifying them as black magic. This is sad, because it deters many people from mastering the use of very powerful and versatile tools for intellectual exploration and enjoyment. With a computer, you can simulate nearly anything you can imagine; having a simulation, you can investigate it.

That assertion deserves some comment. Various uninformed ideas about computers still circulate, for instance

"They are only very good at dealing with numbers."

"A microcomputer is really only capable of games."

"Writing computer programs is for masochists."

The true strength of computers lies in the fact that they manipulate symbols, according to rules provided by the user. The symbols might be represented within the computer as groups of binary digits, but it is the interpretation of the symbols that matters, and that is up to the user — the computer merely obeys the rules. Suppose, for example, that you want to display Russian text on your microcomputer. You could represent the letters of the Russian alphabet as the numbers 1 to 33 and their upper case equivalents as the numbers 34 to 66. Then you could incorporate various rules within a program, such as

- If key A is pressed, store the number 1 (so key A corresponds to the first letter of the Russian alphabet). If key B is pressed, store the number 2. . . .etc.
- To convert all lower case Russian letters to upper case, look at each number. If it is between 1 and 33, then add 33 to it.
- To display the letter corresponding to 1, put dots on the screen at the following (X,Y) co-ordinates and move the origin of co-ordinates so that the next character displayed will be in a sensible place (for example, just to the right of the last one).

These rules are purely to do with numbers, but they could be incorporated into a word processing system for Russian text. The trick of computer programming is to devise rules which operate on numbers, as the computer knows them, such that the content of the rules is consistent with the interpretation you want to put on them. Usually the rules are not as straightforward as these examples suggest. Besides deciding to represent Russian letters as the numbers 1 to 33, you would also have to decide how to represent words, sentences and paragraphs — probably by deciding how to organise sets of representations of letters. One of the important points in the later part of this book will be to do with choosing how to represent what is to be modelled; the choice has a big influence on how easy it is to specify the rules.

Having chosen representations for the ingredients of what you want to model, and thought a little about the rules, the main task is to translate it all into one or more computer programs. Certain maxims are worth remembering at this point. One is that it is better to try to be as general as possible — that way you eventually build yourself a toolkit, and your programming gets easier and faster. Another is that it is better to break the whole task into small bits — they are easier to play about with and to modify. These and many others will be illustrated in this book.

LOGO was designed to avoid most of the initial hurdles in learning to program, and yet to be very powerful. In particular, you need know nothing about the guts of your computer before you start, and you can get interesting results for your efforts almost at once. After all, the whole point of using a computer is to make interesting things happen on your terminal or elsewhere outside the machine. In short, LOGO offers the power in modelling and expression which might be found in other languages, yet avoids much of the bureaucracy and specialised computer science that other languages demand. It is not intended to be the ultimate in programming. In general, what can be done in one language can be done in any other, perhaps more awkwardly and perhaps more simply.

1.2 SOME HISTORY

LOGO was designed at Bolt Beranek and Newman Inc. in Cambridge, Massachusetts, in the late 1960s and so is younger than most other languages. It was created as part of an experiment to test the idea that programming might be a useful educational discipline to teach children. The first research project was closely related to mathematics and the ideas it sought to test were, roughly, these:

- Programming might be the basis for a useful language, not directly linked to computing, in which to talk about problem-solving divorced from the background of any particular school subject.
- Programming might be a good vehicle for illustrating some mathematical concepts which are normally hard to grasp.
- A computer, with the right programming language, could be a wonderful 'mathematical laboratory' in which it would be possible to experiment with abstract ideas it would otherwise be hard to give form to.

The word 'mathematics', being taken in a very wide sense, is the art of being able to analyse and explore rules governing physical or imaginary but logical worlds. The original version of LOGO was designed by Wallace Feurzeig, Daniel Bobrow and Seymour Papert — their design owed much to another language called LISP*, now

---

* LISP is powerful (it was invented in the mid-1960s (at MIT (who still use it for AI research (as do many others (though less so in Europe (where Prolog is a strong rival language))))) and has been much developed since) but tends to be almost unreadable (because its syntax depends so much on parentheses)!

widely used for research in Artificial Intelligence. LOGO was refined at the Artificial Intelligence Laboratory of MIT and at the Department of Artificial Intelligence of the University of Edinburgh, Scotland.

At first LOGO had no provision for computer graphics, the necessary hardware being prohibitively expensive in those days for an education project. Then, fairly early on, graphics were incorporated into the language, in the form of 'turtle graphics'. This is now such a major facet of LOGO for beginners that many people mistakenly assume that 'turtle graphics' is the whole of LOGO.

Graphics have probably contributed most to the success of LOGO. Producing pictures is tremendously appealing, and offers enormous scope for experimenting. Many other programming languages treat graphics as an extra, 'bolted on' afterwards. Although they offer sophisticated ways of generating pictures, it needs a sophisticated user to understand and use their graphics-related parts. For example, they nearly all assume a fair familiarity with Cartesian co-ordinates; this would make them inaccessible to a child who had not yet met them in school. LOGO's 'turtle graphics' avoids such traps, by providing a very simple means of picture construction which demands no prior investment in mathematical or computer knowledge. The essential knowledge is merely an awareness of familiar concepts such as 'forward', 'backward', 'left' and 'right'. This makes it possible for children, even young ones, to start using LOGO.

Various versions of LOGO appeared in the course of time. Most American versions are recognisable as dialects of the MIT LOGO, although the version available for the Texas Instruments TI 99/4 is somewhat unusual compared to others such as IBM PC LOGO and Terrapin LOGO. Nevertheless, it too sprang from an MIT research project. An assumption underlying the work that went into these versions was that LOGO would never easily fit into the conventional maths curriculum — the curriculum would eventually change to incorporate what LOGO had to offer. In the UK a different dialect of LOGO evolved from research work done at the Department of Artificial Intelligence of the University of Edinburgh from 1972 onwards. This was based on the belief that LOGO would best gain acceptance by being used within the conventional curriculum in some way — evolution rather than revolution, so to speak. Thus Edinburgh LOGO was developed, through various research projects, to be even less demanding on the user's understanding and prior knowledge than the MIT versions. Microcomputer versions of Edinburgh LOGO exist for various machines produced by Research Machines Ltd. of Oxford, one of the largest suppliers of microcomputers to British schools.

All the educational research carried out so far suggests that LOGO has a great deal to offer as a means of teaching conceptual thinking, but no survey yet has been on a big enough scale to be conclusive. You may wonder, if it seems to be such a good thing, why it did not become available to the public much sooner than it did? The main reason is this: LOGO requires more from a computer than most other popular languages do. Until the 1980s, a computer powerful enough to provide what LOGO demands would have been too expensive to be a commercial success.

1.3 A DIGRESSION ABOUT ARTIFICIAL INTELLIGENCE (AI)

(You can safely skip this section if you want.)

At first sight it might seem strange that educational research should be done in the world of Artificial Intelligence — a Department of Education, or some such body, might seem more the appropriate place for LOGO. To understand the reasons for this you need to know a little about what Artificial Intelligence is and what it aims to do. It is sometimes defined as the use of computers to study intelligence and, in particular, human thought. The definition does not convey much.

To get a little feel for the subject, consider the following example of the sort of unrealistic 'intelligence test' that often appears in the newspapers:

Which is the odd one out?

When first confronted with such a problem, various ideas spring to mind immediately. Perhaps the Y is the odd one out, because it is the only one which has pretensions to being a vowel. Perhaps it is a code — if you try the usual trick of substituting 1 for A, 2 for B, etc., then it turns out that Y is the only odd number, so it really is the 'odd one out'. At some point you might make the leap of looking at them as geometric figures rather than as letters of the alphabet. In that case you might realise that the Z qualifies as odd one out because it is made up of three straight lines rather than two, or perhaps because it involves two line junctions rather than one. The more you look, the more justifications you can find for any particular one being the answer.

Now imagine that you had to write a computer program to mimic your solution of the problem. The work you would have to put in before starting to write such a program could well be called

Artificial Intelligence (if you did a good job of it). You would, amongst other problems, have to figure out why you made the leap from considering letters to considering shapes, and why you did it when you did. Had you worked through all the letter possibilities? No, there is a huge number of them and you could not possibly try them all. Some obnoxious whiz-kid, for instance, might have been able to claim that the V was the odd one out because all the others were initials of authors of children's books published in 1912! You presumably made the leap because you felt that you were starting to look for possibilities that were too unlikely. But ... how do you embody the notion of 'too unlikely' in a computer program? More-over, how do you encapsulate the knowledge and experience that made you plump for the attribute of shape as a likely factor to explore?

The reason that computers are so vital to the subject of Artificial Intelligence is that you cannot get away with hand-waving about these points in such problems. The computer only obeys instruc-tions; it cannot decide for itself to switch to some new tack, even if the program to explore that new tack exists. The program which mimics your solution to the above problem — do not try writing one, it's a huge can of worms — would have to include regular checks about the likelihood of success with the current approach. Likelihood is not easy to quantify — it depends on past experience. A good program would have to be capable of resuming the explora-tion of a previously rejected avenue if it begins to look more promising after all, as others grow less likely.

The absolute lack of intelligence on the part of a computer makes the act of writing a program to model something a good test of a theory in AI. The problem above is not representative of work in the field — current research (1984) is concerned with more fundamental questions which this problem only hints at. It should help you appreciate, however, that the world of AI has had good reason to spend a lot of effort in developing computer languages specifically for modelling purposes. Those now used in AI, such as LISP and PROLOG, are geared to bring out the aspects of com-puter programming which are most useful in modelling and to play down those aspects which would be least relevant to the aims of the subject. LOGO is one product of that effort; as such, it is a remark-able success.

The studying of how and what people learn through using LOGO also fits in with the interests of workers in AI.

1.4   ABOUT THIS BOOK

What it is not
This book is not a programming manual in the normal sense. It does

not aim purely to teach you how to read and write LOGO — other manuals* already do that well. It is not much concerned with the technical aspects of computers. If you want to know why smoke is coming from your IBM PC, how to make it control your coffee grinder, or why the disk drive is making that grating noise, then look elsewhere...

What it is

On first learning to program a computer, most people estimate their own abilities very badly. Either they plough through a manual or a course and then immediately embark on trying to write a program which will play a decent game of chess, or they find themselves short of inspiration and confidence and rapidly lose interest. Either way, the machine fails to live up to their expectations. Often the problem is that only a hazy distinction is made between knowing the mechanics of programming and knowing how to put it to use.

The purpose of this book is to help you develop the knowledge and experience to be able to make the most of LOGO as a tool. True, to do so involves teaching you to program in LOGO. However, there is a widespread view that good programming is the private preserve of geniuses, that mere mortals cannot aspire to great results, and that a measure of the worth of a program is the amount of ingenuity which went into it. This book should help to demolish that idea. The power to express your ideas well and to develop them thoroughly is not a gift — it is something which can be learned, and LOGO makes it enjoyable.

1.5 THOUGHTS FOR TEACHERS

(You can skip this section too if you are never going to find yourself teaching others about LOGO, even informally.)

Much has been said in magazines and journals about the educational value of LOGO. Not much has been said about the problems. One of the major snags is that, while students can learn a lot from making mistakes and tracking them down, it is extremely disenchanting to make too many mistakes and too little progress towards becoming fluent in the use of LOGO. Your problem is to leave a student along long enough to develop confidence in his ideas, and yet be aware enough to spot when help is necessary. There are asides throughout the book which point out areas of likely trouble.

An aside — apologies now and hereafter to readers who are women — sexist sympathies are not intended by references to 'he'

* For example, the IBM PC LOGO manual, written by LOGO Computer Systems Inc. and provided with IBM PC LOGO, or *Apple LOGO*, by Harold Abelson, published by Byte/McGraw-Hill Publications, 1982.

and 'his', but this book aims to be short and readable. Indeed, you may care to ponder why girls did significantly better than boys in a high school project were LOGO was used to teach the traditional mathematics syllabus.

As a teacher, even if you are not one in the formal sense, you ought to bear one or two points in mind. A beginner is going to have his own ideas about what is really going on inside the computer as he works with LOGO. Usually this is a very simplified version of the truth, but it has the great benefit of making the whole system seem manageable. The habit of simplification is not only used by beginners, of course — for example, just about everyone characterises their government as a sort of collective being with a rather dumb mind of its own. Doing so makes it seem comprehensible.

Such simplification can be useful or it can be obstructive. It is useful only if it helps you to grasp why things are happening and permits you to predict what will happen in response to your actions. A significant part of the art of teaching consists of encouraging pupils to adopt some simplifying and familiar analogy, and then getting them to modify and enlarge it in a reasonably consistent way to take account of new and previously inexplicable details. What has been said above might lead you to think that, in the world of LOGO, this is going to be easier than usual. It is to some extent, but do not imagine you can be complacent about it — being easier does not mean that it is easy. To put you in the mood, consider how you might tackle these two questions from a bright but beginning LOGO user:

> "How can the computer read what is engraved on the keys? If I press 'F' then an F appears on the screen, but the computer has no eyes."

> "If I type a lot, or press ENTER many times, then some of what I have typed goes off the top of the screen. Can I get it back? (Note: the answer is no) and where did it go?"

If you are going to be using LOGO in formal classroom teaching, you will need to do some careful planning. Yes, LOGO can be a vehicle for teaching programming, though there seems little point in teaching programming for its own sake. After all, while LOGO is a powerful and relatively simply language, it is representative of only one of various classes of programming languages, each of which has its own underlying 'programming concepts'. It is the particular approach to expressing ideas which is valuable in LOGO, rather than the computer science aspects.

If you want to use LOGO as a means for teaching topics in some subject such as mathematics or geography (where you could use it for training people in ideas about graphic representations), then you will need a good deal of organised material. This is true no matter what programming language is used. You will also have to figure out how to teach the necessary LOGO programming before getting your pupils to put that knowledge to use in experimenting with your subject.

One neglected approach is to use LOGO to underpin a group discussion. You can do this even if you only have one machine per class, by making the machine the arbiter of who is right and who is wrong in the discussion or by getting the group to plan how to model something, with you as the typist.

Finally — for the moment — do not be put off by articles which try to lay down the law about how LOGO should be used (or even this book). If it suits you to devise LOGO programs which others will use but need not understand, because it is an easy language in which to express your intentions, then go ahead.

1.6 THE LAYOUT OF THE BOOK

As you will have seen, sections within chapters are numbered. The numbering is hierarchical — Section 2.6.1 is Sub-section 1 of Section 6 of Chapter 2. Figures are also numbered by chapter — Figure 2.3 is Figure 3 of Chapter 2. This makes it easier to refer to them, especially because figures might not always appear on the same page on which they are first mentioned in the text. Chunks of LOGO look like this in this book:

```
PRINT 654 * 321
```

although in Dr. LOGO and in Waterloo LOGO what you type in normally appears in lower case instead. You will find that long lines on the screen may look odd — what 'long' means depends on the (selectable) width of the screen. If you type off the end of one line the machine continues for you on the next line. This may cause a word to be split in the middle if it starts close to the end of a line. Long lines of LOGO will be indicated in this book by indenting the continuation. The following example is not LOGO, but you could type it nevertheless (the LOGO system will merely object to it). There are only two lines; you could make it appear on your screen very much as it appears here by the simple step of inserting extra spaces between certain of the words:

```
THIS IS NOT LOGO, JUST AN EXAMPLE OF HOW
        ONE LONG LINE OF TYPING WILL BE
        SHOWN IN THE TEXT OF THIS BOOK.
THIS IS A SECOND LINE.
```

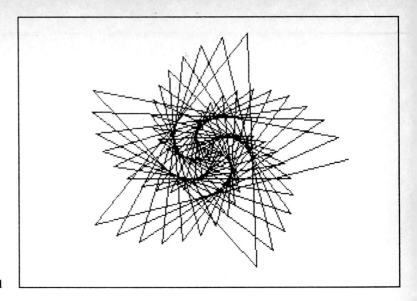

Figure 1.1

Diagrams appear as shown in Figure 1.1. The box around it shows where the useful edges of the screen are, so that you can get an idea of what it ought to look like on your computer. The box will not appear on your screen (unless you add it yourself), as it is an extra included when this book was printed so that you can judge the scale — which is useful if you want to try marrying two or more diagrams.

Some diagrams later in this book contain squares, drawn by LOGO commands. If you look carefully, you will see that they are not accurately square, and that circles are slightly elliptical. On the other hand, the diagrams accurately reflect the appearance of the screen in IBM PC LOGO. Had you not read this paragraph, you might not have noticed. However, IBM PC LOGO and Waterloo LOGO will let you change the ratio of vertical scale to horizontal scale if, for instance, you want to print out geometrically precise shapes.

Appendices describe various versions of LOGO which existed at the time the book was published. They are worth looking at even if you have no chance to use another version; the variations in what they provide might give you some useful ideas about general LOGO commands you can create for yourself.

There are exercises. Those that have a reasonably short and instructive solution are answered at the back of the book. They are not meant to be a graded series to take you through everything that needs to be practiced. Try them as you encounter them or you'll be missing a lot.

2 | TURTLE GRAPHICS

"Suppose it's a figure-picture, and you venture to say 'draws well'. Somebody measure it and finds one of the proportions an eighth of an inch wrong. You are disposed of as a critic! 'Did you say he draws well?' your friends enquire sarcastically, while you hang your head and blush. No. The only safe course, if anyone says 'draws well', is to shrug your shoulders. 'Draws well?' you repeat thoughtfully. 'Draws well? Humph!' That's the way to become a great critic!"

(*Sylvie and Bruno*, LEWIS CARROLL)

Aims: This chapter has two purposes. One is to introduce you to the LOGO drawing commands. They are, individually, remarkably simple; using them with a few of the more generally useful features of LOGO also introduced in this chapter should equip you to produce some fairly elaborate drawings. The other purpose is more general: to show LOGO as an interesting tool for experiment and investigation.

Note: There are examples of LOGO throughout this book. The version of LOGO on which they are based is IBM PC LOGO, developed by LOGO Computer Systems Inc. If you have some other version of LOGO, you will not be able to copy the examples unthinkingly, even though there are more similarities than differences between the various LOGOs that exist. You should treat the examples of LOGO as prototypes of ideas — even if it is this LOGO you have! Anything without a ready counterpart in IBM PC LOGO will be indicated in the text. Dr. LOGO, produced by Digital Research, and Waterloo LOGO, produced by the University of Waterloo in Canada, are fully described in appendixes.

2.1 INTRODUCTION

Suppose that you have just switched on your IBM PC and got LOGO going — if you do not know how, look at the instructions that came with the disk. On the screen you should see, amongst other things, a white square, the cursor. In IBM PC LOGO and Dr. LOGO it is blinking. It will be just to the right of the prompt:

?

This prompt indicates that LOGO is waiting for you to type in a command of some sort. If you have not done so already, try typing a few letters of the alphabet to see what happens, then press the

ENTER key — it is to the right of the alphabetic keys, and on an IBM keyboard it has a down-and-leftward arrow inscribed on it rather than the word 'enter' or the word 'return' as on some other keyboards. Pressing the ENTER key indicates to LOGO that what you have typed is (perhaps) a command that you want obeyed. Unless you were lucky in your choice of letters, LOGO will print an error message on the screen, the gist of which will be that your command is not a known one. There are two points to make here:

- LOGO errors may cost you some time, but they do not damage anything you spent money on.
- Making errors is, as in other subjects, one of the best ways to learn things. It's the normal thing to be doing, rather than the exception!

Initially IBM PC LOGO will only recognise around two hundred commands. However, one of the beauties of the language is that you can extend the set of commands it knows about — this is the main topic of the chapter after this. Around 20% of the commands available at the start are to do with drawing. These are introduced in this chapter.

2.2 THE BASIC TURTLE GRAPHICS COMMANDS

Each time you start LOGO up, you should see a short introductory message, and the prompt. Unless you happen to have a two-screen system, type

    MIXEDSCREEN

(all one word) and press ENTER. [Even at this early point the various versions of LOGO diverge somewhat. In Dr. LOGO and Waterloo LOGO, the word to type is 'splitscreen', in lower case, rather than MIXEDSCREEN. If you skip-read that note at the start of this chapter, you'd better look at it again.] You should now see an arrowhead in the middle of the screen, which points upward. The arrowhead is called the turtle; there are commands that change its location, others that change its direction and one or two that do both. Even MIXEDSCREEN is not really needed before starting to work with the turtle: if you forget it, and just issue a 'turtle command', then LOGO will do a MIXEDSCREEN command for you. A useful characterisation of the turtle, especailly for children, is

    'an animal which crawls across a sheet of paper, towing a pencil or an eraser'

and the screen can be characterised as

'a sheet of paper which you are looking down on from above'

Initially the turtle will draw a line as it moves.

The fundamental commands which control the turtle are FORWARD, BACK, LEFT and RIGHT, and each requires you to supply a number indicating 'how much'. The number gives degrees of rotation (360 is a full turn on the spot) for LEFT and RIGHT, and 'turtle units' for FORWARD and BACK. For example, try typing

    FORWARD 50

(do not forget to press ENTER as well). The turtle will move forward 50 units, drawing a line. One 'turtle unit' does not correspond to some number of inches or centimetres — the physical length of the line depends on the size of your screen. However, the screen has a fixed size when measured in terms of 'turtle units'. If you now type the additional commands

    RIGHT 120
    FORWARD 50
    RIGHT 120
    FORWARD 50

then your drawing should look like Figure 2.1. If you are puzzled by why it should be RIGHT 120 rather than, say, RIGHT 60 then try

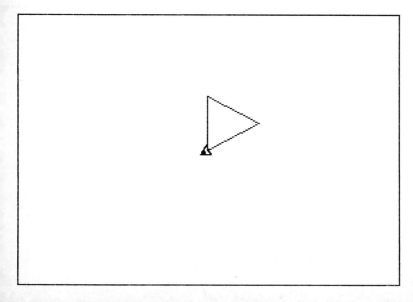

Figure 2.1

the commands with RIGHT 60 instead and see what happens —
experiment! There are commands for cleaning off the drawing and
returning the turtle to where it was (and facing upward) at the start
— in IBM PC LOGO they are

    HOME
    CLEAN

This HOME command will normally have added a line to the screen
— though perhaps on top of an existing one — because the turtle
draws as it moves. If it didn't in this case, it was only because the
turtle was already back at its starting position. Be careful of using it;
it is easy to mess up a beautifully prepared drawing at the last step
by returning the turtle to the centre without thinking first.

Using HOME and then CLEAN to prepare for a new drawing
is such a common occurrence that there is a command specially
provided which subsumes the two. It is

    CLEARSCREEN

2.3 SOME TERMINOLOGY

There is some terminology which it is sensible to mention here.
Things like CLEAN and FORWARD and so on are called procedures; a command is really an instruction to LOGO to execute
(that is, obey) some procedure(s). It is not vital for you to make a
distinction between 'command' and 'procedure' — you should just
be aware of the terminology at the moment.

You may note that, although you must supply a number for
FORWARD (what happens if you do not?), you supply nothing else
with HOME (what happens if you do?). The customary way of
describing this is to say that

    FORWARD takes one input, which must be a number

but

    HOME takes no input

There are other procedures that take more than one input, and even
some for which the number of inputs can be unknown. Examples of
these will appear in Chapters 3 and 4.

Try the command.

    RANDOM 50

— you will get an error message pointing out that you have not said
what to do with some random number less than 50. This is because

RANDOM not only requires one input — in the command it was 50 — it also produces an output. RANDOM's output is a random non-negative integer less than the input number. The output number can be used wherever a number input would be acceptable:

   FORWARD RANDOM 50

would move the turtle forward by a random integer number of turtle units less than 50. FORWARD needs a number for its input, RANDOM 50 outputs a number — if you like, you can choose to think that the expression RANDOM 50 is a number.

The procedures FORWARD, BACK, LEFT, RIGHT, HOME, CLEAN and CLEARSCREEN (and many others) do not produce an output, they merely have some effect. It is one of the fundamental rules about LOGO commands that if something produces an output, it must be used as the input to something else — you cannot leave outputs lying about unused.

2.4 DRAWINGS

There are abbreviations for the most commonly used procedures, to spare your fingertips. In particular, you can use

   MS for MIXEDSCREEN
   FD for FORWARD
   BK for BACK
   LT for LEFT
   RT for RIGHT
   CS for CLEARSCREEN

EXERCISES

There are various things you could now take time to investigate:

1. What happens when the turtle reaches the edge of the screen?
2. What are the dimensions of the screen in 'turtle units'?
3. How much should the turtle be turned from its initial heading so that it points at a corner of the screen (trial and error is the method, unless you want to indulge in trigonometry)?
4. Do FD, BK, LT and RT accept negative numbers, and if so what is the effect?
5. Do those commands accept numbers with decimal parts, or do they just ignore any decimal part? This requires forethought — the decimal part certainly gets ignored when showing lines on the screen; the question is, is the turtle really where it seems to be or is it a fraction of a turtle unit further along the line?

The answers to each of these might be useful to you later on.

You will find, in IBM PC LOGO, the answer to question 1 is that the turtle reappears at the opposite edge of the screen when it moves off any edge. This is called wrapping; you can prevent it happening in subsequent commands by using the command

```
FENCE
```

This puts up an invisible fence at the edge of the screen, which the turtle cannot cross (try it). Instead of having a fence, you can let the turtle move on a square much larger than the screen, by giving the command

```
WINDOW
```

In this case, the screen is just a small window looking onto the middle of the large square. The turtle will then be allowed to get up to 9999 units, horizontally and vertically, away from the centre of the screen before it wraps to the other side of the big square. You can switch back to having the turtle wrap at the edges of the screen by using

```
WRAP
```

When the turtle is allowed to wrap, try the commands

```
CS
RT 50
FD 9000
```

in order to see what happens when you send the turtle forward some distance that is much larger than the dimensions of the screen. There is nothing remarkable about the angle 50 in this trio — try some others (some choices are remarkable). Try a number bigger than 9999 as the input to FORWARD and see what happens.

EXERCISES
You might also like to try your hand at constructing some simple drawings, such as
6. a) some simple polygons — essentially sets of paired FORWARD and RIGHT (or LEFT) commands,
   b) something less regular, such as a drawing of your microcomputer. Keep it fairly simple, unless you are a masochist. Planning the drawing should remind you of those popular challenges 'draw this without lifting pen from paper...'.

At this point you might think, with reason, that LOGO drawings require you to type too many commands for fairly simple results. If more complex drawings were going to be correspondingly more arduous to construct, you would be justified in abandoning the whole enterprise immediately. However, as you might expect — and you ought to have expected that the designers of LOGO would have thought of it — there are ways of making things easier. You can combine several commands into one, by merely putting one after another with space between. For example,

FD 50 RT 90 FD 50 HOME

is one command formed from four. Similarly,

FD 50 RT 120

is one (compound) command, and three such commands in sequence will draw an equilateral triangle. This allows you to make up single commands which are very long; if they spread to the point where they are going to overflow the right-hand edge of the screen, do not worry — just keep typing and what you type will appear on the next line down. An exclamation mark appears at the right-hand end of any line which is continued in this way, in order to remind you what is happening. DON'T press ENTER when your typing reaches the right-hand edge unless you want LOGO to obey the command you've typed so far. So, when drawing a square, part of your screen might look like this (if it is set to be 40 characters wide)

? FD 50 RT 90 FD 50 RT 90 FD 50 RT 90 F!
D 50 RT 90

and LOGO will treat the whole thing as one command. There is a limit to how long a line can be — it is 128 characters, or just over three widths of the screen when set to be 40 characters wide.

What you can do about typing mistakes depends on which version of LOGO you have. In IBM PC LOGO you can use the RUBOUT (or 'back arrow') key, above the ENTER key, to rub out characters. You can use the right and left arrow keys on the numeric pad at the right of the keyboard to move the cursor back and forward in the line, to allow you to pick what you want to rub out. Putting the cursor in the middle of the line somewhere, and then typing, causes what is to the right to be pushed to the right. Some other options are very useful; a few are slightly less convenient because they require you to press the key marked CTRL, and to press another while holding it down (the CTRL key is similar to the SHIFT keys in its use). The options are

Del   which is very like RUBOUT. RUBOUT deletes the character just to the left of the cursor, Del deletes the character which is underneath the cursor. The cursor doesn't move, but all characters to the right get pulled left to fill in the gap.

CTRL-right-arrow

(that is, CTRL and 'right arrow' on the numeric pad) which deletes everything from where the cursor is to the end of the command. Pressing this once is much easier than repeatedly pressing Del till everything gets swallowed.

TAB   (near the left of the keyboard, just below Esc: it has symbols to represent the idea of tabbing engraved on it, rather than the word 'tab') which moves the cursor to the end of the command. Shift-TAB moves the cursor to the start of the command. Therefore, to delete a whole command, type Shift-TAB to get to the start of the command, then CTRL-'right arrow' to delete everything to the right.

There is a variety of other things you can do, but these are the most useful possibilities. Consult the manual that came with your LOGO system to see what powers you can call on for correcting typing — the repertoire may even be amended by the supplier from time to time, so it will not be described in this book. If you are prone to forgetting what the various keys do, it is a good idea to get small sticky labels and use them to embellish your keyboard with suitable reminders.

LOGO has a number of commands which are useful in many situations. One is for those occasions when repetition of some command (perhaps compound) is required:

REPEAT 5 [FD 50 RT 72]

is an example that draws a pentagon. The square brackets are necessary here. They delimit what is called a 'list' in LOGO. Lists are another of the types of object — like numbers — that LOGO is equipped to handle; they form the main topic of Chapter 4.

The general form of the REPEAT command is

REPEAT number [command]

and, using it, you should now be able to draw any regular polygon. It is a very powerful command, more so than might appear at first sight. Think of it as a command with another command inside it — then you should see that the following is legal LOGO, and it will produce an interesting pattern, shown in Figure 2.2.

REPEAT 10 [RT 36 REPEAT 5 [FD 40
        RT 72]]

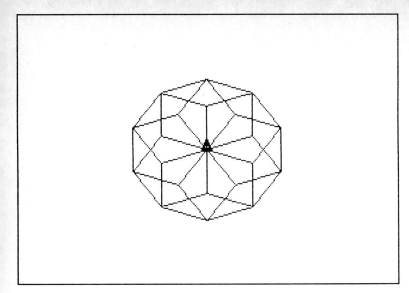

Figure 2.2

This gives you a prototype for all sorts of 'rotated polygon' patterns. There are several noteworthy points about it:

- The REPEAT command on the inside just draws one pentagon, and leaves the turtle as it was before. Such a command, that afterwards has affected neither the turtle's location nor its heading, is sometimes referred to as 'state-transparent'. The turtle's location and heading are together known as the turtle's state.

- The main REPEAT command is thus something of the form

  REPEAT 10 [RT 36 state-transparent command]

  so that the turtle will in effect have turned by $10 \times 36 = 360$ degrees by the end. Thus the whole command is also state-transparent.

- Those numbers 10 and 36 give a pleasingly regular and state-transparent result because they multiply to give 360. How about trying pairs of numbers that multiply to give 720, or some other multiple of 360? For example,

  REPEAT 5 [RT 144 . . .]

  Some are not worth the effort:

  REPEAT 12 [RT 60 . . .]

is just the equivalent of

REPEAT 2 [REPEAT 6 [RT 60 ...]]

and so you would just be repeating a state-transparent procedure twice. Doing that means nothing more than retracing the drawing, because just before the second time, the turtle will be as it was just before the first time. A little thought, and perhaps some experiment, should show you how to spot which pairs of numbers are potentially interesting, and which are not.

- The idea of polygons rotated about one spot may come to seem limited after you've tried a few. A variation that offers further possibilities is

REPEAT x [FD y RT z state-transparent command]

since this too is state-transparent if the numbers x and z are suitably chosen. The drawings in Figures 2.3 and 2.4 were produced by such a command.

All the drawings produced by one such command have a somewhat sterile regularity about them. It should be reasonably clear that this is because in any REPEAT command like those above, the only thing that changes from one repetition to the next is the state of the turtle — its position or heading or both. What the turtle actually does at each repetition is unchanging, and that is because the numbers — distances or angles — are unvarying. There are

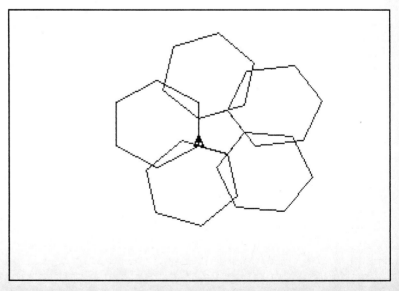

Figure 2.3

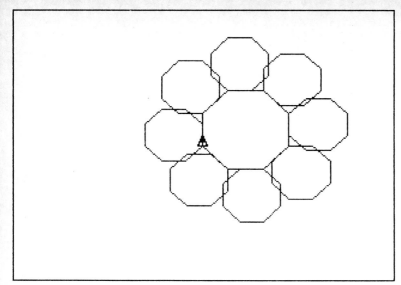

Figure 2.4

some exciting variations on this theme. The first is just to make the command even more elaborate. There comes a point at which there are so many different sorts of regularity in a picture that it is difficult for the eye to grasp what the subsections of the pattern are that have been repeated. Consider the following hypothesis:

It is the state-transparent parts that catch the attention.

The idea of studying such a subjective hypothesis may surprise you if you are of a scientific turn of mind. Nevertheless, you may or may not agree with this, but you can investigate it by trying various sorts of REPEAT combinations (as one or as several commands) where there are several state-transparent ingredients, and various in which there are only one or two at most. The drawing in Figure 2.5 is state-transparent, with only one state-transparent ingredient within it. The command was

```
REPEAT 12 [ FD 30 REPEAT 4 [ FD 15
        RT 90 ] BK 30 RT 30 ]
```

Try experimenting. Get some other people's opinions too — the results may not be as subjective as you think.

Another of the possibilities for variety is to have the turtle erase some parts of a drawing, or to have it not draw at all for some parts. In IBM PC LOGO the turtle cannot erase directly, it can only overwrite something previously drawn with a new line in the same

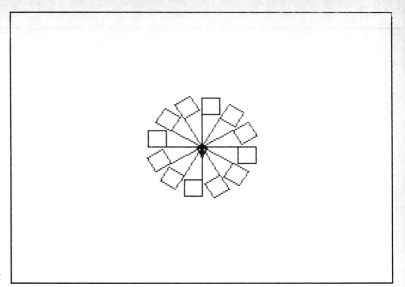

Figure 2.5

colour as the background (so it looks like erasure is happening, to all intents and purposes). There are useful commands for selecting colours — they have some effect even if you only have a monochrome display. The first is SETPC (the PC stands for 'pencolor') which takes an input that must be a number between 0 and 3 and makes the turtle draw in the corresponding colour in future. The default is 3. The colours are selected according to which of two possible palettes of colour is currently in use. You can switch palettes* by using SETPAL 0 or SETPAL 1 — the default is 1. The colour of the background for drawings can be selected by using SETBG, which takes an input between 0 and 15. Each of these 16 backgrounds is different, on a colour display. On a monochrome display the possibilities are limited to black or white.

Try SETPC, SETPAL and SETBG for yourself. On a nonstandard display, especially in countries other than America, the colours may not be exactly as reported in the manual that comes with your LOGO system; such is the standardisation of video technology!

Pen colour 0 is always equivalent to the background colour. Think of it as bleach; it washes out existing lines, letting the background colour show through. Pen colours 1 to 3 are relative to the background, and so will change if you alter it. In order to get the

---

* In Dr. LOGO, there is no explicit choice of palette. Instead there are 64 possible background colours: four sets of 16. This corresponds to the two palettes of IBM PC LOGO but allows two intensities for each as well.

turtle to erase, you could give the command

SETPC 0

Pretty frequently, though, you'll find you want to erase a bit and then resume drawing in the previous colour. To make this easy, there is a command

PENERASE

or PE for short. You can make it resume drawing (with the current pen colour) by the command

PENDOWN

or PD for short. The way to make it neither draw nor erase at all is to use the command

PENUP

or PU for short. This too does not affect the pen colour. The command

PENREVERSE

or PX for short, is curious. It makes the turtle draw in the current pen colour if it is drawing on the background, and draw in the background colour when it is moving over existing bits of drawing. For instance, if there is no drawing yet, the command

PX FD 50

will draw a line, but

BK 25

will erase the last 25 units of it. PX is particularly useful for correcting mistakes: you just back up over them.

Try some of these in a compound command, for example

FD 100 SETPC 0 BK 50 PENUP BK 50

should leave the turtle at its starting point, with a 50-unit line in front of it. You need to give the command

SETPC 3

(or 1 or 2) to get the turtle to resume drawing when it moves.

It is sometimes handy to be able to find out what the pen and background colours have been set to. IBM PC LOGO provides

PC   (PENCOLOR is the full name) which outputs the number of the current pen colour (0–3).

BG   (BACKGROUND is the full name) which outputs the number of the background colour (0–15).

PAL   (PALETTE for long) which outputs the number of the current palette (0 or 1).

These are natural counterparts of SETPC, SETBG and SETPAL. Notice that you cannot expect to get the turtle to draw using the background colour by a command such as

SETPC BG

because there are many more background colours than pen colours. The command

SETBG PC

will work, but it won't make your drawing blend invisibly with the background because the relationship between colours and numbers depends on whether the number refers to background or pen.

Though colours are useful, they enhance drawings rather than add to the repertoire of what's possible. Besides, you may not have colour on your machine or you may — like a surprisingly large proportion of the world — be colour blind in some way. Using colours certainly adds to the amount of work you have to do at the keyboard in order to achieve more elaborate results. Fortunately, the quality and sophistication of drawings does not depend directly on the amount of typing you do. You can greatly extend the potential for drawings by using variables instead of explicit numbers. This idea is so important throughout the rest of the book that it deserves a section to itself.

2.5 VARIABLES

The MAKE command

MAKE "Z 50

gives a variable named Z the value 50 (note the quote mark just before the Z). [WHAT, you were not very sure about variables in your early days of algebra? The image to keep in mind, then, is this:

think of all the numbers, negative or positive, stretching in an orderly line way off into the distance (like railway tracks). Imagine a large luggage label with the name Z written on it, hanging on one of the numbers, 50 for instance. Then you can refer to 50 by the name on the label, rather than as '50'. Moreover, you can move the label around from number to number as the occasion demands. You can also have several labels on one number. Solving algebraic equations is just a matter of deducing which number some label is hanging on...] The name of the variable does not have to be a single letter, it can be anything, such as HIPPOPOTAMUS or HYPOTENUSE, which you find appropriate and not uncomfortably long. You can use most characters apart from ones with special meaning, such as the left and right square brackets and spaces; LENGTH.OF.SIDE and LENGTH__OF__SIDE are perfectly good names for variables.

Then you can use a command such as

```
FORWARD :Z
```

to move the turtle forward 50. Note the colon (:); it means 'the value of the variable called'.

Digression: People often ask two questions about the MAKE command. The first is, what is that quote mark doing there? To answer, consider the command MAKE FORWARD 50. Does this give a variable named FORWARD the value 50, or is it a mangled attempt to move the turtle? The quote mark prevents LOGO mistaking the name as a command — and remember, it was mentioned that in LOGO the user can create new commands (and perhaps create one called Z). To be more precise, the quote mark signifies that what follows is just a word and nothing more than that. Chapter 4 explains various LOGO commands which are concerned with words rather than specifically with numbers. You can PRINT a word by

```
PRINT "HELLO
```

All you need to remember at present is that MAKE expects its first input to be a word, and it takes the word to be the name of a variable. The second input could also be a word if you wanted:

```
MAKE "CLEOPATRA "EGYPT
PRINT :CLEOPATRA
```

will print EGYPT.

The second question is, why is there no matching quote at the end of a word? The answer is that LOGO takes the space after the name to mark the end of the name; it would be wasting your time to force you to put in something which is really superfluous. In IBM PC LOGO, a quote mark at the end, or within a name, will just be taken as part of the name.

Digression for those familiar with another language: LOGO is unusually friendly about variables. You do not have to declare the name or type of variables beforehand, as you would in PASCAL for instance. MAKE looks for a variable of the given name; if there is not one, it creates one. Moreover, the type is the type of the current value.

In most LOGO systems, there is another way to get at the value of a variable. In IBM PC LOGO there is a procedure called THING which expects one input, a word naming a variable, and returns the value of the variable called by that name. For instance, if the variable called Z has the value 50, then

```
FORWARD THING "Z
```

will send the turtle forward 50. Again, the quote mark in that command exists to let the LOGO system know that the Z is merely a name rather than the name of a procedure that it should run.

It might seem that the colon is nothing more than an abbreviation for THING. In fact, it is something even less than that. To illustrate the problem, consider this sequence of LOGO commands:

```
MAKE "FRED 50
MAKE "X "FRED
FORWARD THING THING "X
```

The second command gave the variable called X a value — the value was just a bit of text, namely the word FRED. The FORWARD command is equivalent to

```
FORWARD THING "FRED
```

which is equivalent to

```
FORWARD 50
```

However, the following is NOT the same:

```
FORWARD ::FRED
```

This command would send LOGO looking for a variable called by the name :FRED, but the colon is NOT a procedure (there would need to be a space between the colon and what followed it if it were a procedure). You could always make a variable whose name was :FRED, by

MAKE ":FRED 35

but your FORWARD command would move the turtle 35 units
rather than 50. The colon is only a sort of notational convenience
rather than a procedure; however, it is so convenient that the
procedure THING only gets used where the colon would not do the
job, such as in the example above.

2.6 ARITHMETIC

Introducing the standard arithmetic operations of addition, subtraction, multiplication and division together with MAKE considerably
expands the potential for drawings. For instance, the command

MAKE "Z :Z + 2

gives Z a new value 2 bigger than it previously had. This deserves
some comment. The command is still something of the general form

MAKE "Z number

but the number is :Z + 2 rather than something explicit. In LOGO,
as in real life, the + adds two numbers together. It produces an
output, also a number, that is the sum of the two numbers; such an
expression is acceptable wherever a number is acceptable. The same
applies to other LOGO arithmetic procedures: * for multiplication, /
for division and − for subtraction. You should now be in a position
to understand that a command such as

MAKE "Z 3
REPEAT 50 [FD :Z RT 90 MAKE "Z :Z + 2]

will draw a sort of rectangular spiral.

EXERCISES
Here are various things it would be worth taking some time to
investigate:

7. Nothing has been said about the layout of commands. Where
   are spaces necessary, for instance? Experiment — nothing worse
   than an error message will happen. You will remember better if
   you figure it out than if you clutter up your mental imagery by
   turning to the manual at this point.
8. The MAKE command allows you to alter the sizes of distances
   and angles between repetitions. Try some variants of REPEAT
   commands you tried before. (This might show you that it's a
   good idea to keep notes of your successes.)

9. How do the arithmetic procedures behave when some of the numbers are negative?
10. What happens when you try to divide a number by zero, or try to multiply numbers together to get some colossal result?

Spend some time playing with the arithmetic procedures. The simple way to do this is to use the procedure PRINT — its single input can be also be a number:

```
MAKE "NUM 5
PRINT :NUM * 5
```

will print 25. Try predicting what the commands

```
PRINT 3 * 4 + 5 * 6
```

```
PRINT 12/4/2
```

```
PRINT −4 + 5*6
```

```
PRINT 6/2+4
```

will print, then try them. In IBM PC LOGO, complicated arithmetic expressions are worked out according to the following rules:

a) all the multiplications and divisions are done first (so 3*4+5*6 is really 12+30 rather than 3*9*6);
b) then all the additions and subtractions are done;
c) whenever rules (a) and (b) are ambiguous, work left-to-right (so 6/3*7 is 2*7 rather 6/21);
d) parentheses can be used in the obvious ways.

BEWARE of subtraction — it is easy to get confused between (a) subtracting one number from another, and (b) using a negative number, because the minus sign is used for both purposes. The command

```
PRINT 5 −2
```

does not print 3. It prints 5 and then LOGO complains that you have not said what to do with −2. The safe course is to put a space after the minus sign unless you mean to indicate a negative number.

```
PRINT 5 − 2
```

will print 3.

There are still further possibilities for confusion:

PRINT RANDOM 10 + 12

is the same as

PRINT RANDOM 22

and different from

PRINT (RANDOM 10) + 12

The rule is that LOGO does all the +, *, − and / it can before anything else.

To be absolutely safe, use parentheses to make your meaning clear.

PRINT RANDOM (10+12)
PRINT RANDOM (10   +12)
PRINT RANDOM (10+   12)
PRINT RANDOM (10+12   )

are all the same, and the effort of including the parentheses is only a small price to pay for avoiding arithmetic boobytraps.

2.6.1 Large numbers

Investigate how large and how small a number your LOGO system will let you work with. In IBM PC LOGO numbers with more than a certain number of significant digits — by default, 10 — get printed in a specialised form, and it will also recognise numbers given by you in this form:

1E12	is the same as 1000000000000
1.E12	is also 1000000000000
1E−10	is 1/10000000000, i.e. 0.0000000001
3.7E11	is 370000000000
−4.2E−9	is −4.2/1000000000, i.e. −0.0000000042

The E, for 'exponent', indicates that the number before it is to be multiplied by 10 to the power given by the positive integer after the digit. In the case where there is a negative number after the E, the number before it is to be divided by the appropriate power of 10 instead. In either case the power of ten to use is easily written and thought of as a 1 followed by the given number of 0s. There must be no spaces inside the number, and the integer which follows the E can have at most four digits.

The crucial number of significant figures can be altered if you want. Try

    SETPRECISION 100

100 is not the highest number that SETPRECISION will accept, but some procedures (such as SIN and other trigonometric ones) will not deal with higher precisions. Calculations with a large number of significant digits take a lot longer; the default value of 10 is a very good choice for nearly all purposes. Be careful of the fact that LOGO only remembers numbers to the current number of significant figures. If you try:

    SETPRECISION 5
    MAKE "IT 1/7

then the value of IT will be 0.14286. LOGO does not remember how this value was arrived at — if you increase the precision to, say, 6 and then print :IT, only 0.14286 will be printed, not 0.142857. The procedure PRECISION outputs the current level, should you happen to forget it. The lowest allowable precision is 5.

Sometimes you want a number to be printed in a predictable way, no matter how many significant figures it is known to. For instance, if you want LOGO to print out tables of the results of some calculations, it is handy to be able to get the columns to line up without trouble. For this purpose, there are two special procedures:

EFORM   takes two inputs. It outputs the first, using the number of significant digits given by the second. The command

            PRINT EFORM 1/7 20

        is much more convenient than

            SETPRECISION 20
            PRINT 1/7
            SETPRECISION {whatever it was before}

FORM   takes two or three inputs. The first is the number you want printed (or whatever). The second is the number of digits that you want before the decimal point. The third, if given, is the number of digits that you want after the decimal point. Thus

            PRINT FORM 1/7 3 8

will print something that is 3+8+1 (the 1 is the decimal
point) characters wide.

2.6.2 Other arithmetic procedures

Mainly for the sake of completeness, here are the other arithmetic
procedures in IBM PC LOGO. If your LOGO system does not have
them don't despair — you will (eventually) find that it is almost
certainly possible to create them for yourself.

There are three trigonometric procedures. COS and SIN take
one number as input — an angle in degrees — and output the cosine
or sine of that angle:

PRINT SIN 30

prints 0.5. The procedure ARCTAN normally takes two inputs,
though you are allowed to give it just one, and outputs the angle in
degrees whose arctangent is the second input divided by the first —
try making the first input 0. The angle is always between 0 and 360.
If you give only one input, the missing second input is assumed to
be 1. With two inputs, it is convenient to think of them as being
respectively the base and height of a right-angled triangle.

There are various procedures which are concerned with integers
(whole numbers) in particular, in one way or another. They are

INT   This procedure takes one input and outputs the
               integer part of it; that is, it gets rid of any fractional
               part.

ROUND   This takes one input and outputs the nearest integer
               to it:

                       PRINT ROUND 2.6   prints 3
                       PRINT ROUND 2.47   prints 2
                       PRINT ROUND −2.6   prints −3

REMAINDER   This takes two inputs. If they are not integers it
               ROUNDs them first; it then outputs the remainder
               left when the first input is divided by the second:

                       PRINT REMAINDER 75 11   prints 9

POWER   This expects two inputs. It outputs the result of
               raising the first input to the power given by the
               second input. The second input does NOT have to

be an integer, nor does it have to be positive. Unless it IS a positive integer, it does take a short while to calculate the result. Examples:

PRINT POWER 5 3   prints 125 (that is,
                                         5*5*5)
PRINT POWER 5 −3   prints 0.008
PRINT POWER 2 −0.5   prints 0.7071067811
                                         (if precision is 10)
PRINT POWER 2 −1/2   prints the same.

EXP   This expects one input. It outputs the mathematical constant 'e' raised to the given power. In effect, EXP :X is POWER 2.7182818284... :X

LN   This expects one input, and outputs the logarithm of the given number to the base 'e'. It is the inverse of EXP; if :X is bigger than 0, then

PRINT EXP LN :X

should print the value of X, unless you've been monkeying with the precision.

SQRT   This takes one input and outputs its square root. The input must of course be positive.

RANDOMIZE This takes no input and does not output anything. Its effect is to make the values produced by RANDOM even less predictable than they are. If you do not use RANDOMIZE, then whenever you start up LOGO and use RANDOM you will get the same sequence of random numbers.

There are also four procedures — SUM, DIFFERENCE, PRODUCT and QUOTIENT — which expect two numbers and output the appropriate result. In the case of DIFFERENCE, this means (first input) — (second input) rather than vice-versa.

2.7 MORE ABOUT DRAWINGS

All this knowledge can be put to use for constructing more elaborate and interesting drawings. However, there is one further LOGO topic that is worth knowing about first.

2.7.1 Controlling how the screen is used

On the IBM PC, when you have text and graphics visible at the same time (after MIXEDSCREEN), it is possible to have text and drawing overlapping, so that neither is readily comprehensible.

Figure 2.6 shows an example. Fortunately this is only one of the ways of utilising the screen permitted by the machine's electronics. Table 2.1 shows the choices, together with the corresponding IBM PC LOGO commands that select them. On other machines, with other LOGO systems, the possibilities and commands will be different and you should read your manual to find out more. If you forget to use one of these so that only text is visible, your first drawing

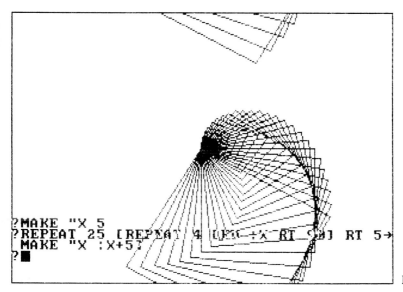

Figure 2.6

Table 2.1   Using the IBM PC screen

MIXEDSCREEN (MS for short)	Visible area: 320 wide 250 high (overlaps text) Text area: bottom 4 lines
FULLSCREEN (FS for short)	Visible area: 320 wide 250 high Text area: none
TEXTSCREEN (TS for short)	No drawing at all Text area: full 24 lines

command will also cause a MIXEDSCREEN to happen. Using TEXTSCREEN does not erase your drawing, it just makes it invisible for the time being. When you are doing drawing, these F-key functions (at the left of the keyboard) are extremely useful:

F4   This has the effect of FULLSCREEN

F2   This has the effect of MIXEDSCREEN

F1   This has the effect of TEXTSCREEN

When the screen is entirely devoted to text, it is possible to change the colours of characters. The procedure SETTC expects one input, but it should not be a number. Instead, it should be an entity called a list; lists were mentioned earlier, in connection with the REPEAT command. The list it expects should contain two numbers, for example

SETTC [2 6]

The first number inside the square bracket is taken to be the colour of the character itself. The second is the colour of the background to the character — each character comes with a small bit of background, as though it were a pattern on a tile. Instead of setting out what the numbers mean in some boring table, you should try SETTC for yourself. In exploring SETTC, it matters whether the graphics are being displayed or not.

2.7.2 Putting variables and arithmetic to use

If you have had some fancy graphics ideas in mind already, you may now be equipped to tackle them. Try them. If you find them still impossible, read on — there are yet more drawing commands to come. If you do not have a pet project, don't worry — there is no reason why you should, and there are many ways to get inspiration. One is to think about what you have recently learnt about LOGO, and consider whether you can apply it to make interesting variations on what you had done previously. To make the most of this,

KEEP NOTES OF SUCCESSES
KEEP NOTES OF FAILURES — and what went wrong
KEEP NOTES OF IDEAS — especially half-baked ones

so that you can look back at them later. It is good practice to keep a notebook, or at least a supply of paper, close at hand for this. (Note for teachers: it is VERY IMPORTANT to get people to do this. Do not be influenced by articles in the press suggesting that using a computer is a big step towards getting rid of paper.)

Here are two examples of the approach.

Spirals

In Section 2.4 it was hinted that one way out of the sterile regularity which comes from overworking REPEAT is to vary some lengths

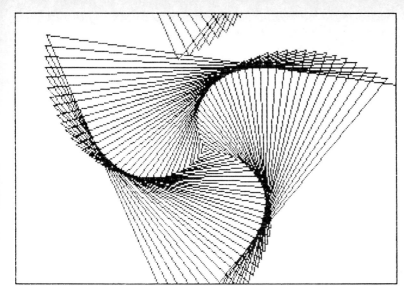

Figure 2.7

from one repetition to the next. Variables are the way to do this. Figure 2.7 was produced by

```
MAKE "X O
REPEAT 100 [FD :X RT 121 MAKE "X :X+ 3]
```

The angle of 121 degrees is close to, but not equal to, the angle of 120 degrees used in drawing an equilateral triangle. Try some others:

44 or 46	(close to an octagon)
89 or 91	(close to a square)
71 or 73	(close to a pentagon)
143 or 145	(close to a pentagram)

but remember to MAKE "X 0 or some small number first, and to centre the turtle and clear the screen with CS.

(Note for maths teachers: this exercise could be used to motivate the idea of experimenting with small changes in familar situations.)

There is nothing special about the number of repetitions — 100 seems a reasonable number. If it is too small the spiralling effect is not very clear. If it is too big the drawing overflows the screen, and if the turtle is being allowed to wrap the outcome can be very messy. It can be beautiful too, so try some examples nevertheless.

There are endless variations on spiralling. In the example above the length the turtle moves increases by 3 at each step while the angle it turns remains constant. What happens if it is the angle that increases, while the length stays constant? For instance,

```
MAKE "ANGLE 0
REPEAT 1000 [FD 3 RT :ANGLE
        MAKE "ANGLE :ANGLE + 7]
```

draws Figure 2.8. The number of repetitions does need to be large here. Notice that there are 8 blobs, and the angle is increased by 7 degrees at each step. If the angle is increased by 11 degrees instead there are 12 blobs. With an increment of 13, there are 14 blobs. This suggests a simple rule relating the increment to the number of blobs. However, it is not

blobs = increment + 1

but something a bit more complex.

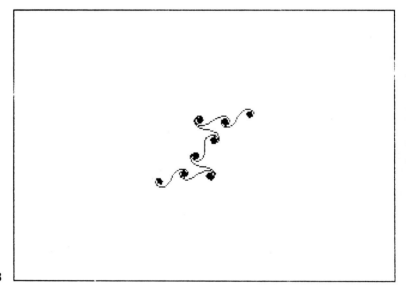

Figure 2.8

EXERCISES
11. What is the rule?
12. Investigate what happens when both the length and the angle vary. Try decrementing as well as incrementing.

Random figures
To draw a rectangle of some random size it is not enough to

```
REPEAT 4 [FD RANDOM 50 RT 90]
```

because each side in the drawing would be of random length, whereas rectangles have two pairs of equal sides. These commands do the
trick:

```
MAKE "W RANDOM 50
MAKE "H RANDOM 50
REPEAT 2 [FD :W RT 90 FD :H RT 90]
```

Therefore the following monster command will produce a sort of
'instant Mondrian' picture*:

```
REPEAT 100 [MAKE "W RANDOM 50 MAKE "H
      RANDOM 50 REPEAT 2 [FD :W RT 90 FD
      :H RT 90] FD RANDOM 100 RT 90 FD
      RANDOM 100 LT 90]
```

The anatomy of this is:

```
REPEAT 100 [{set up W} {set up H}
      {rectangle W units by H units}
      {move the turtle somewhere else}]
```

Figure 2.9 was drawn this way, with the turtle allowed to wrap. The
final four commands (FD, RT, FD, LT) in the repetition are included to move the turtle away from the first corner of the rectangle
it has just drawn. A PU and a PD command inserted on either side
of these four commands would ensure that only complete rectangles
appear in the drawing. However, after a hundred repetitions it
should be almost impossible to see the extra lines where the turtle
moved from one rectangle to the next.

As an example of making constructive use of unsuccessful
ideas, look again at the first attempt to draw a single random
rectangle. It did not draw one, and it was not state-transparent. The
'instant Mondrian' command had to include some means of making
sure that the repeated commands were not state-transparent. Repeating the 'unsuccessful' command might be an easy way to achieve
similar results:

```
REPEAT 25 [REPEAT 4 [FD RANDOM 50
      RT 90]]
```

This is the same as

---

* This isn't fair to Piet Mondrian, whose paintings are anything but random.

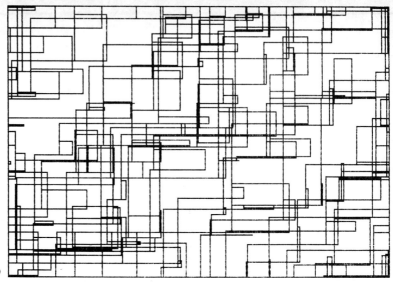

Figure 2.9

REPEAT 100 [FD RANDOM 50 RT 90]

a sample of which is shown in Figure 2.10. (Note for teachers: this works because the intersection of two rectangles is a rectangle. It also works for triangles provided they are all of the same shape. It

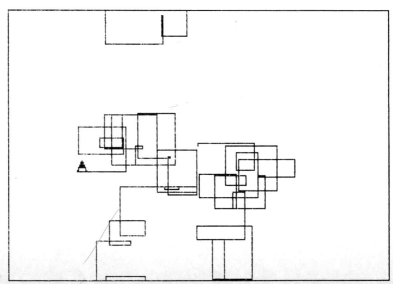

Figure 2.10

does not apply in quite the same way to pentagons, hexagons, etc.)

There is nothing special about 100 as the number of repetitions. There is also nothing particularly vital about 90 as the turning angle in such a random figure. If the angle is made random and the length fixed the resulting drawing (such as Figure 2.11) is a kind of random walk: Figure 2.11 was drawn by the following command. Try this with a much larger input to FORWARD as well.

```
REPEAT 1000 [FD 3 RT RANDOM 360]
```

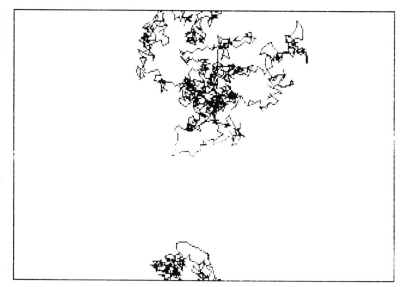

Figure 2.11

A non-graphic example

In IBM PC LOGO, the TONE command controls a loudspeaker inside the computer. Two inputs are needed. The first should be a number giving the desired frequency of the tone, and the second should be a number giving the duration of the tone in terms of clock ticks. There are 1092 ticks per minute, or roughly 18 per second. Both inputs get rounded to the nearest integer. Thus

```
TONE 440 18
```

produces a one second tuning note — an A. The note is reasonably accurate, but not of concert standard! If you give a second TONE command, it waits till the previous one ends, unless the duration is 0 in which case the effect is to end the previous tone prematurely.

These two commands will produce a long descending sound, appropriate for a lead-in to some dramatic visual effect:

```
MAKE "FREQ 10000
REPEAT 950 [TONE :FREQ 5 MAKE "FREQ
        :FREQ-10]
```

You may hear a short gap at some point. This is because LOGO has to do some internal reorganisation every so often (the jargon is 'garbage collecting'). You can postpone this inevitable brief hiccup by forcing one immediately when it doesn't matter so much, and so delaying the next; the command to do this is RECYCLE. This applies as much to drawings as to sound.

By compounding REPEATs, you can produce a variety of siren effects. The limit on the length of a command stops you from producing really complex sounds, but the material in Chapter 3 will help you get round this snag.

EXERCISES

There are some interesting questions about random walks:

13. In a two-dimensional random walk, does the turtle tend to return to the starting point? Use WINDOW to prevent wrapping, as that could cause confusion about whether the turtle had really returned to its start.

14. If so, roughly how many steps does it take? If not, does varying the range of angles make a difference, for example using RANDOM 90 or 90 * (RANDOM 4) instead?

15. Investigate one-dimensional random walks, by using the expression 180 * (RANDOM 2) for the angle.

2.7.3 Cartesian drawing procedures

Most LOGO systems include procedures which control the turtle in a Cartesian way; that is, according to an (X,Y) co-ordinate system. In IBM PC LOGO the origin of co-ordinates is at the centre of the screen, so that the turtle's position co-ordinates can lie (give or take a small amount) in the ranges

X: −160 to 160 inclusive   Y: −125 to 125 inclusive

It is possible to change either of the turtle's co-ordinates, or both at once. The effect of doing any of these is to make the turtle leap to a new position on the screen. If the turtle's pen is down it will draw a straight line between the old position and the new one. The commands are

SETX   This takes one number, the turtle's new X co-ordinate, as input. If the pen is down a horizontal line will be drawn.

SETY   This takes one number, the turtle's new Y co-
            ordinate, as input. If the pen is down a vertical line
            will be drawn.

SETPOS   This takes one list as input. For example,

            SETPOS [140 105]

            will move the turtle in a straight line (drawing, if
            the pen is down) to the point given by X=140,
            Y=105. Unfortunately, except for a few specific
            commands like REPEAT, LOGO does not treat
            the contents of a list as something to be worked
            out. So

            SETPOS [139+1 110−5]

            will only earn you the message

            SETPOS DOESN'T LIKE [139 + 1 105 − 1] AS
                INPUT

            However, the procedure LIST (described in
            Chapter 4) normally expects two inputs, and
            outputs a list containing them. Thus

            SETPOS LIST 139+1 110−5

            will work.

SETHEADING (or SETH for short). This takes one number, the
            turtle's new heading, as input. It turns the turtle on
            the spot to point along that heading.

The following command should help you to get the feel of it:

REPEAT 50 [SETPOS LIST (RANDOM 160)
    (RANDOM 125)]

The parentheses are included only for clarity. The command draws
a cat's cradle of lines, but only in the top right quarter of the screen
where both co-ordinates are positive. To cover the whole screen a
random X co-ordinate between −160 and 160 is needed, and also a
suitable Y co-ordinate. One possible way to do this is

REPEAT 50 [SETPOS LIST (160 − RANDOM 320)
    (125 − RANDOM 250)]

The Cartesian commands also provide a simple means of

checking on the randomness of RANDOM. The idea is to use RANDOM to scatter small blips onto the screen; if it is done at random they should be evenly spread rather than clustered in places. The command FD 1 BK 1 draws a small blip, so

```
REPEAT 500 [PU SETPOS LIST (160 − RANDOM
          320) (125 − RANDOM 250) PD FD 1 BK 1]
```

draws 500 blips at random places on the screen. It takes a while. A faster way to achieve this effect is to use the procedure DOT. It expects, like SETPOS, a list as input. It puts a single dot at the specified place, but it doesn't move the turtle at all! Therefore the PU and PD are not needed:

```
REPEAT 500 [DOT LIST (160 − RANDOM 320)
          (125 − RANDOM 250)]
```

The SET− commands by themselves are not very convenient to use. They deal with absolute rather than relative positions on the screen and working in terms of absolute positions needs forethought. There is a complementary set of procedures which help to make the SET− ones much more useful. They are

XCOR
:   This takes no input, but outputs the turtle's current X co-ordinate. The command SETX XCOR thus does nothing at all. Note that the turtle's X co-ordinate cannot lie outside the range −160 to 160, even if the turtle has wrapped round an edge of the screen. If the turtle is at the right-hand side of the screen and it wraps round to the left-hand side, the X co-ordinate does not change smoothly as you do it. It jumps from around 160 to around −160.

YCOR
:   This takes no input, but outputs the turtle's current Y co-ordinate. It behaves much like XCOR.

HEADING
:   This takes no input, but outputs the turtle's current heading. The heading is measured in degrees, in the range 0 to 360. A heading of 0 is directly up the screen, and the heading increases clockwise.

TOWARDS
:   This takes a list of two numbers as input, which it treats as the X and Y co-ordinates of a point on the screen. It outputs the heading that the turtle must have to aim at that point from its current location.

POS
:   This outputs a list of two numbers, the X and Y co-ordinates. Until you know how to take a list to bits (covered in Chapter 4) this isn't much use except for printing for information.

This set of procedures frees you from having to work in terms of absolute positions. The command

    SETPOS LIST XCOR + 10 YCOR + 10

moves the turtle — drawing, if the pen is down — in a straight line to a point 10 units right and 10 units up. It does not change the heading. The command

    SETX XCOR + 2 SETX XCOR −2

makes the turtle draw a small horizontal blip in a state-transparent way. It is also possible to record a position on the screen for later use, for instance

    MAKE "X XCOR MAKE "Y YCOR
    MAKE "H HEADING
    {do some drawing}
    SETPOS LIST :X :Y
    SETH :H

This is a very useful trick when constructing a drawing which requires many commands, such as Figure 2.12. It was drawn using only Cartesian commands. Even simple drawings like this demand quite a lot of typing. You would naturally hesitate to repeat this effort every time you wanted to include a church or a house or

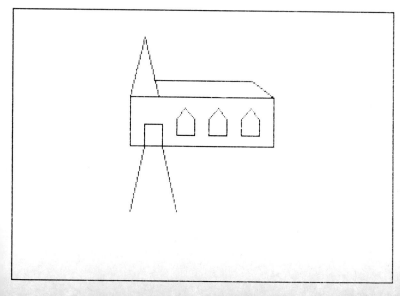

Figure 2.12

whatever in a drawing. There is a means of encapsulating a sequence of commands as one (new) procedure, which can then be used in exactly the same way as existing procedures. Computer programming, after all, is supposed to help you avoid undue work rather than create it. Chapter 3 is about defining new procedures.

2.7.4 Curves

All the diagrams in this chapter have been composed of straight lines. There are no built-in IBM PC LOGO procedures immediately available to you for curve drawing (there are in some other LOGO versions). The material in Chapter 3 will explain how to define some; this section is about the ideas involved.

Figure 2.8 suggests how curves can be simulated. The trick is approximation. Consider circles or arcs of circles, for example. The command

```
REPEAT 360 [FD 1 RT 1]
```

draws a 360-sided polygon (very slowly). It is also as good a representation of a circle as the machine is going to allow. How big is this circle? Well, the circumference is 360 units so the radius must be 360 divided by 2π, or roughly 57.296. In general the circumference of a circle of radius R is $2\pi R$. To approximate to such a circle, therefore, the turtle must move FORWARD by $2\pi R/360$ for each step, and turn by 1 degree. Now $2\pi/360 = 0.01745\ldots$, so a circle of a particular radius can be drawn by

```
MAKE "R {radius}
REPEAT 360 [FD :R*0.01745 RT 1]
```

If that messy number offends you, you can do without it. There is a procedure PI which outputs the value of π. To draw an arc of a circle just reduce the number of repetitions. To draw a rightward-bending arc which subtends a particular angle at the circle's centre,

```
REPEAT {angle} [FD {radius}*0.01745 RT 1]
```

By looking at the command itself rather than what it drew, it should be easy to see that the turtle will change its heading by the chosen angle in drawing the arc. A leftward-bending arc can be drawn by substituting LT for RT.

The drawing of a circle can be speeded up a bit, by commanding LOGO not to bother showing the turtle. The command is

```
HIDETURTLE (or HT for short)
```

and the complementary command is

SHOWTURTLE (or ST for short)

It is possible to approximate to curves other than circles, but it is usually much harder. Spirals probably represent the next step up in complexity — just make the radius increase slowly at each repetition. For instance,

```
MAKE "R 50
REPEAT 720 [FD :R*0.01745 RT 1 MAKE "R
     :R + 1]
```

draws two turns of a linear spiral. There is considerable scope for experimentation. Try changing the distance the turtle moves at each repetition as well, although stop it before this gets too big or it will become obvious that the curve is really made up of straight line segments. Another thing to do is to change the length or angle by multiplying by a constant less than 1 at each step, instead of adding a constant.

3 | PROCEDURES

> "Then we must be somewhere in the Third Act," said Eric.
> "You don't expect the mystery to be cleared up till the Fifth
> Act, do you?"
> "But it's such a long drama!" was the plaintive reply. "We must
> have got to the Fifth Act by this time!"
>
> (*Sylvie and Bruno*, LEWIS CARROLL)

Aims: Defining your own procedures offers an enormous range
of possibilities. This chapter explains how to create and modify
them. Doing so offers a great deal of power for experimenting
with ideas. Later in the chapter, some advice and general principles are described that should help you to make the most of
this.

3.1 CREATING NEW PROCEDURES

IMPORTANT NOTE: Before starting work on this chapter, read
the technical manual that came with the LOGO system to find out
how to prepare a floppy disk (if your system uses them) so that it
can be used for storing things in LOGO that you want to keep. You
need to do this NOW because you cannot prepare one while running LOGO.

Suppose you wanted to draw a scene such as the one shown in
Figure 3.1. (Maybe it is not something you would want to do, but

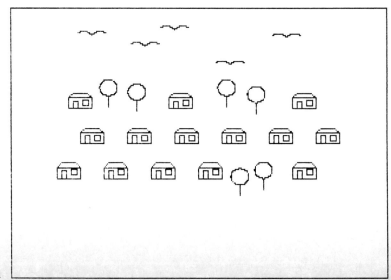

Figure 3.1

just suppose for the sake of argument...) Drawing each house, tree and bird using only the basic turtle graphics commands would be extremely tedious. It would be easier if there were commands HOUSE, TREE and BIRD: the only difficulty might then be ensuring that the turtle was in the right place at the right time for each of these commands.

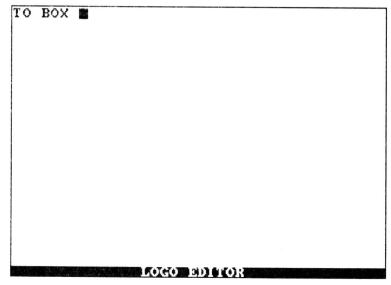

Figure 3.2

The ability to define such new commands, in terms of other commands, is an essential part of every version of LOGO. In IBM PC LOGO the procedures TO and EDIT let you do this. The same commands, with minor variations of detail, are used in most other versions of LOGO. Unlike most other LOGOs, they are not synonymous in IBM PC LOGO. The procedure TO provides an elementary but very limited way to define a new command, but it won't let you correct mistakes easily and it won't let you modify a command that you defined earlier on. It is as well to start with EDIT. Although there is more to learn about it, it is very much more useful and yet not difficult. TO is really intended for the very young. A brief outline appears near the end of Section 3.2.

To see how to use EDIT, consider the following example. It is often convenient to have a command that will draw a box of some kind. Suppose the command is to be called BOX. The LOGO command

```
EDIT "BOX
```

will cause any drawing to vanish (unless you have two screens) temporarily, and will cause any text on the screen to disappear permanently. Instead you should see essentially what is shown in Figure 3.2. The line at the top is the title line of the new procedure BOX. It begins TO rather than EDIT for historical reasons. Essentially, it is indicating that you are about to give a recipe for 'how to ...' — in this case, 'how to BOX' when you give the command BOX in future. The cursor is one space beyond the end of the title line, and LOGO is now waiting for you to specify the sequence of commands that will make up the definition of BOX. Press ENTER to move it to the start of the next line. You can now type commands, but LOGO will not obey them yet, even when you press ENTER — the cursor merely moves to the start of the next line. This is because you are now using a piece of the LOGO system called the editor. It helps to think of the editor as a tool for writing out the definition of a command which, when you finish editing, becomes known to the LOGO system. Try typing

```
REPEAT 4 [FD 50 RT 90]
END
```

and then pressing the 'Esc' key (at the top, near the left). The screen should clear and the message

```
BOX DEFINED
```

should appear, perhaps after a short pause, followed by the normal prompt. You can now use BOX as a normal command. Type

```
BOX
```

and press ENTER, and the turtle will draw a square of side 50. If it did something else instead then you may have made some mistake in typing the definition — read on...

When you use the editor you will find in at least three cases out of four that you want to change something or correct some typing mistake in an earlier line. Whatever the version of LOGO you are using, there are ways of moving the cursor around the screen, deleting parts of what you have typed and inserting new material. If you have already finished the editing of the definition you can get it back to modify it by the command

```
EDIT "BOX
```

IBM PC LOGO gives you the following powers when using EDIT:

- A single LOGO command line can, as before, stretch over

several lines of the screen. However, when this happens (i.e. you type off the end of a line and onto the next line) the editor puts an exclamation mark at the right-hand side of the screen as a reminder that the line continues. In fact, lines can be much longer than the 128 characters allowed for a directly entered command. The only limit, inside the editor, is that the whole procedure definition must fit into 4096 characters.

- The arrow keys (on the 'pad' to the right of ENTER) move the cursor left or right, up or down. If the cursor is at the start of a line and is moved left, it jumps to the end of the line above. If the cursor is at the end of a line and is moved right it jumps to the start of the next line. If it is moved up or down, but the line it would move onto is not long enough, then the cursor springs across to the end of the line rather than remaining floating in empty space. The general principle is that the cursor abhors a vacuum. (If the 'arrow keys' don't move the cursor but print numbers instead, then you've pressed the 'NumLock' key at some point. Just press it again.)

- Typing bits of LOGO inserts them at the point where the cursor is. Anything underneath or to the right of the cursor gets pushed to the right as you type.

- The 'back arrow' key, as before, can be used to delete the character just to the left of the cursor. Stuff to the right gets pulled leftward to fill the gap. If the cursor is at the start of a line, so that there is no character left of the cursor, then that whole line gets joined onto the end of the previous one — think of it as deleting the ENTER you pressed to move from the line above.

[The keys are somewhat different in Dr. LOGO. The whole concept of the editor is radically different in Waterloo LOGO — see Appendix C.] Various other options exist, but they depend on which LOGO you are running. These are the ones provided by IBM PC LOGO:

- MOVING about, locally:
  Tab   (near the left, by the F4 key) jumps the cursor to the end of the current line.
  BackTab (same as the 'Tab' key, but 'shifted') jumps the cursor to the beginning of the current line.
- MOVING about, in big leaps:
  PgUp   (by the 'arrow keys') moves you back a screenful, if possible.
  PgDn   (by the 'arrow keys') moves you forward a screenful, if possible.
  CTRL-PgUp moves you to the very beginning.
  CTRL-PgDn moves you to the very end.
  Home   (beside the 'arrow keys') moves you to the top of the screen.

End   (beside the 'arrow keys') moves you to the bottom of the screen.

- Modifying the text:

Del   (below the 'arrow keys') deletes the character on which the cursor is standing. If it is just past the end of a line, then it causes the next line to be married with it.

Ins   (below the 'arrow keys') splices in a blank line.

CTRL-left-arrow
             causes a copy of the most recently typed-in line to be inserted, where the cursor is now standing. The F3 key does this too.

CTRL-right-arrow
             deletes everything from the cursor to the end of the line.

A very common operation is to remove a complete line. The easy way to do this is:

- move the cursor onto the line,
- if necessary, use BackTab to get the start of it,
- use CTRL-'right arrow' to delete all of it,
- use CTRL-'right arrow' again to remove the empty gap.

As was mentioned earlier, 'Esc' is the way to end editing if you are satisfied with the definition. If you are not satisfied and want instead to abandon editing and discard the definition, type CTRL-Break, alias CTRL-ScrollLock. This feature makes it easy to practice using the editor: just type

        EDIT "JUNK

or whatever, to get 'into' the editor and then try typing anything at all — a limerick, your name and address, rows of numbers. You can play around with the editing keys to your heart's content and eventually throw away all the messy results by typing CTRL-Break — only do not type 'Esc' first! It is a very good idea to spend a little while doing this practice; everyone develops their own style of working with an editor and it is better to get a feel for it before using it in earnest.

Therefore, PRACTICE NOW.

(Notes for teachers: (a) Get people to do this as an abstract exercise before they move on to defining procedures. It can be hard to think about editing and about the LOGO commands making up a definition at the same time. (b) Be careful about how you introduce LOGO procedures. Many beginners have trouble grasping the distinction between defining and running a procedure. They often expect the commands typed in as part of a definition to be obeyed at once — after all, they may never have articulated the notion of 'postponed action' to themselves before in any subject, and not just computer programming. (c) If you have read the instructions above you may have noticed that the description of how to use the editor is based on a particular image, although it is not made explicit. The image is that of typing on a roll of paper seen through a window. The roll can be wound on (downward) by 'PgDn', and back (upward) by 'PgUp'. Strips of blank paper can be spliced in by 'Ins'. It helps beginners to have some such analogy, though it is best not to press it too far if the reality cannot sustain it. Joining two lines into one using 'Del' is something that does not fit the analogy well, which is why the analogy is not explicitly stated above. It might still be worthwhile to use it if you are careful about the order in which the editing functions are introduced.)

3.2 PROCEDURES WITH INPUTS

The procedure BOX defined above can be put to use as though it were a normal LOGO command, e.g.

    REPEAT 36 [RT 10 BOX]

After a short while BOX will seem fairly limited. It would be better if it took an input which gave the size of the BOX. Procedures such as FORWARD and RIGHT take an input, so why not BOX? It can, once the definition is suitably changed. To do this, give the command

    EDIT "BOX

and the definition of BOX will reappear. Remember that any drawing which was visible before the EDIT command will vanish, temporarily. [The drawing won't reappear immediately, either, when you finish editing. Instead, IBM PC LOGO assumes (a bit unreasonably) that you'll be using the whole screen for text and won't be wanting the drawing back straight away. Fortunately, any drawing command will make the drawing reappear.] Use the editing functions to change the definition to look like this:

    TO BOX :SIDE
    REPEAT 4 [FD :SIDE RT 90]
    END

The first line, called the title line, has been changed by the addition of ':SIDE'. This informs the LOGO system, when you finish the editing, that BOX will in future take one input which, for the purposes of the definition, will be a variable called by the name SIDE. This variable only exists while BOX is being run, and it temporarily supersedes any previously existing variable called SIDE. Therefore the last of the commands

```
MAKE "SIDE 100
BOX 50
PRINT :SIDE
```

will print 100, because the command BOX has finished by the time the PRINT command is given.

A procedure can have as many inputs as you like, though they must all appear on the title line. Once into the editor, you are free to change the title line as you like, provided that there is a valid title line when you finish the editing.

To reinforce the point about inputs, look at these two procedures:

```
TO JUNK1 :N
JUNK2
END

TO JUNK2
PRINT :N
END
```

(It is legal and commonplace to define two or more procedures in one piece of editing. That is the only real significance of END, to mark where one definition ends and where another should start. You can leave out the last END, if you're really lazy — LOGO will insert it for you.) With these,

```
MAKE "N 100
JUNK1 50
```

will result in the number 50 being printed. Although it is JUNK2 that is responsible for a number being printed, JUNK1 is still running when JUNK2 gets obeyed (because the command JUNK2 is part of the definition of JUNK1), so the variable called N whose value is printed is really the input to JUNK1.

A 'box' does not have to mean a square, it can mean anything polygonal. Here is BOX modified to take two inputs, the first of which is to be the side length and the second is to be the number of sides:

```
TO BOX :SIDE :N
REPEAT :N [FD :SIDE RT 360/:N]
END
```

Now the command

```
BOX 50
```

will result in an error message saying that there are not enough inputs for BOX. The command

```
BOX 50 6
```

will draw a hexagon, and

```
MAKE "N 3
REPEAT 18 [BOX :N 6 RT 10 MAKE "N :N+3]
```

will draw Figure 3.3. The example used in this chapter so far, drawing a box, may not look like a particularly good advertisement for procedures as labour-saving devices. The next sub-section should help to dispel doubts.

Digression: As promised, a comment about TO. If you type the title line of a procedure in response to the normal ? prompt, instead of using EDIT, then LOGO will expect you to enter the procedure line by line. The prompt becomes >. To end your entering

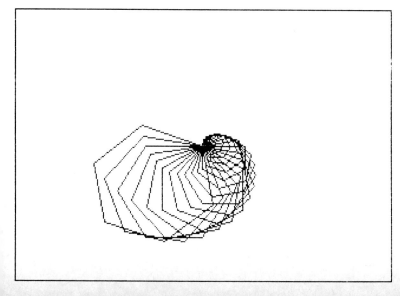

Figure 3.3

of a procedure, use END on a line by itself. You can't backtrack to revise earlier lines — only EDIT can help you there.

3.3 CRUDE ANIMATION — A STUDY

It is possible, in IBM PC LOGO, to achieve a crude form of animation. In some versions of LOGO it is not really possible, and in others it is very much easier. The difference is mainly caused by differences in computer hardware rather than software.

At this point, the value of LOGO as a tool for experimenting starts to appear — for there are a variety of ways to set about animating something. Suppose that the objective is to animate a small square to make it appear to move around the screen. There are at least two ways this might be done:

1. a) draw the box on the screen,
    b) move the turtle a little, with the pen up,
    c) clear the screen,
    d) repeat steps (a) to (c) many times.

2. a) draw the box on the screen,
    b) erase the box by redrawing it in the background colour, perhaps after a short pause,
    c) move the turtle a little, with the pen up,
    d) repeat steps (a) to (c) many times.

At first sight there is not much to choose between these as basic methods. It would be nice if the basic method could be extended, for instance

- to allow acceleration or deceleration of the shape,
- to allow motion along curves,
- to allow size changes so that the shape appears to be getting nearer or further away.

The rest of this sub-section will be devoted to showing one typical route for the investigation and development of one of these methods, namely method 2. The question of whether method 1 has any relative advantages or disadvantages will be left as an exercise.

Assume that the background colour is 0, the pen is down and the pen colour is unknown. Then step (a) is

```
SETPC 3 BOX 10 4
```

The initial SETPC (that's 'set the pen colour', remember?) ensures that the turtle will draw the box, in colour 3. Step (b) is just

```
SETPC 0 BOX 10 4
```

Forget about the business of a delay before erasing, for the moment at least. Step (c) is just

```
PU FD 10 PD
```

This assumes that 'a little' means 10 units. Remember that PU is short for PENUP and PD is short for PENDOWN. All these can be combined in one procedure called ANIMATE:

```
TO ANIMATE
SETPC 3 BOX 10 4
SETPC 0 BOX 10 4
PU FD 10 PD
END
```

Now tidy up the screen and then try it, by

```
CS
REPEAT 50 [ANIMATE]
```

The result is remarkably disappointing. It is not at all fast, and the turtle leaping about all over the drawing spoils any impression of motion by the box itself. This does not mean that animation is impossible. In such a situation, there are two things you should do. The first is to remind yourself that in 90% of cases it will turn out that there is more to the problem than appears at first glance. The second is to analyse why the result is disappointing. Writing down what the snags are helps a lot; then, when other difficulties appear later on, your notes will help you to avoid falling into the same old traps. In this case, perhaps the two difficulties — slowness and the mad dancing of the turtle — are related. It may be that the time spent by LOGO in drawing the turtle at the end of each FD and RT command is why it is so slow. The cure is to dispense with the turtle somehow. Is there a way of doing this? Yes, the command HT (short for HIDETURTLE) instructs the LOGO system not to bother showing the turtle. Try it:

```
CS
HT REPEAT 50 [ANIMATE]
```

It is better, but still poor. There are two 'motions' visible — the turtle round the square in the BOX command, and the jerky motion of the square. The second might be made less jerky by reducing the turtle motion between one square and the next, by changing the FD 10 in the last line of ANIMATE to FD 5 or thereabouts. Doing this helps the situation a little, but also makes it clear that the motion of the turtle around the square in BOX is the main snag.

Getting round this looks impossible. There is no IBM PC LOGO command to make the turtle draw faster. One possibility is to make the box even smaller — say 5 units on a side — but it is rather weak-willed to have to accept that it is only possible to animate tiny shapes. Therefore the question comes down to this: is there any other way to draw a square, a way that does not use FD? Presumably BK is just as inadequate for the task as FD, although it is worth a try. The answer is yes, there are the Cartesian commands. You may have noticed that they are fast, though that is only an impression at this stage. However, how can BOX be modified to use Cartesian commands? Drawing a hexagon, for example, must be difficult because the co-ordinates will never be straightforward integers.

A useful principle to call on at this point is

If you cannot crack the problem, avoid it.

The command BOX is too general for this investigation. A command that draws a small square is all that is required. The way forward is to edit ANIMATE to replace the BOX commands by (say) SQUARE and to define SQUARE suitably using Cartesian commands. SQUARE can be defined in the same editing session as changing ANIMATE, by moving the cursor past the end of the definition of ANIMATE and typing in the definition of SQUARE, or it can be defined separately:

```
TO ANIMATE
SETPC 3 SQUARE
SETPC 0 SQUARE
PU FD 10 PD
END

TO SQUARE
SETX XCOR + 10
SETY YCOR + 10
SETX XCOR − 10
SETY YCOR − 10
END
```

Each of the four lines in SQUARE draws one side of the square. The square it draws has its sides parallel to the sides of the screen whatever the heading of the turtle, but that is not a particular handicap. In fact, it could be an advantage; in the earlier version the motion of the square was always parallel to a side of the square. If you try this version of ANIMATE you should find that it is somewhat better. In IBM PC LOGO the Cartesian commands are a bit faster than FD and BK, even with the turtle hidden.

At last the basic idea, method 2, looks workable. Having established this, it is time to think about embellishments. Look once more at the definition of ANIMATE. Having cut out the use of FD in drawing the square, it might well be advantageous to cut out the use of FD there too. Replacing it by a SETX command is too restrictive, but a SETPOS command should do. The amount by which to change the X and Y co-ordinates could be inputs to ANIMATE:

```
TO ANIMATE :X :Y
SETPC 3 SQUARE
SETPC 0 SQUARE
PU SETPOS LIST XCOR + :X YCOR + :Y PD
END
```

Try various values for the inputs. Beware of this, however:

```
CS
HT REPEAT 50 [ANIMATE 10 − 10]
```

If, as here, you have accidentally put a space after the minus sign, LOGO will tell you that ANIMATE needs more inputs, because it takes the ANIMATE command to be ANIMATE (10−10) rather than ANIMATE 10 (−10). The way to avoid this trap, if your typing isn't very reliable, is to use parentheses to make the meaning clear.

ANIMATE can be further improved. At present it does only one movement of the square. Suppose that a final line is added:

```
TO ANIMATE :X :Y
SETPC 3 SQUARE
SETPC 0 SQUARE
PU SETPOS LIST XCOR + :X YCOR + :Y PD
ANIMATE :X :Y
END
```

This is legal because, at the time ANIMATE is run, the LOGO system knows how to obey the ANIMATE command in the last line! This idea of a procedure invoking itself, whether in the last line or elsewhere, is called recursion. It is a very powerful technique, and it will be used a lot later in this book. The new version of ANIMATE does one movement of the square, then invokes ANIMATE. So, what it does is to move the square once, then ... move the square once, then ... move the square once, then ... etc. Before you try it you had better make sure that you know how to stop it. In IBM PC LOGO, the way is to type CTRL-Break. This always stops whatever is happening and gets you back to the prompt. (Note for teachers: 'Break' for 'break off'? Whichever mnemonic you choose, use it. There is no virtue in trying to use computer jargon such as 'CTRL-Break causes an execution interrupt'.) With recursion, all that is needed to start the animation is

```
CS
ANIMATE 10 2
```

for example. The REPEAT command is unnecessary. If it is used, only the first repetition will happen. Typing CTRL-Break will stop everything, including the REPEAT.

Another embellishment is the 'zoom lines' effect common in early Walt Disney cartoons. An easy way to achieve it is to have several (say three) squares always visible. Whenever one is added to the screen, the idea is not to delete it but to delete the fourth square back instead. Here is one way to do this:

```
TO ANIMATE :X :Y
SETPC 3 SQUARE
PU SETPOS LIST XCOR − 3*:X YCOR − 3*:Y PD
SETPC 0 SQUARE
PU SETPOS LIST XCOR + 4*:X YCOR + 4*:Y PD
END
```

The first SETPOS in this leaps the turtle from the latest square, back past the previous two to the starting position of the third last square. That square is deleted. The second SETPOS leaps the turtle past the newly added square to the starting position for the next ANIMATE. The whole effect is much more pleasing, even if very crude as an example of computer animation.

There is one further possibility to explore, at least in IBM PC LOGO. You can change the shape of the turtle! There are 256 choices, and 128 of them can be modified by you. The choices are identified by the numbers 1 to 255 and the final choice is the default shape, TURTLE. The command to give the turtle one of these shapes is SETSHAPE — for instance,

```
SETSHAPE 207
```

or

```
SETSHAPE "TURTLE
```

Shapes 1 to 127 correspond to the characters found on the keyboard. Shapes 128 to 255 are meaningful, but you can overwrite them by using SNAP:

SNAP 153

would make shape 153 a copy of what was in the 9×9 box around the turtle at that moment. SNAP copies that little bit of drawing to LOGO's internal table of shapes. It doesn't become the turtle's shape until you then select it by a SETSHAPE.

You can therefore make a miniscule drawing, then hide the turtle so that SNAP doesn't pick up part of the turtle's shape too. Use SNAP to copy it to one of the changeable shapes. The use SETSHAPE to make this the turtle's current shape. By this means, you can 'animate' very small drawings. One advantage is that, by using a command STAMP, you can stamp the turtle's current image onto the drawing. One disadvantage is that only the default turtle shape visibly responds to turning commands such as LEFT or RIGHT. All other shapes do not alter their orientation visibly, though LEFT and RIGHT do still work.

EXERCISES

1. How can acceleration and/or deceleration of the square be simulated?
2. Is it practicable to make the square grow or shrink as it moves? Can motion toward or away from you be simulated by this?
3. Is it practicable to make the square change orientation as it moves? (It might help you to remember that LOGO provides procedures for SIN and COS.)
4. Does moving along a non-linear path spoil the animation effect? One way to start on this would be to consider changing the inputs to the recursive ANIMATE command within the definition of ANIMATE, by a small fixed amount each time it invokes itself.
5. What are the relative merits of using basic method 1 for animation instead?

3.4 THOUGHTS ABOUT WORKING WITH PROCEDURES

Look again at Figure 3.1, which showed some houses, trees and birds. There are various ways to set about the task of making such a drawing. Each way has its pros and cons. The next two sub-sections will consider fundamentally different approaches.

3.4.1 A bottom up approach

One way to start is to get a sheet of graph paper and plot roughly where everything is to go. Going to the lengths of actually drawing the whole scene on paper is too much like real work; the point is to make sure that none of the houses and none of the birds overlap any other. To do this it is necessary to decide on the size of a house and on the size of a bird (are different sizes of bird to be allowed?). Thereafter you can start on defining the procedures which will be used for a house. A house in this scene will have a body (the main rectangular part), a roof, a door and a window. Suppose the body is to be 20 units across and 10 units high. The door ought to be near one side (the left, say) and perhaps 4 wide and 7 high. The window will be perhaps 5 square. Assume that the turtle is to start at the lower left corner of the body and with a heading of 0 degrees. Some playing might get you to this definition, or something similar:

```
TO HOUSE
REPEAT 2 [FD 10 RT 90 FD 20 RT 90]
RT 90 FD 4 LT 90
REPEAT 2 [FD 7 RT 90 FD 4 RT 90]
LT 90 FD 4 RT 90
RT 90 FD 12 LT 90 PU FD 3 PD
REPEAT 4 [FD 5 RT 90]
PU BK 3 PD LT 90 FD 12 RT 90
FD 10 RT 45 FD 5.66
RT 45 FD 12 RT 45 FD 5.66 RT 135
FD 20 RT 90 BK 10
END
```

This is almost incomprehensible. It is easier to break it up into suitable chunks, like this:

```
TO BODY
REPEAT 2 [FD 10 RT 90 FD 20 RT 90]
END
```

```
TO DOOR
RT 90 FD 4 LT 90
REPEAT 2 [FD 7 RT 90 FD 4 RT 90]
LT 90 FD 4 RT 90
END
```

```
TO WINDOW
RT 90 FD 12 LT 90 PU FD 3 PD
REPEAT 4 [FD 5 RT 90]
PU BK 3 PD LT 90 FD 12 RT 90
END
```

```
TO ROOF
FD 10 RT 45 FD 5.66
RT 45 FD 12 RT 45 FD 5.66 RT 135
```

```
FD 20 RT 90 BK 10
END


TO HOUSE
BODY DOOR WINDOW ROOF
END
```

This is slightly easier, although exactly the same basic commands are used and in the same order. Each of the procedures assumes the same starting place for the turtle, and requires some care to define considering the simplicity of the resulting drawing of a house. Are you convinced that the definitions are correct? Did you check them or did you sensibly baulk at that mundane task? On the other hand there is this to be said; each of the ingredients is state-transparent and so the definition of HOUSE in terms of BODY, DOOR, WINDOW and ROOF is child's play. This sort of approach, where the ingredients are tackled separately, and almost in isolation, and are combined only at the last stage, is widely known as bottom up. Progress of the work is from the bottom (or specific) level up towards the top (or general) level.

3.4.2 A top down approach

Instead of diving straight into the fine detail you could start with generalities. For example, a house in this scene consists of a body, a door, a roof and a window and so the definition of HOUSE can be

```
TO HOUSE
BODY DOOR ROOF WINDOW
END
```

and it remains to define these four ingredients. The body, door and window are all rectangles even though the window is a special case, viz. a square. Thus BODY can be defined as

```
TO BODY
RECTANGLE 10 20
END
```

provided that RECTANGLE's first input is going to be its height and its second is going to be the width. In HOUSE, the BODY is followed by the DOOR. This could be expressed as

```
TO DOOR
MOVE.FROM.BODY.TO.DOOR
RECTANGLE 7 4
END
```

where MOVE.FROM.BODY.TO.DOOR does what its name suggests. Note that it is acceptable to have full stops within a name, and it makes a compound name more readable. Similarly,

```
TO WINDOW
MOVE.FROM.DOOR.TO.WINDOW
RECTANGLE 5 5
END
```

```
TO ROOF
MOVE.FROM.WINDOW.TO.ROOF
RT 45 FD 5.66 RT 45 FD 12 RT 45 FD 5.66
MOVE.FROM.ROOF.TO.BODY
END
```

There are still five undefined procedures, but assumptions have already been made about each of them. For instance, in MOVE. FROM.DOOR.TO.WINDOW the turtle starts from where it finished after DOOR, and must end at the starting place for drawing the rectangular outline of the window. (Note for pedants: all those MOVE.FROM.somewhere.TO.somewhere could indeed have been incorporated explicitly in the definition of HOUSE, for example

```
TO HOUSE
BODY MOVE.FROM.BODY.TO.DOOR
DOOR MOVE.FROM.DOOR.TO.WINDOW
WINDOW MOVE.FROM.WINDOW.TO.ROOF
ROOF MOVE.FROM.ROOF.TO.BODY
END
```

and that makes it slightly easier to remember the necessary assumptions. But it requires more forethought at the start and it does not save any work. An exhaustive discussion would be exhausting.)

You can define the extra procedures for yourself. This sort of approach goes by the name of top down; progress is from the top (or general) level towards the bottom (or specific) level.

3.4.3 Comparing the two approaches

The 'bottom up' approach often leads to defining unduly elaborate procedures, such as those on page 62. Three of these four contain a LOGO command to draw some size of rectangle, and it would have been neater to define a general rectangle procedure to use in those three. Doing that is not much less work, but at least the rectangle procedure would thereafter exist as a general tool for other uses as well. For example, you could decide, in due course, that the house is really in need of a chimney. It would be much easier to experiment with its size if there were a general rectangle procedure available.

Another point against working 'bottom up' is that your procedures are harder to read and harder to extend later on. The decisions made while defining the procedures are not even hinted at by anything visible within them, they are only recorded elsewhere — on paper at best, more commonly solely in your head. On the other hand working 'bottom up' is 'natural' and easy to start with. When visualising a drawing, the semantically complete components such as 'door' and 'window' are what catches the attention rather than incomplete ingredients such as 'side of door' and 'top of roof'. But, when you start defining the sequence of LOGO commands, it is the details such as angles and lengths which are the focus of attention and this makes 'bottom up' working the 'natural' way.

Working 'top down' is much cleaner once you are used to it. Unfortunately it does take a while to get used to. However, because you begin by representing general chunks of the drawing by procedure names before defining the procedures themselves, it is natural to choose the names so as to remind you of the decisions, such as MOVE.FROM.BODY.TO.DOOR. When you return later to extend or change the drawing, it is easier to pick up the threads. It is also easier to do the actual modifications. Take an example: suppose that HOUSE is not the right size for some particular purpose. You resolve to give HOUSE an input which is a scale factor, so that HOUSE 1.5 is half as big again as HOUSE 1. In both the 'top down' and 'bottom up' cases the new HOUSE procedure might be

```
TO HOUSE :SCALE
BODY DOOR WINDOW ROOF
END
```

(Note that it is unnecessary to give BODY, etc., an input, though it is up to you. The temporary variable SCALE will exist while they are being run, so the definition of these procedures can use it.) In the 'bottom up' versions of BODY, etc., you need to append the LOGO phrase '* :SCALE' to every FD and BK command — a total of sixteen times. In the 'top down' case you need only do this twelve times — twice inside the definition of rectangle, three times inside ROOF, once in MOVE.FROM.BODY.TO.DOOR and twice each in the other MOVE... procedures.

Contrary to popular programming folklore, the 'top down' approach is not appreciably easier to work with, although it is easier to read and understand once the whole thing works. There is just as much scope for mis-remembering decisions made at an earlier stage of the enterprise, or perhaps even more. A very common occurrence is to forget to define some procedure at all first time round, although this is not hazardous but merely frustrating in LOGO. Getting used to 'top down' working calls for some effort, particularly in learning to plan and analyse first then act later. This does not mean that you have to map out the entire campaign beforehand; it merely means learning to remind yourself to take a second look at what you are visualising, and learning to generalise.

Very few people, even sampled from professional programmers, stick purely to one approach or the other. The vast majority use a hybrid of the two and the ease and flexibility of the solution depends on the particular mix. As a general principle, if one is needed,

top down   is the one to choose if you are tackling something unknown or if you expect to want to generalise your work later on;

bottom up is for when you are on familiar ground.

3.4.4 Afterthought
Adding the birds is the major hurdle on the way to finishing Figure 3.1. Each is made of two arcs, and arcs were the topic in Section 2.7.4. It is worthwhile to define procedures for arcs; for instance

```
TO ARCRIGHT :RADIUS :ANGLE
REPEAT :ANGLE [FD :RADIUS * 0.01745
      RT 1]
END
```

Notice that the angle has to be positive (LOGO will object if it is negative) but the radius can be any number. An ARCLEFT procedure is useful even though ARCRIGHT with a negative radius will do the trick.

Drawing a bird by joining two arcs is still not entirely trivial — try it — but it is fairly easy to experiment with, once you have a tool such as ARCRIGHT at your command. You can reasonably expect to get it wrong two or three times before getting it right, so don't kick yourself the first time! The rules are

a) make procedures which are tools, when you can, and
b) in general, generalise.

3.5 ANOTHER STUDY — A TICKING CLOCK
The aim of this is to draw a clock face, and make it keep to time. There are three separate chunks clearly involved: drawing the clock

face, drawing the hands and making the clock work. Figure 3.4 shows a simple clock face, drawn by

```
TO MARK
PU FD 50 PD FD 10 PU BK 60 PD
END

CS
REPEAT 12 [MARK RT 30]
```

The procedure MARK is state-transparent, and it is assumed that the turtle starts and ends at the centre of the clock face. A better face might have the marks for 12, 3, 6 and 9 o'clock slightly longer than the rest. A further refinement would be to add Roman numerals — much easier to draw than arabic numerals — but it is best to start with something very simple.

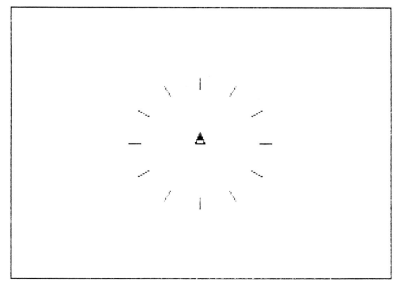

Figure 3.4

The other two chunks are not so easy. It is tempting to launch into the task of drawing the hands and give no thought to the other one. Doing so will probably get you into a mess, because making the clock tick involves redrawing the hands once per minute. Consider that first, therefore. A command such as

```
REPEAT 1000 [TICK]
```

would be all that is needed, if TICK advances the hands by a minute and then takes a minute to finish. The clock will wind down after 1000 minutes, but if you seriously want to leave your computer switched on and doing nothing else for much longer than 16 hours you can simply increase the number of repetitions. Thus the problem is only how to define TICK. Look at the phrase 'advances the hands'. Where are they advanced from, and where to? This suggests having two variables, one concerned with the minute hand and one with the hour hand. Call them MINUTE and HOUR. The value of MINUTE will be the heading of the minute hand; it would have been equally reasonable to elect that the values should be the number of minutes since the clock was started. TICK must do this at least:

- erase the minute hand,
- erase the hour hand,
- update the MINUTE and HOUR variables,
- draw the minute hand in its new place,
- draw the hour hand in its new place

The minute hand must not be long enough to reach the hour marks on the face or it will erase them as it moves; let it be 40 units long, and let the hour hand be 20 units long. Then the erasing of the minute hand can be done by

```
SETPC 0
SETH :MINUTE FD 40 BK 40
```

The hour hand is erased in the same way. The next task is updating MINUTE and HOUR. As there are 60 minutes in an hour, and 360 degrees to be swept by the minute hand, the command is

```
MAKE "MINUTE :MINUTE + 6
```

and, for the hour hand,

```
MAKE "HOUR :HOUR + 0.5
```

Here is a prototype for TICK:

```
TO TICK
SETPC 0
SETH :MINUTE FD 40 BK 40
SETH :HOUR FD 20 BK 20
MAKE "MINUTE :MINUTE + 6
MAKE "HOUR :HOUR + 0.5
SETPC 3
SETH :MINUTE FD 40 BK 40
```

```
SETH :HOUR FD 20 BK 20
END
```

Unfortunately it only takes moments rather than a full minute, when it is run. What is needed is a delaying command, something that does nothing but takes a while. Tests will show you that

```
REPEAT 61000 [ ]
```

is such a command (even doing nothing takes a little time!), and that 61000 is approximately the right number if you add the command as the last line of TICK. You will need to adjust it slightly to make the clock accurate. There is, alternatively, a command WAIT, which expects a positive integer as its input. It waits for (about) that many 1/18ths of a second, so

```
WAIT 1080
```

should be about right. However, using REPEAT gives you a finer degree of control.

Digression for computer junkies: Running the REPEAT command above doesn't use up lots of workspace, so it shouldn't cause any of those discordant, one-second pauses that you will occasionally find happening during prolonged drawing work. However, the repeated redrawing of the clock hands does use workspace, so at some point the system will pause to tidy up internally — this is called 'garbage collecting', and is the cause of the hiccups. You need to leave the clock running long enough to be sure to take account of this if you are going to be really fussy about making it accurate.

One oddity of TICK is that the first time it is used, it erases non-existent hands, but this does not matter. It only remains to put all the ingredients together. Remember to set the values of MINUTE and HOUR before starting the clock.

EXERCISE
6. Is it practicable to include a second hand?
7. Define a procedure which takes two numbers as input, representing the time of day, and draws the clock and starts it.
8. Create a clock that runs backwards, or only has six hours on its face. Find out if other people can get used to using such a clock.

3.6 MORE ABOUT PROCEDURES
Inputs to a procedure, as you should by now appreciate, behave just

like ordinary variables, except that they supersede any other variable of the same name while the procedure is actually running. The jargon for this is that ordinary variables are called *global* variables, whereas inputs to a procedure are called *local* because they are only meaningful to that procedure and to any it calls. The fact that inputs leave any global variable of the same name undisturbed is often very useful. It saves you having to invent new unique names. On occasion, however, you will find a need for such a means of temporary 'storage' but don't want to have a superfluous input just for the sake of this feature. For instance, suppose you want to make all your drawing procedures state-transparent. A simple way to do this is to record the turtle's position and heading at the start, then do the drawing, then lift the pen and return the turtle to its initial state as recorded:

```
TO DRAWING.A
MAKE "START.POS POS
MAKE "START.HEADING HEADING
{do some drawing}
PU SETPOS :START.POS
SETH :START.HEADING
PD
END
```

The trouble with this is that you might want to use a similar procedure, say DRAWING.B, inside the procedure DRAWING.A. When the turtle's state is recorded at the start of DRAWING.B, it will change the variables START.POS and START.HEADING so that at the end of DRAWING.A the turtle gets returned (wrongly) to where it was at the start of DRAWING.B. If START.POS and START.HEADING were inputs to DRAWING.A and DRAWING.B then the problem wouldn't arise. On the other hand, you would need to specify some values, even if only some random rubbish, for the inputs when you called these procedures.

To get round this, IBM PC LOGO provides the procedure LOCAL which normally takes one input, a name (with a quote mark before it). It creates a local variable having that name, which will exist only as long as the procedure is running and which will temporarily supersede any other variable of the same name. This gets round the problem:

```
TO DRAWING.A
LOCAL "START.POS
LOCAL "START.HEADING
END
```

```
TO DRAWING.B
LOCAL "START.POS
LOCAL "START.HEADING
END
```

The START.POS and START.HEADING used in DRAWING.B will not interfere with those in DRAWING.A, they will merely supersede them while DRAWING.B is running. As you will discover, such local variables are extremely useful.

All the examples in this chapter so far have been concerned with drawing. Some have used inputs, others have not. None have output anything. It is reasonable to want to define procedures that output, and LOGO, being a very reasonable language, provides a means of doing so. In IBM PC LOGO there is a procedure OUTPUT, which takes one input. Its effect is to end the procedure in which it appears, and make it output whatever OUTPUT's input was. Here is an example:

```
TO SQUARE :N
OUTPUT :N * :N
END
```

The command

```
PRINT SQUARE 7
```

will print 49, because the OUTPUT procedure has input 49, and causes SQUARE to end and output 49. Note that SQUARE does not resume (so to speak) — if SQUARE were instead

```
TO SQUARE :N
OUTPUT :N * :N
PRINT "CLOWN
END
```

then PRINT SQUARE 7 would still only print 49, because obeying the OUTPUT is taken by LOGO to be a sign to stop obeying the definition of SQUARE.

Digression: Suppose that were not so? Then you could put two OUTPUTs in a procedure definition, and LOGO would get very confusing. If you have ever fancied trying your hand at specifying a new programming language, this suggests an intriguing possibility on which to base something...

Another common factor of all the examples so far is that all the commands in a procedure definition are obeyed, none depend on any kind of circumstance. Being able to do one thing if some condition prevails and another thing if not, is what makes computers so useful. A facetious but comprehensible example, which never-theless calls for a sophisticated computer system and a lot of pro-gramming work, is

> if . . . . . it is Friday
> and . . . it is near the end of the day,
> then . . remind the users that the computer closes down at
>   6 p.m.

Note that there is an implied 'else . . . do not remind them' here. This example would require that the computer can find out the date and time, that it has a means (expressed in the form of a program) of judging what 'near the end of the day' means, and that it has a means of reminding users. Of course, nobody would be single-minded enough to do all the programming work needed to make this example possible, unless the work could also be put to many other such uses.

    In LOGO, and in most programming languages, the kind of conditions which it is possible to make some action or command depend upon are very simple. What complicates the matter is that it is very handy to be able to compound conditions, such as 'this condition and that condition' or 'this or that'. Since these are themselves conditions it must also be possible to have conditions such as 'this condition and (that condition or another condition)' and so on.

    In IBM PC LOGO conditional commands look like this:

> IF :N > 0 [MAKE "Z :N]

This says that 'if the value of N is greater than 0 then give Z the value of N'.

> IF :N = 0 [PRINT "HELP] [MAKE "N :N − 1]

This is 'if the value of N is 0 then print the word HELP, else make N one less than its present value'.

    In general such commands must be of the form

> IF condition [commands to do if it's TRUE]

or

> IF condition [commands to do if TRUE] [commands if FALSE]

although there is one further way of expressing the idea which will be mentioned shortly.

There are numerous possibilities for the condition in these commands. As the examples above suggest, it can be

Something > AnotherThing
Something = AnotherThing
Something < AnotherThing

where the 'Somethings' and 'AnotherThings' are numbers. In the case of 'Something = AnotherThing' they can also be words, or even lists — examples will appear in Chapter 4. In fact, in LOGO a condition is really just the word TRUE or the word FALSE or any expression that outputs TRUE or FALSE; each of the above conditions does that, so

PRINT 3 > 4

prints FALSE, and

PRINT 7 * 7 > 30

prints TRUE.

There are other possibilities for conditions. They can be any procedure which outputs the word TRUE or the word FALSE. For instance, suppose a number is to be deemed huge if it is bigger than 1000. The procedure

```
TO HUGE :NUMBER
IF :NUMBER > 1000 [OUTPUT "TRUE] [OUTPUT
      "FALSE]
END
```

can be used as a condition:

IF HUGE :X [PRINT "COLOSSAL!]

Conditions can be compounded by using the procedures AND and OR. Each of these normally takes who inputs, which must be TRUE or FALSE, and outputs one of TRUE or FALSE, for example

PRINT AND 4 > 2 71 < 70

prints FALSE because not all are true.

However, it is sometimes necessary to check whether all, or perhaps any, of a fair number of conditions are true. There is, accordingly, a convenient way of doing this in LOGO. The rule is that AND and OR can actually have any number of inputs provided that the whole collective condition is enclosed in parentheses, for example

```
IF (AND XCOR > 135 YCOR > 115 XCOR <
     -135 YCOR < -115) [PRINT "OOPS!]
```

If parentheses are not used then there must be exactly two inputs for AND or OR. The same kind of rule happens to apply to the procedure PRINT, and to a very few other procedures that will appear in Chapter 4.

There are some procedures built into IBM PC LOGO for checking certain kinds of condition. The procedure NUMBERP takes one input, and outputs TRUE only if the input is a number (rather than, say, a word). The procedure WORDP outputs TRUE only if its input is a word. The procedure NAMEP expects a word as its input, and outputs TRUE only if there is a variable by that name. [In other LOGO books you will find this expressed another way, namely that NAMEP only outputs TRUE if the variable has a value. The notion implied by this is that every possible variable exists, but most have no value! (Note for teachers: beware of such a notion. There are an immense number of possible variables, and an IBM PC is physically quite small ... so where are they?)] The procedure NOT is very useful. Its input must be the word TRUE or the word FALSE — whichever it is, NOT outputs the other one.

EXERCISES

Suppose you have typed in the commands

```
MAKE "ALPHA 6
MAKE "BETA 9
MAKE "GAMMA -12
```

9. What does this do?

```
IF NOT :ALPHA < 10 [PRINT "RATS]
```

10. What does this do?

```
IF ( OR :ALPHA < 5 :BETA < 5 :GAMMA <
     5 ) [PRINT "OK] [PRINT "HAGGIS]
```

11. What does this do?

```
PRINT AND :ALPHA > :BETA 0 > :GAMMA
```

12. What does this do?

   PRINT :GAMMA / :ALPHA + :BETA = 7

13. What does this do?

   IF THING "GAMMA [PRINT "EXISTS] [PRINT
        "NON-EXISTENT]

3.6.1 An example — bouncing the turtle

The aim of the experiment in this sub-section is to make the turtle appear to bounce back from the edges of the screen as it moves around (see Figure 3.5). One way to start is to figure out how to make the turtle seem to move continuously. This need be nothing more sophisticated than repeating the command FD 5 (the number 5 being just a typical small number). What happens near the edge?

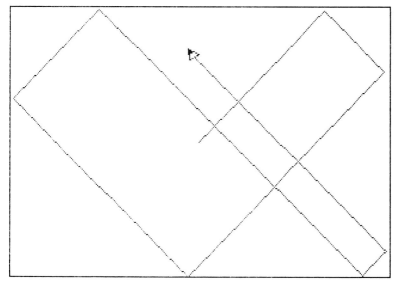

Figure 3.5

Clearly, the turtle's heading has to change, but by what? Take a specimen case: the turtle is moving along a heading of 73 degrees and comes to the right-hand side. A nice effect would be if the turtle's heading changed to −73 degrees. Thinking about some more specimen cases suggests the following rules

• if the turtle 'hits' either side its heading H should change to −H,

- if the turtle 'hits' the top or bottom, its heading H should change to (180−H).

The remaining problem is how to find out when the turtle is nearing a side. The easy way is to check its co-ordinates. Rather than redirecting the turtle exactly when it hits the edge, do the simple thing and redirect it if it is close to the edge, for example if XCOR > 155. Testing whether the turtle is close to an edge ought to be done at every move, since any move might be the one which takes it near an edge. Here is a procedure STEP to make one 5-unit turtle step; the turtle motion will be done by repeating STEP:

```
TO STEP
IF OR XCOR > 155 XCOR < −155 [SETH
      ( − HEADING )]
IF OR YCOR > 120 YCOR < −120 [SETH
      ( 180 − HEADING )]
FD 5
END
```

Before trying this, think a minute. There seems to be a possibility not accounted for — what if the turtle comes to two edges simultaneously, when it approaches a corner of the screen? As it happens this is a red herring — the definition of STEP is adequate for this circumstance too (or is that wrong?).

Try STEP, but give the turtle an unusual heading first, for example

```
CS
SETH 37
REPEAT 500 [STEP]
```

You can modify STEP by adding the command ṠTEP to the end of the definition. Then the REPEAT command can be replaced by the command STEP alone, because it will repeat itself.

One of STEP's deficiencies is that the screen fills up with diagonal lines pretty swiftly and it becomes hard to see the bouncing effect. A cure is to change things so that the turtle appears to be towing a piece of string — as the turtle moves, the line 50 units back along its path must be erased. Since the task of figuring out where the turtle was some distance back along a path which might have corners in it looks hard, do it another way. Instead, imagine that there are two turtles moving independently, with one drawing and one erasing. Because there is only one turtle in IBM PC LOGO, it must leap about a lot to achieve this effect; the position and heading of each hypothetical turtle can be recorded by variables, and updated at each leap of the real turtle. You can work out the details for yourself. Do try it, because many of the mistakes you can make in this project give you different and very pleasing effects!

3.6.2 Another sort of conditional command

IBM PC LOGO has a useful alternative to IF .. [...] [...]. Instead of

```
TO VASTP :N
IF OR :N > 10000 :N < −10000 [OUTPUT
      "TRUE] [OUTPUT "FALSE]
END
```

you can redefine it as

```
TO VASTP :N
TEST OR :N > 10000 :N < −10000
IFTRUE [OUTPUT "TRUE]
IFFALSE [OUTPUT "FALSE]
END
```

The TEST command takes one input, TRUE or FALSE, and causes LOGO to note what it was. The IFTRUE command, IFT for short, causes a command inside the list to be obeyed only if the outcome of the previous TEST was TRUE. The IFFALSE command, IFF for short, works similarly.

Although TEST, IFTRUE and IFFALSE can make a procedure neater and more comprehensible, be careful with them. The TEST and the associated IFTRUE and/or IFFALSE must appear in the same procedure definition; you cannot have the IFTRUE or IFFALSE in a sub-procedure. Also, note that there is no point in having IFTRUE inside the list given with an IFFALSE or vice-versa.

3.7 MORE ABOUT RECURSION

Recursion, defining a procedure partly in terms of itself, is a very powerful technique and well worth mastering. It is not especially difficult to use and it can make many problems almost magically easy to solve. This section contains some examples and two or three simple rules of thumb for checking that you are getting it right.

Look at this:

```
TO JUNK
PRINT "HOHO
JUNK
```

END

It is recursive; if you run it HOHO will be repeatedly printed until you stop it. Make sure you know how to stop it, though if the worst comes to the worst you can always switch the machine off. In IBM PC LOGO the way to stop anything is to type CTRL-Break (remember, that means press the CTRL key and then, while still pressing that, press 'Break'). The motto suggested by tbe JUNK procedure is that

> Recursion can be an easy way to make something repeat indefinitely.

There are examples in earlier sections where this was or could have been applied, such as ANIMATE in Section 3.3 and TICK in Section 3.5.

Sometimes what a problem requires is repetition ending when some condition is satisfied, rather than repetition forever or for a known number of times. For instance, suppose that a problem requires that the turtle should move straight ahead until it reaches either side of the screen. The way to formalise what the turtle must do is

- If at either side of the screen then do no more.
- Otherwise FD 1 (or 5 or whatever is the chosen step size) and think again.

There is an IBM PC LOGO procedure called STOP which, like OUTPUT, causes the procedure being run to finish at that point. If some other procedure called it, that one then resumes. STOP allows you to turn the plan above into LOGO:

```
TO TRUNDLE
IF OR XCOR > 159 XCOR < −159 [STOP]
FD 1
TRUNDLE
END
```

To see how this works, imagine that the turtle is at X=157.5, Y=0 (say) and its heading is 90 so that it is only three units from hitting the right-hand edge. If TRUNDLE is run, then

> in line 1, the condition is not satisfied so, line 2: the turtle moves FD 1 (now X=158.5) line 3: TRUNDLE is obeyed
>
> . . .
>
> :
>
> : line 1: the condition is not satisfied, so

```
:   line 2: the turtle moves FD 1 (now X=159.5)
:   line 3: TRUNDLE is obeyed . . .
:   :
:   :   line 1: the condition holds, so STOP
:   :   causes this procedure to finish . . .
:   :
:   . . . and there is no more to do in this
:   TRUNDLE, so it ends . . .
:
```
so the command is complete.

The turtle is at X=159.5, Y=0. True, this is not quite the edge of the screen, but you cannot have everything. TRUNDLE at least gets the turtle to within a 1-unit-wide band at either side. To get it exactly to the edge there are only three possibilities:

a) Move it by 0.001 at a time. This is horribly slow.
b) Do some trigonometry. This is messy.
c) With no wrapping (after FENCE) try to send it past the edge. This causes an error, which stops everything and returns LOGO to waiting for your command.

None of these is entirely satisfactory; the unit-at-a-time way is a reasonable compromise. (Note for teachers: it would be possible to base a whole mathematics course on the art of reaching an acceptable compromise. LOGO would make a good vehicle for it.) The principle which TRUNDLE hints at is that

> Recursion can be an easy way to cause repetition subject to some conditions.

3.7.1 Filling areas with colour

A very satisfying variation on the line drawings normally associated with LOGO is to have the turtle fill in whole areas on the screen. There are many ways to do this. As is often the case, one way is relatively easy and many are ghastly. An easy way is to imagine that the turtle is repeatedly drawing a line between its current position and some anchor point. To phrase it another way, imagine the turtle is anchored by an elastic thread to some point. As the turtle moves, what the thread sweeps over is filled in.

The SETPOS command makes the turtle jump from one place to another, drawing a line in the current colour. Thus, to draw a line from its current place all it needs to do is to jump to the anchor point and then back to where it was. To turn this idea into LOGO, suppose that the X co-ordinate of the anchor point is stored as the value of a variable called ANCHORX, and the Y co-ordinate is

similarly stored. There will need to be two more variables to record
the turtle's proper position while it is at the anchor point: call them
REALX and REALY. Then the following procedure is a sort of
counterpoint to FD, which does what FD does but also fills in the
area between the drawn line and the anchor point:

```
TO FILL.FD :N
IF :N=0 [STOP]
MAKE "REALX XCOR
MAKE "REALY YCOR
SETPOS LIST :ANCHORX :ANCHORY
SETPOS LIST :REALX :REALY
FD 1
FILL.FD :N−1
END
```

It moves the turtle fairly slowly; hiding the turtle first (with HT)
speeds it up a bit. To make it easy to shift the anchor point around,
define

```
TO ANCHOR
MAKE "ANCHORX XCOR
MAKE "ANCHORY YCOR
END
```

It is possible to make this a little neater, by using the procedure
POS which outputs a list giving the turtle's co-ordinates. Since there
is no need here to take the list to bits, it is possible to redefine
ANCHOR as

```
TO ANCHOR
MAKE "ANCHORPOS POS
END
```

and to change FILL.FD to be

```
TO FILL.FD :N
IF :N=0 [STOP]
MAKE "REALPOS POS
SETPOS :ANCHORPOS
SETPOS :REALPOS
FD 1
FILL.FD :N−1
END
```

This is also slightly faster.

Whenever ANCHOR is used, the turtle's current location becomes the anchor point. Figure 3.6 used FILL.FD and ANCHOR — it looks better in colour!

FILL.FD works because SETPOS does not affect the turtle's heading, so when the second SETPOS is done the turtle is back to where it was when the procedure was started. Suppose that the IF command were left out. Then FILL.FD would invoke itself endlessly and the turtle would not stop moving until you typed CTRL-Break, if it were being allowed to wrap. Therefore, obviously,

> A recursive procedure which is not to run indefinitely must include some conditional command that may stop it. The conditional command must come before the recursive use of the procedure in the definition.

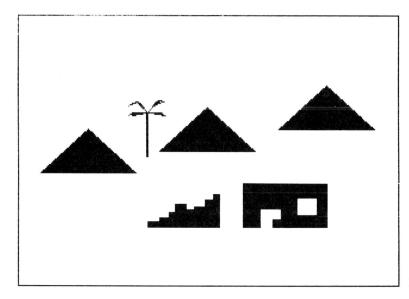

Figure 3.6

A basic safeguard is to check a recursive procedure by eye, and see what its inputs are used for. If the IF command were missing from FILL.FD, then the :N would not be used for anything other than part of the input to the final recursive use of FILL.FD, and that should at least arouse your suspicions.

A final word about filling areas with colour: IBM PC LOGO has a primitive named FILL, which takes no input and produces no output. It causes the area within which the turtle is standing to be flooded with the current pen colour. It is much faster than FILL.FD, but there are one or two drawbacks. 'Flooding an area' is exactly what it does — if there is some way for the flood to get out onto the rest of the screen, then the whole screen will be filled with the colour. FILL is also very fussy. If the turtle is not standing on background — for example, if it is standing at the end of a line it has just drawn — then FILL will do nothing.

3.7.2 Output by a recursive procedure

The overworked example used in 99% of all known programming books is the 'factorial' function, written

$$n!$$

and meaning the product of all the integers from 1 to n inclusive — so 3! is 6, and 4! is 24. Rather than spoil your expectations, here it is in LOGO — it is very concise:

```
TO FACTORIAL :N
IF :N=1 [OUTPUT 1] [OUTPUT :N *
      FACTORIAL :N−1]
END
```

This is based on the straightforward observation that if you know the product of the integers from 1 to :N−1 (which is FACTORIAL :N−1) then FACTORIAL :N is just :N times that. The observation transliterates readily into pseudo-LOGO as

```
FACTORIAL :N is :N * FACTORIAL :N−1
```

but this has no conditional command, so that recursion never stops. Recursion can only stop if at some point the procedure outputs the result of some expression which does not itself involve FACTORIAL. For example, you could always note that FACTORIAL 3 is 6, and begin the definition with

```
IF :N=3 [OUTPUT 6] . . .
```

but then you would find, perhaps by experience (like everyone else), that it did not work if N was 1 or 2.

EXERCISE
14. What if N is not an integer?

A much less well aired example is the finding of the cube root of a number. Although there is a cunning algorithm usable by someone who excels at mental arithmetic, it is somewhat elaborate and unnecessary when you have an obedient computer to do some brute calculations for you. The method to be applied here is the honourable and ancient mathematical one of inspired guesswork. Take an example: what is the cube root of 9? Clearly it lies between 1 and 9. Perhaps it is the average of 1 and 9, namely 5. No, 5 cubed is 125. Moreover, 1 cubed is 1, so it must lie between 1 and 5. Perhaps it is their average, 3? No, 3 cubed is 27, so it is between 1 and 3. Perhaps it is their average, 2? No, 2 cubed is only 8 so it must lie between 2 and 3 ... and so on. In theory this process never ends. However, LOGO cannot deal with more than so many significant digits in a number. When the calculation has reached that digit accuracy then as far as LOGO is concerned the average is equal to one of the numbers — and that is when to stop. It would be a lot of effort if you were going to do it on paper, but it is no skin off your nose if it is LOGO that does the work. To formalise the method, define a procedure that has three inputs, namely the number whose cube root is to be found, a low guess and a high guess. Its title will be

```
TO CUBE.ROOT :N :LOW :HIGH
```

The first step is to average the guesses:

```
MAKE "AV ( :LOW + :HIGH ) / 2
```

If this is at the limit of accuracy, output it:

```
IF OR :AV = :LOW :AV = :HIGH [OUTPUT
      :AV]
```

If it is not then, if it is too high look again between :LOW and :AV, otherwise look again between :AV and :HIGH, like this:

```
IF :AV * :AV * :AV > :N [OUTPUT
      CUBE.ROOT :N :LOW :AV] [OUTPUT
      CUBE.ROOT :N :AV :HIGH]
```

and that is all there is to it. If you are doubtful, try it and see. If it offends your eye to have to give three inputs then you can always beautify the whole affair this way:

```
TO CU.RT :N
OUTPUT CUBE.ROOT :N 1 :N
END
```

You should find this works surprisingly fast.

EXERCISES

15. Is it sensible to use the same method for fourth roots?
16. There is still a problem if the input to CU.RT is negative, or between 0 and 1. How can you fix it?
17. Why is the stopping test in CUBE.ROOT not :AV * :AV * :AV = :N ?
18. For keen mathematicians: define ARCSIN, the inverse of SIN.

3.8 DIAGRAMS DRAWN BY RECURSION

Many of the best mathematicians of all time have devoted a significant amount of their effort to studying figures drawn by essentially recursive methods. Although there are interesting theorems to be dug out, much of the motivation has been purely the beauty of the results. The power of LOGO makes the area readily accessible to your exploration.

To start with, consider the command FORWARD 90. The turtle, afterwards, is 90 units away but has the same heading. It is rather mundane for the turtle to get there along a straight line. Make it take a more devious route, such as that in Figure 3.7. A procedure to do this, for any input as well as 90, is

```
TO DOODLE :N
FD :N / 3
RT 90 FD :N / 3
```

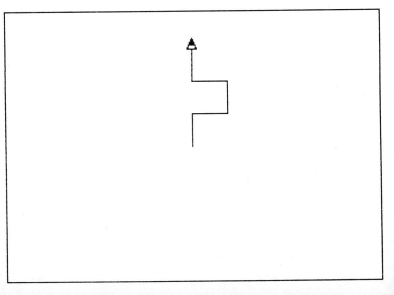

Figure 3.7

```
LT 90 FD :N / 3
LT 90 FD :N / 3
RT 90 FD :N / 3
END
```

This can be thought of as a 'more interesting' sort of FORWARD; it has the same overall effect on the turtle's state. Therefore, why not use it instead of FORWARD — in particular, inside the definition of DOODLE?

```
TO DOODLE :N
DOODLE :N / 3
RT 90 DOODLE :N / 3
LT 90 DOODLE :N / 3
LT 90 DOODLE :N / 3
RT 90 DOODLE :N / 3
END
```

Either by looking at this, or by trying it, you ought to see that this is not quite good enough. The recursion never stops because there is no conditional command involved. To get round this, include at the start a command to say that if the input is suitably small then just do FORWARD rather than the fancy path:

```
IF :N < 5 [FD :N STOP]
```

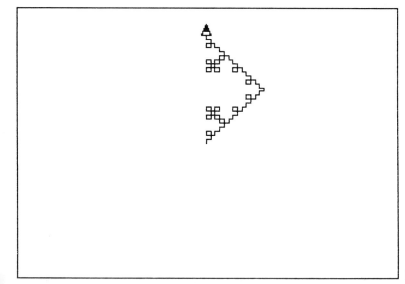

Figure 3.8

Remember, this has to come before the first recursive use of DOODLE in the definition. It is also a good idea to use a variable, say one called MIN, instead of 5. That way if 5 turns out to be not quite the right choice of a small number, you need only change the value of MIN rather than edit DOODLE. This is yet another application of the principle that you should really try to make things easy for yourself... Figure 3.8 shows the result of DOODLE 100.

Spend some time trying other variations, other choices for the indirect path to replace the straight line. But note: each segment of the path must be shorter than the whole. If not, the input to one of the DOODLEs in the definition will not be any smaller than the input to the main DOODLE, and so when it is run it will not be progressing towards the point at which the 'halt recursion' condition is satisfied. Apart from this, your most likely problem is to forget to include the STOP.

Here is a variant of the idea, shown in Figure 3.9:

```
TO BRANCH :N
IF :N < 3 [STOP]
FD :N
RT 45 BRANCH :N * 0.6
LT 90 BRANCH :N * 0.4
RT 45
BK :N
END
```

An interesting thing about this definition is that if the sub-procedures BRANCH :N * 0.6 and BRANCH :N * 0.4 are state-transparent, then the whole thing is. Now, certainly, if the input is very small (less than 3), BRANCH is state-transparent because all it does is STOP and nothing else. Having seen this, you can convince yourself that BRANCH is state-transparent whatever its input. Again there is a vast selection of variations on this idea, for example you can have three or more BRANCH commands within the definition. An area to experiment with is to see if a procedure can meaningfully be 'nearly but not quite' state-transparent — make the first line

```
IF :N < 3 [FD 1 STOP]
```

and see what happens.

Finally, here, without further comment, is a famous example first suggested by the German mathematician David Hilbert:

```
TO LHAND :S :N            TO RHAND :S :N
IF :N=0 [STOP]            IF :N=0 [STOP]
LT 90                     RT 90
```

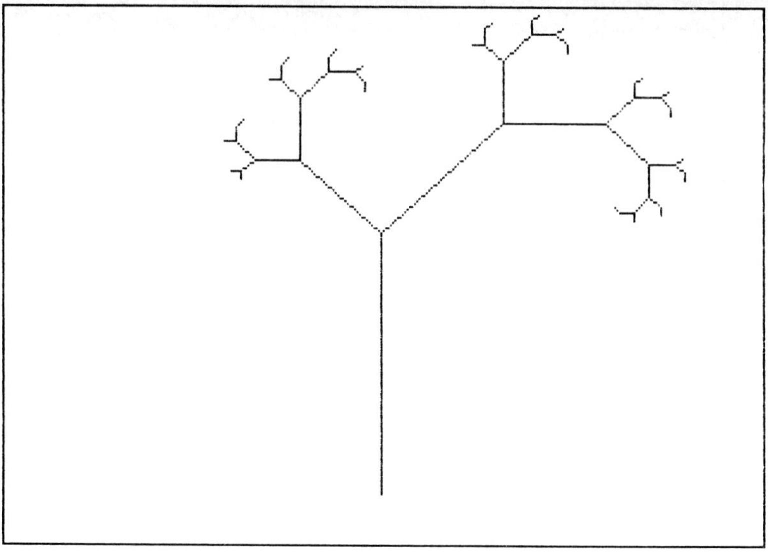

Figure 3.9

```
RHAND :S :N − 1          LHAND :S :N − 1
FD :S                    FD :S
RT 90                    LT 90
LHAND :S :N − 1          RHAND :S :N − 1
FD :S                    FD :S
LHAND :S :N − 1          LHAND :S :N − 1
RT 90                    LT 90
FD :S                    FD :S
RHAND :S :N − 1          LHAND :S :N − 1
LT 90                    RT 90
END                      END
```

There is no accompanying diagram, you will just have to try it! To start with, try LHAND 30 2 and LHAND 18 3 with the turtle at the centre of the screen.

3.9 AFTERTHOUGHT

This chapter has provided you with nearly all the ingredients for some sort of 'turtle billiards'.

3.10 FILING AND OTHER CONVENIENCES

If you have worked through this chapter, you should now have several procedures, some of which are worth keeping for the future. Of course you may by this time have lost track of what you have defined. The way to find out what you have is to use the IBM PC LOGO procedure PO (back in the mists of time, it used to be called 'printout'). It expects one input, which can be a name (quoted, as usual) or a list. For instance:

    PO "LHAND

or

    PO [LHAND RHAND]

In addition to PO, these exist:

POTS   This prints the title lines of all procedures.
PONS   This prints the names and values of all (global) variables.
POPS   This prints the definitions of all procedures.
POALL This prints everything!

The procedure ERASE gets LOGO to discard a procedure. Normally the input is the name of a procedure, or a list of them. Correspondingly, there are also:

ERPS   This erases all procedures.
ERNS   This erases all variables.
ERN   This erases the named variable or list of variables.
ERALL This is cataclysmic.

It is possible to preserve a copy of all the current procedure definitions on a disk (if you are unsure about using a disk, check with the technical manual). The procedure is SAVE; it expects as its input a word by which you wish to name the whole collection of current procedures. For example,

    SAVE "CURVES

This command would save the procedures in a file on the disk, called CURVES.LF (the LF stands for 'LOGO file'). If the name you specify contains a dot —

    SAVE "THREE.D

then LOGO doesn't add the '.LF'. The file will be called THREE.D instead. It is very important to know that a filename can only have eight characters before the dot, and only three afterward.

In a similar fashion to saving procedures, you can save a picture by using SAVEPIC:

```
SAVEPIC "LEONARDO
```

— the file will be called LEONARDO.PF (the 'PF' is for 'picture file'). To fetch a group of procedures from the disk at the start of the next session (or any other time), use READ. For example,

```
READ "CURVES
```

would fetch all the procedures you had previously saved with that SAVE command above. Any procedures existing before the READ in the current session will still exist, provided that their names were not the same as any of those procedures fetched by READ.

To fetch a picture from the disk, use READPIC:

```
READPIC "LEONARDO
```

This will destroy any current drawing. It will not affect the turtle, and in particular the turtle will not necessarily be where you left it when you did the SAVEPIC.

Eventually you will forget what is on a disk. You can find out what files exist by using the command DIR. This looks at the default disk drive (normally A: with IBM PC LOGO) though you can look at, say, drive B by the command

```
DIR "B:
```

If you want to throw away one or more files (disks do have limited though large capacity) use ERASEFILE to get rid of a procedure collection or a picture. The commands

```
ERASEFILE "CURVES
```

```
ERASEFILE "LEONARDO
```

will irrevocably discard what had been saved under these names.

Here are some useful guidelines:

a) Make the names sensible. It might be fun to call something RABBIT, but it is not very helpful a few days later.
b) At the end of a session, use POTS to check on what exists. Use ERASE to prune out unwanted procedures before using SAVE.
c) You can merge two SAVEd collections by READing in first one then the other, and then SAVEing the combined collection under a new name. If you use an existing name you will lose what was previously stored under that name.

d) There is no easy way to merge two pictures.

3.10.1 Packaging and burying

In order to make it a bit easier to administer your collections of procedures, IBM PC LOGO provides tools for wrapping up collections of procedures, and hiding them from the view of procedures such as POTS. The way to bundle up a collection of procedures is to use PACKAGE:

PACKAGE "HILBERT [LHAND RHAND]

would create a package, called HILBERT, containing the procedures LHAND and RHAND. If you then

BURY "HILBERT

the procedures LHAND and RHAND won't appear in the information displayed by any of the printing-out procedures mentioned above, and won't be SAVEd. To reverse this effect, use UNBURY. Sometimes it can be tedious to specify all the things you want included in a package. PKGALL may help; it packages, using the name it is given, anything that hasn't so far been packaged elsewhere.

Packages are very useful, largely because the procedures

POALL
PONS
POTS
ERALL
ERNS
ERPS
SAVE

can all be given an input — the name of a package, or a list of package names — and will then restrict their attention to those packages. LOAD can be given a second input, after the filename, and will load all the procedures (and variables) from that file into the named package.

In time, you will develop your own style and tricks for making use of packages. It is a bit tedious to set up experiments so that you can get the feel of them, because you ought to define some junk procedures to work on rather than risk your valuable ones at the start. Nevertheless, try it. The payoff, in being able to administer your sets of procedures in future, is very definitely worth the effort. Create two or three sets of procedures, say

JUNK1, JUNK2, . . .

```
TRIPE1, TRIPE2, . . .
TRASH1, TRASH2,. . .
```

and experiment.

4 | WORDS AND LISTS

"In Science — in fact, in most things — it is best to begin at the beginning. In some things, of course, it's better to begin at the other end. For instance, if you wanted to paint a dog green, it might be best to begin at the tail, as it doesn't bite at that end. And so —"

(*Sylvie and Bruno Concluded*, LEWIS CARROLL)

Aims: Chapters 2 and 3 have been almost entirely concerned with graphics. This one is not. It has more to say about words, and it introduces a third kind of entity called lists. It also develops the idea of creating a 'toolkit' of procedures.

4.1 WORDS

Words in LOGO look similar to printed words in English, although they are not formed according to quite the same rules. In particular, there are precise rules in LOGO whereas in English rules, if they exist at all, are very flexible. LOGO words were introduced in Chapter 2, as names of variables. A word in IBM PC LOGO is composed of any sequence of printable characters except for a space or one of the characters

$$[\,]\,(\,) + - / * < = >$$

Even these can be part of a word if you precede each such exceptional character by a backslash — \. The backslash alerts LOGO that the following character does *not* have any special significance. (IBM PC LOGO will, in a few circumstances, let you do without the backslash. The rules about it are, however, a bit fussy. Use the backslash if you are ever in doubt.)

WHO??	FATIMA
!?. **	LESSER\ FLAMINGO
23907	PRICE. OF. BUTTER
PRINT	TIME\+MOTION
THIS. IS. A. LONGISH. WORD	

are all acceptable words. One of these looks like two words though it is really one (because of that backslash), another looks like a number, a third looks like a LOGO procedure. In general, the way to distinguish a word from something it might be confused with —

such as the name of a not-yet-defined LOGO procedure — is to put a double quote mark before it. [The phrase "double quote mark" (there goes two of them) troubles some people. They may know it as "the quotation mark", not to be confused with the 'apostrophe' alias the 'single quote mark'.] So,

    PRINT FATIMA

will, in IBM PC LOGO, produce the error message

    I DON'T KNOW HOW TO FATIMA

whereas

    PRINT "FATIMA

will do just what it suggests. The initial quote mark, being an indication to LOGO, will not be printed, though

    PRINT " "FATIMA

will print "FATIMA rather than FATIMA. Similarly,

    PRINT "TIME\+MOTION   prints   TIME+MOTION
    PRINT "!?. **   prints   !?. **
    PRINT "LESSER\ FLAMINGO   prints   LESSER FLAMINGO
    PRINT "239   prints   239
    PRINT "PRINT   prints   PRINT

The PRINT "239 example is surprising. In fact, IBM PC LOGO is somewhat woolly-minded about the difference between numbers and words. In particular,

    PRINT "23 + 24

will print 47, and so will

    PRINT "23+24

The + is one of the special characters which are normally regarded as a complete, separate word in themselves. Moreover, a word with only digits in it is still a perfectly good name for a variable:

    MAKE "2 397

Then

```
PRINT 2     prints 2
PRINT :2    prints 397
```

Also,

```
PRINT :2 + 3
```

prints 400, and so does the command

```
PRINT :2+3
```

On the other hand, be cautious about putting spaces around + and −, which both have two meanings. They can stand for an arithmetic operation on two numbers, or they can indicate the sign of a number. The commands

```
PRINT :2−3    PRINT :2 − 3
```

will both print 394, whereas

```
PRINT :2 −3
```

will first print 397 and then complain

```
I DON'T KNOW WHAT TO DO WITH −3
```

Unfortunately, they don't quite behave the same when used with parentheses:

```
PRINT (−3)
```

will do that, but

```
PRINT (+3)
```

will complain

```
NOT ENOUGH INPUTS FOR +
```

To summarise, the rules are

- Use a double quote before a word, if it might be confused with something else (there is only one place where confusion cannot arise, and that is inside a list — see Section 4.4).
- If you want to use an unusual character as part of a word, put a backslash before it.

(Note for teachers: the idea of 'rule' is not the same as 'formal definition'. Where the formal definition is a mess, it is much better to give some examples and then emphasise that caution is needed.)

There is a procedure WORDP which takes one input, and outputs TRUE only if the input is a word or a number (whereas NUMBERP only outputs TRUE for a number). If you are in doubt, use it.

There is one unusual case of a word which is worth knowing about, which follows from the definition. A word need have no characters at all! The command

    PRINT "

prints a blank line. This case is called the 'empty word'.

So far, all the printing has been one word per line, which is next to useless for practical purposes. To get round this, there is a version of PRINT called TYPE. It behaves like PRINT except that it does not start a new line after printing its input(s). If you use only TYPE then the prompt which appears after the command has finished will appear on the same line as your printing. Here are some examples:

    TYPE "HELLO TYPE "THERE

prints HELLOTHERE and the next prompt appears immediately next to the final E.

    TYPE "HELLO PRINT "THERE

prints HELLOTHERE and the next prompt will be on the line below. Notice that TYPE does not put any space after what it prints. To separate words by space you need quite explicitly to print a word consisting of spaces:

    TYPE "HELLO TYPE "\ PRINT "THERE

prints HELLO THERE. Notice the two spaces before the PRINT. The first is a single character word, because of that backslash. The second is the normal gap between commands on the same line.

It can be very tedious to use one PRINT or TYPE command per word. As a convenience, IBM PC LOGO allows you to use just one PRINT or TYPE command for any number of inputs, provided that you surround the whole printing command with parentheses. Thus

    (PRINT "HELLO "THERE)

prints HELLO THERE. Also, quite reasonably,

    (PRINT 2 −3)

prints 2 −3.

The LOGO jargon used to describe a procedure such as PRINT, which can take many inputs, is that it 'can be greedy'. In this book you have already met eight procedures so far which can be greedy: PRINT, TYPE, AND, OR, LIST, LOCAL and two lesser-used ones, PRODUCT and SUM. You will meet one or two others in this chapter.

4.2 BEAUTIFUL PRINTING, PART 1

All this opens up the possibility of printing text on the screen in fancy ways. However, the effect of having an exotically printed display of information would be marred by having all those previous command lines on the screen. You can reset the displaying of text on the screen by using the procedure

    CLEARTEXT

(CT for short). This wipes away all the text; the next prompt will appear at the top left of the area in which text can appear. If you specified MIXEDSCREEN recently, this means the twentieth line, first column. If you specified TEXTSCREEN recently, this means the top left of the screen.

You can make printing appear where you like, within reason, by using the procedure SETCURSOR. Like the turtle command SETPOS, this takes a list of two numbers as inputs; the first is the line number where printing is to start next, counting from line number 0, and the second is the column number, counting from column 0. [In Dr. LOGO, the column comes first. Waterloo LOGO does not have any form of direct cursor control.] Line 0, column 0 is at the top left of the screen whether or not the graphics are being displayed. The line number must lie in the range 0 to 23, and the column number must be in the range 0 to the current maximum screen width. [You can change the screen by using the SETWIDTH command, and find out the current value by printing the output of the procedure WIDTH. Changing the screen width doesn't make characters fatter or thinner. Setting the width to more than 40 on a single-display system means that you cannot use graphics.] A further restriction is that SETCURSOR rounds its inputs to be integers, so you cannot use commands such as CURSOR 12.5 20.5 to produce fancy subscripts or superscripts.

Within these restrictions, SETCURSOR is very useful. For instance,

```
TO CRAWL
CURSOR [21 10]
(TYPE "X\ \=\ XCOR)
CURSOR [22 10]
(TYPE "Y\ \=\ YCOR)
FD 1
CRAWL
END
```

makes the turtle crawl along its current heading, while a display of its X and Y co-ordinates is continually updated. If the heading is not a multiple of 90 degrees the co-ordinates will have decimal parts, and the display will be changing so much that it is pretty confusing. It would be better to ROUND the co-ordinates first. If you edit CRAWL to be this,

```
TO CRAWL
CURSOR [21 10]
(TYPE "X\\=\ ROUND XCOR)
CURSOR [22 10]
(TYPE "Y\\=\ ROUND YCOR)
FD 1
CRAWL
END
```

you may be puzzled to find that sometimes either or both co-ordinates seem to be much too big. What is happening is this. Imagine that the X co-ordinate is just above 100, and decreasing. When it is 100 the number 100 will be printed starting at column 14 of line 21. When the X co-ordinate drops to around 99, the 99 will be printed starting at column 14 of line 21. However, 99 is only two digits long whereas 100 was three. The final 0 digit of 100 will not be overwritten when the 99 is printed, so the coordinate will appear on the screen to be 990. The cure is to print as many spaces after the number as are necessary to guarantee that the previous number is fully overwritten, for example

```
TO CRAWL
CURSOR [21 10]
(TYPE "X\\=\ ROUND XCOR "\\ )
CURSOR [22 10]
(TYPE "Y\\=\ ROUND YCOR "\\ )
FD 1
CRAWL
END
```

The SETCURSOR procedure was also used in this procedure to

produce Figure 4.1, with the command shown at the top left, previously defined.

The procedure CURSOR can be used to find where the cursor currently is. It outputs a list of two numbers, which is not very useful until you find out later in this chapter how to take a list apart to get at the constituents.

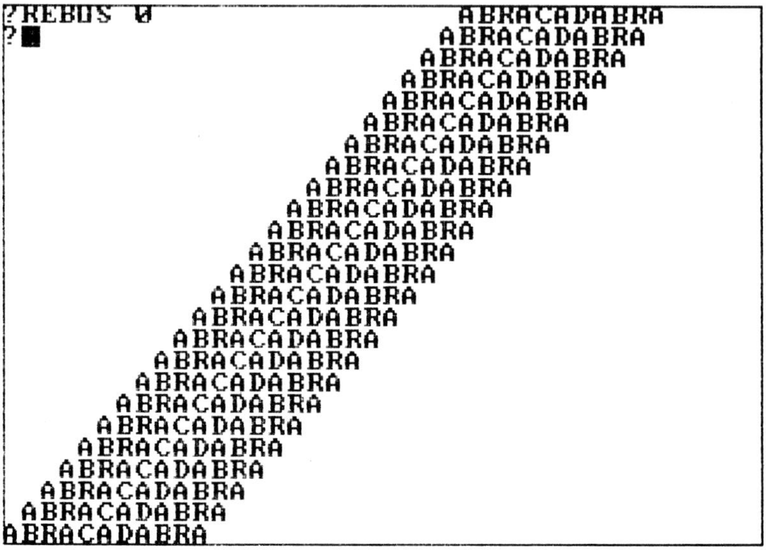

Figure 4.1

4.3 NEW WORDS FROM OLD

There are times when, in a problem, you need to be able to assemble a word from some constituent parts. In IBM PC LOGO there is a procedure WORD which normally takes two inputs, thought it can be greedy, and concatenates the characters of its inputs to form one larger word. The resulting word is output. An example:

    PRINT WORD "CAN "DID

prints CANDID, and

    MAKE "FATHER "DOMINIC
    PRINT THING WORD "FAT "HER

prints DOMINIC. (Note: this is a case where the colon cannot be used in place of THING.) An example of greedy use is

```
PRINT (WORD "IN "TERM "IN "ABLE)
```

prints INTERMINABLE.

There are other circumstances for which WORD is useful, besides playing about with English words. One sometimes arises in large LOGO procedures when you need to use a substantial number of variables. You do not want to type in all their names, or perhaps you do not know how many will be needed when you are only at the stage of defining the procedures. For instance, you may be creating a game suitable for any number of players, and you want to keep some detail about each player as the value of a variable called PLAYER1, or PLAYER7, or whatever. However, you also want to be sure that none of the variables already exists, because if one did it might already be in active use for some other purpose. The variable named X, for instance, tends to be overused. The idea, then, is to define a procedure which generates, at each successive use, the next word in the sequence PLAYER1, PLAYER2, PLAYER3 ... provided that word is not already in use as the name of a variable. This procedure, say called GENVAR, will be used with MAKE, for instance

```
   . . .
   MAKE "NEWNAME GENVAR
   MAKE :NEWNAME 87
   . . .
```

The logical ingredients for defining GENVAR are:

a) Get the next unused number in the sequence 1, 2, 3 ... which could form part of the word to be output. The easy way to do this is to store it as the value of a variable, say GEN.NEXT, and increment its value each time GENVAR is used.

b) Concatenate 'PLAYER' and this number to form a possible word to output.

c) Use NAMEP to see if this word is the name of an existing variable. If not, output it. If it is, do all the steps again (by recursion?).

This translates fairly directly into LOGO as

```
MAKE "GEN. NEXT 0
TO GENVAR
MAKE "GEN. NEXT :GEN. NEXT + 1
TEST NAMEP WORD "PLAYER :GEN. NEXT
IFFALSE [OUTPUT WORD "PLAYER :GEN. NEXT]
IFTRUE [OUTPUT GENVAR]
END
```

There are interesting details in this procedure. The variable GEN.NEXT does not have to be incremented first of all, but it will have to be at some point and this way is neat (try it another way and see). You may also be surprised to see IFFALSE appearing before IFTRUE, but there is no reason why not. Because of this, the TEST/IFTRUE/IFFALSE method of defining conditionals is more flexible, although more verbose, than IF … […] […]. A third point to note in GENVAR is that the OUTPUT is needed in the last line. If you cannot see why, try the experiment of leaving it out.

GENVAR can be tested easily:

```
MAKE "PLAYER3 "SOMETHING
REPEAT 4 [PRINT GENVAR]
```

should print PLAYER1, PLAYER2, PLAYER4 and PLAYER5 because PLAYER3 is already in use.

4.4 LISTS

In addition to numbers and words, LOGO also deals with a third sort of entity, lists, which have already appeared in various contexts. In particular, the commands REPEAT, SETPOS, SETCURSOR and IF all expect a list as one of their inputs, if not their sole input. Lists are the most versatile and elaborate of the three. A list is just an ordered collection of numbers, words and … lists. The word 'ordered' means that it does matter which number, word or list in the collection comes first, which comes second and so on. A list is expressed in LOGO by writing the members of the collection in order and enclosing the whole lot in square brackets. For example,

    [23 6 1 99]

is a list with four members. The word 'element' is a common synonym for 'member'. Because a list is ordered, the list

    [23 1 6 99]

is not the same as the example above. Here are some more examples of lists:

[PIES 1 75]	This has three elements, a word and two numbers.
[THIS IS A LIST]	This has four elements, all words.
[[0 0][29 76]]	This has two elements. The first is the list [0 0] and the second is the list [29 76].
[[[A Q][R T]]]	This has one element, the list [[A Q][R T]] which itself has two elements.

[ ]   This has no elements at all. This is a very com-
                       mon example called the empty list. There can be
                       space between the brackets.

Lists can be used to represent almost any kind of information,
whether that information has some order to it or not. The first
example above shows how a list might be used to represent pricing
information. The second shows how a list can represent an English
phrase or sentence. The third shows how a list might be used to
represent a set of X and Y co-ordinate pairs.

Try PRINTing examples of lists. You will find that PRINT, in
IBM PC LOGO at least, omits the outermost pair of square
brackets. [If you want the outermost brackets printed, use SHOW
instead. This is the only difference between PRINT and SHOW.]
For example

```
PRINT [HELLO BOSS]   prints HELLO BOSS
PRINT [EH? [OUCH]]    prints EH? [OUCH]
PRINT [ ]             prints a blank line
```

Try using lists as values for variables:

```
MAKE "TRY [THIS IS A TEST]
PRINT :TRY
```

will print THIS IS A TEST. You will find that you are never obliged
to separate a square bracket from anything else by spaces, though
you can if you like.

You should now see that the REPEAT command, introduced
in Chapter 2, just takes two inputs. The first is a number, the
second is a list representing an ordered sequence of commands.
Therefore

```
MAKE "X [FD RANDOM 30 RT 90]
REPEAT 5 :X
. . . move the turtle . . .
REPEAT 3 :X
. . . move the turtle . . .
REPEAT 12 :X
. . . etc . . .
```

saves a lot of repetitive typing. Another useful tip that saves lots of
typing is the following. Suppose you have just typed a very long
command, and run it. You realise that you want to make some
minor adjustment — say, change the value of a variable — and then
run the command again. To save typing the command in again,
press the F3 key which retypes that last command, leaving the

cursor at the end. Rather than pressing ENTER, use the 'BackTab' key to get to the start of the command, insert

MAKE "BIG.COMMAND [

and then use the 'Tab' key to jump to the end, and insert a closing square bracket. Your command should now be

MAKE "BIG.COMMAND [your original very long command]

so that when you press ENTER, your command is stored for later re-use. To re-use it, just

REPEAT 1 :BIG.COMMAND

or equivalently

RUN :BIG.COMMAND

A list can never be mistaken for the name of a procedure to be run; procedure names must always be words. Because of this, words do not need an initial double quote when they are used within a list. Consider this faulty pair of commands:

MAKE "X 100
PRINT [:X IS 100]

This does not print [100 IS 100]. Because the :X is within a list, LOGO treats it just as a word rather than 'the value of the variable called X'. Remember that :X is a legal possibility for a word, for instance

MAKE "Y ":X
PRINT :Y

prints :X. But note, REPEAT treats lists as commands.

4.5 USING LISTS

4.5.1 Informative messages

In the factorial procedure in Section 3.7.2, it was assumed that the input was a positive integer. If it was 0 or negative the procedure recursed happily until stopped by CTRL-Break. If the input was not a number but a word, IBM PC LOGO would give the unappetising message

— DOESNT LIKE word AS INPUT:
JUST BEFORE LEAVING FACTORIAL

(Note that the phrase 'JUST BEFORE LEAVING ...' means that
it was in the last line of the procedure or it was about to OUTPUT.
Otherwise the offending line would be included in the message.
There isn't any especially strong argument for this, rather than
printing the offending line in all circumstances.) You can make your
assumptions about FACTORIAL explicit by introducing some conditional commands to check that the input is what you intended:

```
TO FACTORIAL :N
IF NOT NUMBERP :N [PRINT [SILLY INPUT TO FACTORIAL] STOP]
IF :N<1 [PRINT [INPUT LESS THAN 1] STOP]
IF :N=1 [OUTPUT 1] [OUTPUT :N * FACTORIAL :N−1]
END
```

Here lists are used to provide short informative messages to make
the procedure more foolproof. Alas, it is still not perfect. Consider
the command

```
PRINT FACTORIAL 2.5
```

The procedure FACTORIAL 2.5 will try to output 2.5 *
FACTORIAL 1.5. The procedure FACTORIAL 1.5 will try to
output 1.5 * FACTORIAL 0.5. The procedure FACTORIAL 0.5
will print INPUT LESS THAN 1 and stop, not outputting anything.
Thus the expression 1.5 * FACTORIAL 0.5 will be an error — IBM
PC LOGO will tell you that

```
FACTORIAL DIDNT OUTPUT TO PRINT
```

As is so often the case, there is an easy repair. There is a
command THROW "TOPLEVEL (the procedure THROW is
explained later) which, like STOP, immediately ends the procedure
it appears within. Unlike STOP, it ends every other unfinished
procedure as well, so that LOGO immediately returns to waiting for
your next command. Putting a THROW "TOPLEVEL at some
point in a procedure is very much like telling LOGO "imagine I
type a CTRL-Break at this point". The repair to FACTORIAL is to
use THROW "TOPLEVEL instead of STOP. Indeed, because of
what THROW "TOPLEVEL does, you can define a generally
useful procedure called ERR which takes one input — usually to be
a list — and use it in conditional commands that check for errors:

```
TO ERR :MESSAGE
```

```
PRINT :MESSAGE
THROW "TOPLEVEL
END

TO FACTORIAL :N
IF NOT NUMBERP :N [ERR [SILLY INPUT TO FACTORIAL]]
IF :N<1 [ERROR [INPUT LESS THAN 1]]
... etc ...
```

A procedure such as ERR is a very useful tool. You may wonder, why is it not provided as standard? Fundamentally the answer is that LOGO is really a kit of useful procedures from which to assemble procedures to suit your own particular needs. ERR, taking only one input, could be too specific for some purposes. For example, you might choose to start each session of LOGO with

```
MAKE "ERROR.COUNT 0
```

and define ERR as

```
TO ERR :MESSAGE
PRINT :MESSAGE
MAKE "ERROR. COUNT :ERROR.COUNT + 1
TYPE [THAT WAS BLUNDER NUMBER]
TYPE "\
PRINT :ERROR.COUNT
THROW "TOPLEVEL
END
```

The aim of LOGO's designers has been to provide a collection of procedures which was sufficiently general and yet sufficiently complete for users to put it to a very wide variety of uses.

4.5.2 Constructing lists from bits
Wide though the possibilities suggested by this last section are, it is ultimately limiting if every list used in any procedure is one that had to be typed in at some point. LOGO provides ways of assembling lists from bits, and for turning sentences typed by you into lists. For the latter, IBM PC LOGO provides READLIST, or RL for short. READLIST takes no input; it waits till the user has typed a line, and then outputs that line as a list:

```
TO HELLO
(TYPE [WHO ARE YOU?] "\ )
MAKE "REPLY READLIST
(TYPE "HELLO "\ :REPLY)
END
```

If you give the command HELLO you might see something like this on your screen:

```
?HELLO
WHO ARE YOU? ATTILA THE HUN
HELLO ATTILA THE HUN
?
```

IBM PC LOGO also provides two procedures for constructing lists:

LIST   This takes two inputs normally, though it can be greedy. It outputs a list formed from its inputs.

SENTENCE   This procedure, SE for short, also takes two inputs normally and can also be greedy. It too outputs a list formed from its inputs. However, if any input is a list it first breaks it up into its elements, for example [THIS LIST] would be treated as the two words THIS LIST. It does not do this recursively; lists within lists are not broken up.

Some examples should help:

```
LIST "HELLO "SIR
```

outputs [HELLO SIR].

```
LIST 2*5 "COMMANDMENTS
```

outputs [10 COMMANDMENTS].

```
(LIST [HO HO] "HE "SAID)
```

outputs [[HO HO] HE SAID].

```
(LIST 1 2 3 4 5)
```

outputs [1 2 3 4 5].

```
SE "MICHAEL "MOUSE
```

outputs [MICHAEL MOUSE].

```
(SE [HO HO] "HE "SAID)
```

outputs [HO HO HE SAID].

```
SE [WHAT IS] [THE QUESTION]
```

outputs [WHAT IS THE QUESTION].

A simple mnemonic is that LIST puts square brackets around the collection of its inputs, and SENTENCE strips the outer square brackets off any of its inputs before putting square brackets around the lot.

As the names suggest, SENTENCE is the more useful in applications where lists are to be used essentially as sentences. LIST is often the more useful in other cases. As an example of the former here is a simple and educationally hopeless quiz procedure:

```
TO QUIZ
MAKE "N1 RANDOM 50
MAKE "N2 RANDOM 50
TYPE (SE [WHAT IS] :N1 "TIMES :N2 "?)
IF (SE :N1 * :N2) = READLIST [PRINT [YES]] [PRINT SE [SHAME IT
      WAS] :N1 * :N2]
QUIZ
END
```

It is educationally useless because if you give any wrong answer at all it tells you the correct answer! Note the line

```
IF (SE :N1 * :N2) = READLIST [. . .
```

SE has only one input, so (SE :N1 * :N2) is just the list whose sole element is the right answer. The READLIST outputs a list formed from what the user types. If he types the right answer and nothing extra, the two lists will be equal.

As an example of using LIST, here is a simple fault-tracing aid called CHECK. Its input is assumed to be a word which is the name of a variable:

```
TO CHECK :QXRZ
PRINT (LIST :QXRZ "HAS "VALUE THING :QXRZ)
END
```

It can be used like this:

```
. . .
MAKE "X [120 110]
. . .
CHECK "X                           (Note, not CHECK :X)
```

— it will print

```
X HAS VALUE [120 110]
```

CHECK could be used within a procedure to print the values of the inputs if you were not sure what was going on and needed to make some basic checks. If SENTENCE were used here instead of LIST then CHECK would have printed the more confusing message

    X HAS VALUE 120 110

The input to CHECK was called QXRZ because the name is unlikely to be used elsewhere. The name must be an unlikely one:

    CHECK "QXRZ

will print QXRZ HAS VALUE QXRZ, which is true but unhelpful if you want to examine the value of some other variable called QXRZ. You may find it more useful to give CHECK a second input, a list to be included in the message which will identify the place where that CHECK was used:

    CHECK "X [THIRD LINE OF PROCEDURE HILL]

4.5.3 Dissecting lists

LOGO also provides procedures for getting at bits of lists. In IBM PC LOGO there are five:

FIRST
: This takes a list as input, and outputs the first element. Obviously, the input list must not be the empty list.

BUTFIRST
: This procedure, BF for short,takes a list as input and outputs a list formed by removing the first element. The input must not be the empty list. If the input list has only one element then the output list will be the empty list.

LAST
: This is the opposite of FIRST. It takes a list as input, and outputs the last element. The input list must not be empty.

BUTLAST
: This procedure, BL for short, is the opposite of BUTFIRST. It outputs a list consisting of all but the last element of the input. The input list must not be empty.

ITEM
: This expects two inputs, a number and a list. It outputs that element of the list, counting from 1 as the first element.

These five procedures can also accept a word as input, and do the corresponding action with the appropriate character of the word. Examples:

FIRST [HELLO SIR]	outputs	HELLO
BF [HELLO SIR]	outputs	[SIR]
FIRST "HELLO	outputs	H
BF "HELLO	outputs	ELLO
LAST [ONE TWO THREE]	outputs	THREE
BUTLAST [ONE TWO THREE]	outputs	[ONE TWO]
LAST "CLAMP	outputs	P
BUTLAST "CLAMP	outputs	CLAM
ITEM 3 [A B C D]	outputs	C
ITEM 2 "HELLO	outputs	E
ITEM 6 1/7	outputs	8 (1/7=0.142857 ...)

There is also a procedure LISTP which outputs TRUE or FALSE depending on whether its single input is a list or not.

It may seem perverse that there is no way directly to replace the seventh (or whichever) element by something else, or to splice in a new element somewhere. It is somewhat perverse. Failing to provide some such procedures is taking the aims of generality a little too far, especially since it is not a wholly trivial task to define them for yourself. There is a historical reason for it, but it is no longer valid. It was this: LOGO is descended from the language LISP. In LISP and in LOGO, there was and still is a commonplace requirement to be able to compare two lists. LISP users also frequently wanted to be able to make more elaborate checks, such as 'is [A B C D] a list containing only letters of the alphabet?'. In the early days of LISP, both software and hardware ideas were much less sophisticated. In particular it was conceptually more taxing, although not impossible, to handle whole entities such as lists where the size was unknown in advance. It was much easier, and mathematically more satisfying, to look on a list as though it had precisely two constituents — a 'first element' and a list, which was the BUTFIRST bit. In those terms the list

[A B C D]

might have been written as

{A, {B, {C, {D, { } } } } }

However the square bracket notation, or an equivalent of it, was adopted instead, being much easier to read and write. Unfortunately for you, the notation disguised the fact that a list really had exactly two constituents. Since those days both hardware and software science have made a lot of progress. Now, various versions of LOGO do provide procedures which allow you to deal directly with elements other than the first or last of a list. IBM PC

LOGO, for compactness, has only provided LAST and BUTLAST as the symmetrical counterparts of FIRST and BUTFIRST, and has provided ITEM since it is so very useful. Anything beyond these you must create for yourself.

This brings out the notion of building yourself general toolkits of procedures. It is almost always much easier to step from a general case to a specific one than it is to do the reverse. This is because moving from the specific to the general requires you to articulate what the generalisation is, each time; in the other direction no such articulation is needed. The next section and its sub-sections are concerned with defining a small but very useful kit of tools for working with procedures. You would be well advised to spend one whole LOGO session working through it, so that at the end you could SAVE all the procedures as one collection (as a file) called, say, LISTKIT. Then in future, when you want to work with lists, you can ease the burden by giving a command

```
LOAD "LISTKIT
```

at the start.

4.5.4 What is needed?

When you embark on the construction of such a toolkit, the first step is to plan what will be in it. Remember that it is always possible to add to the collection at a later date. It is also very sensible not to let the size of the collection get out of hand. The planning usually demands imagination and some past experience of what is useful, and takes hours or days rather than minutes. If at this point you have not spent much time playing with lists in LOGO then the following thoughts should be helpful. They might also serve to set you thinking about some involved projects to do with lists.

Needs: ˙

- It is useful to be able to test whether something is a member of a specified list. Suppose a procedure asked a question; the user could reply 'I THINK YES' or 'YES PERHAPS' or 'MY ANSWER IS YES' or 'YES INDEED' as well as plain 'YES'. If you used READLIST to capture the answer, it would be nice to check whether YES was part of it. This could go wrong, the user might answer 'CERTAINLY NOT YES', but it is impossible to cater for every possibility. IBM PC LOGO provides MEMBERP which does the job:

```
PRINT MEMBERP "YES READLIST
```

will print TRUE if YES is a word in the reply.

- It is useful to be able to find out how many elements there are in a list (and how many characters there are in a word). The procedure COUNT outputs this. It is also useful to be able to find out how many times a given element occurs in a list. Think of certain kinds of games in which it matters to know how many times a particular type of move has been made. The moves can be recorded by appending each to a 'history' list.
- It is useful to be able to update one particular element of a list. Imagine your aim is to devise LOGO procedures to play tic-tac-toe, otherwise known as noughts-and-crosses. You could represent the state of play as a list with nine elements, for example

[BLANK X X BLANK O BLANK O BLANK BLANK]

to represent Figure 4.2. If the O player were to play in the top left cell, you would have to update the first element of the list from BLANK to O. (Note for those interested in the ideas of artificial intelligence: it is much harder to devise a procedure which plays badly but believably than it is to devise one which plays perfectly.) As another example, suppose you wanted to count letter frequencies in text typed by a user. You could represent the count for each character as one element of a large list. Each time a letter appeared you could make the corresponding element one larger than before. This is easier than having one variable per character because there are at least 57 likely characters, excluding lower case letters. There is a procedure

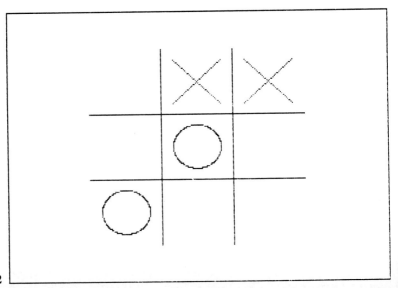

Figure 4.2

ASCII which expects a one letter word as input and outputs a number which uniquely stands for that letter. The correspondence between numbers and characters is defined by the American Standard Code for Information Interchange — ASCII for short. Incidentally there is a procedure CHAR which does just the reverse. The IBM PC LOGO procedure READCHAR, RC for short, outputs a single character word representing one keystroke by the user; you can type a certain number of characters ahead of a program that uses RC, and the LOGO system will preserve them so that RC can catch up. The procedure KEYP outputs TRUE if there are any characters currently available for RC to read without waiting for the user's next character to be typed. The procedure RCS takes a number as input and collects up that many characters; it outputs the word consisting of that sequence of characters. Like RC, it will wait for more characters if necessary.

- It is useful to be able to delete a (numerically) specified element from a list, or to delete all occurrences of a given element. This often arises when using lists to hold sets of related details, in database-type applications.
- It is useful to be able to construct a list consisting of all the elements common to two lists. Suppose that you are using LOGO to experiment with set theory and you are representing sets by lists. The 'intersection of two sets' will be the list of elements common to the two lists.
- It is useful to be able to construct a set which contains any element in either of two lists, but only once. In set theory this would be the union of two sets.
- It is useful to be able to generate a new list from a given one, in which every occurrence of some specified element has been replaced by a new element. An example of this will be given in Chapter 7, in a project to create a simple database of facts.
- It is very useful to be able to sort a list.

This forms an adequate basic collection. In due course you will think of some others which are worth including, but remember to keep notes of what they do and what they do not do.

Counting the number of occurrences of an element

If you do not see at once how to do this, try an example: how many times does the element A appear in [A B A C D]? There are six basic list-handling tools at your disposal: FIRST, BUTFIRST, LAST, BUTLAST, COUNT and ITEM. Of these, FIRST and BUTFIRST are useful for dealing with a list starting at the front. LAST and BUTLAST are complementary — they relate to the back, or end, of a list. If you are familiar with another programming language, you should be able to spot that COUNT and ITEM could be used together for counting the occurrences, like this:

- set a variable indicating the number found to be 0 initially;
- use COUNT to find how many elements there are;
- cycle through that many elements, using ITEM to look at each. If that element is the one sought, increment the count of the number of occurrences.

Resist the temptation to do it this way. In LOGO, it would be a mess, because there is a much neater and quicker way, not available in more conventional languages. The idea is as follows. Is A the first element of [A B A C D]? Yes, so the number of occurrences is one more than the number of occurrences in the BUTFIRST of the list, namely [B A C D]. If A had not been the first element, then the number of occurrences would just have been the same as the number in the BUTFIRST of the list. The algorithm this suggests is

a) Is the element sought equal to the FIRST of the list? If so, output 1 + the number of occurrences in the BUTFIRST of the list.
b) If not, output the number of occurrences in the BUTFIRST of the list.

The algorithm is not quite complete. If the list is empty, then FIRST will object. Moreover, only the number 1 appears explicitly in this algorithm, but the answer 0 must be a possible result. An extra step is needed. The full solution, in LOGO, is

```
TO OCCURS :ELEMENT :LIST
IF :LIST = [ ] [OUTPUT 0]
IF :ELEMENT = FIRST :LIST [OUTPUT 1 +
        (OCCURS :ELEMENT BF :LIST)] [OUTPUT
        (OCCURS :ELEMENT BF :LIST)]
END
```

(The parentheses here are only for legibility.) This may be the first time you have seen a procedure which invokes itself recursively in one of two possible places in its definition, rather than in just one possible place. If you are in doubt, try it out.

It is easy to extend it so that it can also be used to count the number of times a character appears in a word or number. The only change needed is to replace the test

```
IF :LIST = [ ] . . .
```

by

```
IF EMPTYP :LIST
```

since EMPTYP outputs TRUE if its input is the empty word or the empty list. FIRST and BUTFIRST work equally on words and on lists.

Updating an element of a list

IBM PC LOGO provides two procedures which are really specialised and restricted forms of SENTENCE. One, FPUT (an acronym for FirstPUT), is for glueing some element onto the front of a list. It takes two inputs, the second of which must be a list, and outputs a list whose first element is the first input and whose remainder is the second input, for example

    FPUT "A [B C]

outputs [A B C]. The other procedure, LPUT (an acronym for LastPUT), works in a predictably similar way. You can safely opt to forget about both of these; however, for the sake of showing them in use they will both be used in the remainder of this chapter.

When updating an element of a list you need to know three things: what the list is, which is the element to update and what its new value is to be. Again it is best to think about the simplest case first of all. To update the first element of a list, just output the list formed by glueing the new value onto the front of the BUTFIRST of the given list (that is, prune off the old value, glue on the new). If it is not the first element that is to be updated then it becomes a matter of updating the (N-1)th element of the BUTFIRST of the given list, for instance to update the third element of [A B C D], update the second of [B C D]. Forethought, or one or two misfiring experiments, will remind you that it is also necessary to glue the FIRST element of the given list onto the result of updating the BUTFIRST of it.

This is the bones of it in LOGO:

```
TO UPDATE :N :LIST :NEW
IF :N = 1 [OUTPUT (FPUT :NEW BUTFIRST
     :LIST)]
OUTPUT (FPUT (FIRST :LIST) (UPDATE
     (:N − 1) BUTFIRST :LIST :NEW)
END
```

(Note for teachers: the inputs to UPDATE appear in the order shown for a good reason, namely that it makes the use of UPDATE easier to verbalise. The expression UPDATE 2 [A B C] "Z could be read as 'update the second element of [A B C] to be Z'. It pays to get people into this habit.) The procedure could be improved a little — what if there were too few elements in the list? With careless typing it would be easy to produce something like

```
... UPDATE 22 [A B C] "Z ...
```

A remedy would be to include an extra line at the start of UPDATE:

```
TO UPDATE :N :LIST :NEW
IF :N > COUNT :LIST [ERR [UPDATE:  LIST
     IS TOO SHORT]]
```

This uses the procedure ERR defined in Section 4.5.1.

Since both FPUT and SENTENCE always output a list, it is trickier to make UPDATE work for words too. It is undoubtedly neater to define a whole new procedure if you want to be able to do this operation on words. The corresponding procedure to FPUT or SENTENCE is WORD.

Deleting the Nth element

If N is 1 it is easy — output the BUTFIRST of the list. If N is not one, what is wanted is to delete the (N-1)th element of the BUTFIRST of the list. Look at an example. Suppose you want to delete the third element of the list [P Q R S]. The answer will be [P Q S]. The BUTFIRST of the given list is [Q R S], and deleting the second element of it gives [Q S]. The answer is obtained by glueing the first element of the given list, namely P, onto the front. In LOGO:

```
TO DELETE :N :LIST
IF :N = 1 [OUTPUT BF :LIST]
OUTPUT FPUT (FIRST :LIST) (DELETE :N-1 :LIST)
END
```

(again, the parentheses are purely for legibility). This is capable of improvement — what if :N is zero or negative, or the list is too short? Here is a better version:

```
TO DELETE :N :LIST
IF OR (:N < 1) (EMPTYP :LIST) [ERR [SILLY
     INPUT FOR DELETE]]
IF :N = 1 [OUTPUT BF :LIST]
OUTPUT FPUT (FIRST :LIST) (DELETE :N-1 :LIST)
END
```

This, too, uses the ERR procedure defined in Section 4.5.1. If you wanted a version of DELETE which worked equally on words and on lists, you'd need to do something like this:

```
TO DELETE :N :OBJECT
```

```
IF LISTP :OBJECT [OUTPUT DEL. FROM. LIST
        :N :OBJECT] [OUTPUT DEL. FROM. WORD
        :N :OBJECT]
    END

TO DEL. FROM. LIST :N :LIST

...

TO DEL. FROM. WORD :N :WORD

...
```

The intersection of two lists

Consider some examples: the intersection of [A B C] and [C A R] ought to be [C A] or [A C]. The intersection of [A B] and [C D] ought to be the empty list. It is reasonably clear that the thing to do is to work through the first list, and include each element that also features in the second list in the answer. Yet again, the tools for working through the first list are FIRST and BUTFIRST. To check whether an element features in the second list, you have MEMBERP available. The only time that the answer is the empty list is when you have checked all the elements of the first list and are left with an empty first list.

In LOGO this could be expressed as

```
TO INTERSECT :L1 :L2
IF :L1 = [ ] [OUTPUT [ ]]
TEST MEMBERP (FIRST :L1) :L2
IFTRUE [OUTPUT FPUT (FIRST :L1)
        INTERSECT (BF :L1) :L2]
IFFALSE [OUTPUT INTERSECT (BF :L1) :L2]
END
```

It may help to work through an example on paper first.

The union of two lists

The union of [A B] and [A C] ought to be [A B C] or some permutation of it, rather than [A A B C]. The union of [A B] and [C] ought to be [A B C] or some permutation of that. The important point is to avoid unnecessary duplication of elements in the answer. As with INTERSECT the obvious method is to work through the first list, using FIRST and BUTFIRST. If the first list is empty the answer is just the second list, even if that is empty. If the first list is not empty, consider its first element. If it features in the second list, ignore it because that would otherwise lead to duplication. If it is not in the second list, glue it onto the union of the BUTFIRST of the first list, and the second list.

In LOGO this could be expressed in a manner very like the

example of INTERSECT:

```
TO UNION :L1 :L2
IF :L1 = [] [OUTPUT :L2]
TEST MEMBERP (FIRST :L1) :L2
IFTRUE [OUTPUT UNION (BF :L1) :L2]
IFFALSE [OUTPUT FPUT (FIRST :L1) UNION
      (BF :L1) : L2]
END
```

Compare this carefully with INTERSECT; the similarities are surprising.

Replacing all occurrences of an element

Once more, the tools for working through the list are FIRST and BUTFIRST. If the list is empty, output the empty list. Otherwise, look at the first element. If it is an occurrence of what is to be replaced, use FPUT to put the new value onto the front of the result of processing the rest of the list. If not, FPUT the first element instead. In LOGO this is

```
TO REPLACE :OLD :NEW :L
IF :L = [] [OUTPUT []]
TEST :OLD = FIRST :L
IFTRUE [OUTPUT FPUT :NEW REPLACE :OLD
      :NEW (BF :L)]
IFFALSE [OUTPUT FPUT FIRST :L REPLACE
      :OLD :NEW (BF :L)]
END
```

Sorting a list

Almost any book on any programming language gives examples of sorting. The most widely used algorithm is the Quicksort, invented by C. A. R. Hoare in 1960. It is very easy to express in LOGO. The idea is as follows:

a) Take the first element. Split the rest of the list into two others: a 'less' list of all those elements less than the first, and a 'more' list of all those that are not less than the first.
b) Sort the 'less' and the 'more' lists. Join the results, with that first element in between, to get the answer.

Here is the definition of SORT. It uses a procedure LESSP whose inputs should be any two elements and which outputs TRUE if the first is less than the second. The definition capitalises on the fact that LOCAL and SENTENCE can be 'greedy' procedures:

```
TO SORT :L
```

```
IF EMPTYP :L [OUTPUT [ ]]
(LOCAL "LESS "MORE)
MAKE "LESS [ ]
MAKE "MORE [ ]
SPLIT BUTFIRST :L FIRST :L
OUTPUT (SENTENCE SORT :LESS FIRST :L
      SORT :MORE)
END


TO SPLIT :L :E
IF EMPTYP :L [STOP]
IF LESSP :E FIRST :L [MAKE "MORE FPUT
      FIRST :L :MORE] [MAKE "LESS FPUT
      FIRST :L :LESS]
SPLIT BUTFIRST :L :E
END
```

Note that this needs a little modification if the elements of the list to be sorted are themselves lists, since SENTENCE will replace a list by the collection of its elements. A suitable change to SORT is

```
. . .
OUTPUT (SENTENCE SORT :LESS (LIST FIRST
      :L) SORT :MORE)
END
```

since SENTENCE will happily treat a list with one element as though it were that element!

A version of LESSP that works for words or numbers is

```
TO LESSP :W1 :W2
IF EMPTYP :W2 [OUTPUT "FALSE]
IF EMPTYP :W1 [OUTPUT "TRUE]
IF (FIRST :W1) = (FIRST :W2) [OUTPUT
      LESSP BUTFIRST :W1 BUTFIRST :W2]
OUTPUT (ASCII FIRST :W1) < (ASCII FIRST
      :W2)
END
```

The ASCII codes determine the ordering. A complete list of the standard characters in IBM PC and their ASCII codes can be found in Figures 8.2, 8.3 and 8.4.

EXERCISES

If you have worked carefully through this chapter you should be able, with care and perhaps one or two false starts, to do these exercises. They are hard. Do not expect to do them in a few minutes. If you have not been following this chapter you are now on your own . . .

1. Devise a procedure REVERSE that outputs a list formed by reversing its input:

    REVERSE [A B C]   should output [C B A]

    (Hint: LPUT might help.)
2. Devise a procedure REVWORD that reverses a word:

    REVWORD "STRAP   should output PARTS

3. Devise a procedure which tests whether a word or a list is palindromic, that is, reads the same backwards as forwards. Try to do it more directly than by using the results of the first two exercises.

    PALINDROME "REFER   should output   TRUE
    PALINDROME [A B B A]   should output   TRUE
    PALINDROME [A B A B]   should output   FALSE

4. Devise a procedure which prints out a list reasonably elegantly. What this means is for you to decide. As a suggestion, printing out the list

    [HERE [WITH [A FEW] FRILLS] IS A LIST]

    might be nicely printed as

    HERE
            WITH
                A
                FEW
            FRILLS
        IS
        A
        LIST

    Remember the procedure LISTP which tests whether its input is a list or not; it is analogous to WORDP and NUMBERP.

4.6 LISTS AND TURTLE GRAPHICS

Putting together your knowledge of lists and your knowledge of

turtle graphics can expand your programming horizons considerably. Chapter 5 is largely concerned with a project in this area;
Chapter 7 suggests several others. This section describes two small
projects for the sake of demonstrating some basic practical uses of
lists.

4.6.1 Playing with scale

This project was originally motivated by the idle thought that it
would be fun to be able to shrink or enlarge shapes easily, and to
turn them over. One way is to edit a procedure such as

```
TO BOX
REPEAT 4 [FD 100 RT 90]
END
```

so that it has an input, which is used as a multiplying factor for the
100. This permits change of scale, but not turning over.

What is involved in turning over a shape? Some playing about
with simple non-symmetric shapes ought to convince you that what
is needed is to replace FORWARD by BACKWARD and RIGHT
by LEFT, and vice-versa. BACKWARD 100 is just the same as
FORWARD −100, and LEFT 90 is the same as RIGHT −90. So,
all that is needed is to reverse the signs of the numbers involved.
The awkward point about this is that the definition of BOX will
come to look cumbersome — it will need two inputs, one for the
side length and one for the angle. It will also be an unreasonable
amount of work to incorporate this feature in each new shape, and
this would stop the whole enterprise from being fun or easy.

There is another approach. The key idea — which you may not
feel is the best or even much use, but this is only a demonstration —
is to represent simple shapes as lists of lists. Each list will contain
two numbers, an amount to go FORWARD and an amount to turn
RIGHT. For instance, the basic BOX would be

```
[[100 90] [100 90] [100 90] [100 90]]
```

It must be possible to define a procedure, say called DO, which
takes such a list as input and draws the shape. The steps involved
are:

a) If the list is empty just STOP.
b) Otherwise look at the FIRST of it (in the case of the box its
   [100 90]). Go FORWARD by the FIRST of this, turn RIGHT
   by the second element.
c) Now just DO the BUTFIRST of the list of lists.

Here is the LOGO definition:

```
TO DO :LL
IF :LL = [ ] [STOP]
FORWARD FIRST (FIRST :LL)
RIGHT ITEM 2 (FIRST :LL)
DO BUTFIRST :LL
END
```

It is easy to give DO a second input which will be a scale factor:

```
TO DO :LL :SCALE
IF :LL = [ ] [STOP]
FD :SCALE * FIRST (FIRST :LL)
RT ITEM 2 (FIRST :LL)
DO (BUTFIRST :LL) :SCALE
END
```

To draw the shape turned over, use a separate procedure:

```
TO FLIP :LL :SCALE
IF :LL = [ ] [STOP]
BK :SCALE * FIRST (FIRST :LL)
LT ITEM 2 (FIRST :LL)
FLIP (BUTFIRST :LL) :SCALE
END
```

The beauty of DO and FLIP is that it is easy to express shapes as lists of lists. These two procedures could form the basis of a simple kit for experimenting with rotations and reflections.

An entirely different approach to playing with scale and orientation is possible in IBM PC LOGO. Suppose you created a global variable called SCALE whose value was the scale you wanted drawings to be. It would be handy if you could, so to speak, redefine FORWARD and other such procedures as, say, this:

```
TO FORWARD :DISTANCE
FORWARD :DISTANCE * :SCALE
END
```

If you try to redefine FORWARD by using EDIT, then you will be told

```
FORWARD IS A PRIMITIVE
```

meaning it's one of the procedures built into LOGO and available right from the start. Even if you could redefine it to be the procedure above, it wouldn't help, because the FORWARD above is recursive. What the procedure ought to say is 'define FORWARD to invoke the old version of FORWARD, with an input changed by a factor of :SCALE'. To do that, you'd need to be able to have the old version available — but not called FORWARD, because you want to use that name for the new version so that all your procedures that use FORWARD now deal with your new version.

IBM PC LOGO has two special provisions for precisely this situation. If you want to change the built-in procedures using EDIT, you must first have given the command

```
MAKE "REDEFP "TRUE
```

The variable called REDEFP is itself built into the system, and at the start has the value FALSE. You can change the built-in procedures only when its value is TRUE. To preserve the old version of FORWARD before you change it, you can use the procedure COPYDEF, which takes two words as input. The effect of COPYDEF is to make the system give the same meaning to the first word, in future, as it currently gives to the second word. Therefore, the command

```
COPYDEF "OLD. FORWARD "FORWARD
```

will ensure that OLD. FORWARD is a command that behaves just like FORWARD. Now you can redefine FORWARD as

```
TO FORWARD :DISTANCE
OLD. FORWARD :DISTANCE * :SCALE
END
```

Beware, though — redefining FORWARD does not automatically redefine its abbreviation FD, or its opposite BACK. If you redefine FD, BACK and BK (and perhaps SETX, SETY, SETPOS and so on as well) then you can start playing with the value of the variable SCALE without having to change all your own carefully defined drawing procedures. To start playing with turning shapes over, you would need to redefine LEFT and RIGHT (and LT and RT and SETH and so on), like this:

```
MAKE "TURNED. OVER "FALSE
COPYDEF "OLD. RIGHT "RIGHT
COPYDEF "OLD. LEFT "LEFT

TO RIGHT :ANGLE
IF :TURNED. OVER [OLD. LEFT :ANGLE] [
```

```
        OLD. RIGHT :ANGLE]
END


TO LEFT :ANGLE
IF :TURNED. OVER [OLD. RIGHT :ANGLE] [
       OLD. LEFT :ANGLE]
END
```

COPYDEF and the variable REDEFP give you a lot of power to adjust what your own procedures do without having to edit them.

4.6.2 Simple shape recording

When playing with SETX, SETY and SETPOS, it often happens that you give values which are not quite correct and this mars the drawing. Either you accept the blemish or you start again. What motivates this project is the thought that it would be useful to be able to manoeuvre the turtle into the right spot, making mistakes on the way, and then record the spot somehow. Then it would be easy to clear the screen and draw a perfect shape by replaying the recording.

The main idea is to have a variable, say called RECORDING, whose value will be a list of lists each containing the X and Y co-ordinates of one spot, and POS conveniently outputs such a list. A procedure RECORD will be used to append the turtle's current co-ordinates to the end of the recording and update RECORDING. Another procedure, REPLAY, will be used to replay the recording. RECORD will only be used when the turtle is on a wanted spot.

RECORD is simple:

```
TO RECORD
MAKE "RECORDING LPUT POS :RECORDING
END
```

REPLAY is only slightly harder. You only need to SETPOS to the position given by the FIRST of RECORDING, then REPLAY the BUTFIRST of it. However, it would be pleasing if REPLAY took no inputs at all. It ought not to change RECORDING itself, because then you could only use REPLAY once. Here is one solution: use a sub-procedure with an input.

```
TO REPLAY
PU
SETPOS FIRST :RECORDING
PD
PLAYBACK :RECORDING
END
```

```
TO PLAYBACK :L
IF :L = [ ] [STOP]
SETPOS FIRST :L
PLAYBACK BUTFIRST :L
END
```

The first line in REPLAY gets the turtle to the starting position; therefore it would be slightly more economical if the last line were PLAYBACK BF :RECORDING instead. Before trying the procedures, remember to

```
MAKE "RECORDING [ ]
```

at the start.

4.6.3 The state of the turtle
If you want to play about with other such projects it may help you to know that IBM PC LOGO provides procedures called PEN and SHOWNP. They take no input. SHOWNP outputs TRUE if the turtle is normally visible. In particular, only the procedures SHOWTURTLE and HIDETURTLE affect what SHOWNP outputs.

PEN outputs a list of three elements:

- the mode of the pen, one of the four words PENUP, PENDOWN, PENERASE or PENREVERSE;
- a number (0−3) giving the pen colour;
- a number (0 or 1) giving the palette currently in use.

The procedure SETPEN is complementary to PEN. It expects such a list as input.

These procedures, together with XCOR, YCOR, HEADING and SHAPE, tell you all there is to know about the state of the turtle at any time.

4.7 TWO NON-GRAPHIC EXAMPLES
This section gives two examples of the use of lists. The comments are brief.

4.7.1 A calculator
This section describes a simple set of procedures which together form a 'reverse Polish' calculator, mimicking the way some pocket calculators work. The name 'reverse Polish' refers to a particular notation for arithmetic. Instead of expressing the product of 23 and 34 as

23 * 34

the 'reverse Polish' form is

23 34 *

that is, you enter the number 23 first, then the number 34, and only then do you say what is to be done with them — in this example, they are to be multiplied together. The principle behind the notation is that you are working with an ordered sequence of numbers, initially empty. Any number you enter is appended at the end of the sequence. If you specify an arithmetic operation it is carried out using the last (that is, most recent) two numbers of the sequence; those numbers are deleted from the end of the sequence by the operation, and the result is put there instead. Therefore you need to keep in mind what the sequence is. For example:

```
              sequence: nothing
enter: 7    ... sequence: 7
enter: 9    ... sequence: 7 9
enter: 6    ... sequence: 7 9 6
enter: *    ... sequence: 7 54
enter: +    ... sequence: 61
enter: +    ... error! There is only one number.
```

The sequence will be stored in LOGO as a list, the value of a variable called SEQ. The main work will be done by a procedure R.POLISH, which will use READLIST to get a number or an operation from the user. If it is a number it will be appended to the list, otherwise the appropriate operation will be done. It is convenient to have a fifth operation called P which prints the sequence, and to have the last number in the sequence printed whether you specify a number or an operation.

In the definitions below, the procedure PUT puts its input onto the end of the sequence and the procedure GET takes one number off the end and outputs the number. The effect of the operation of addition is therefore just to PUT the sum of the outputs of two GETs — that is, in LOGO,

PUT (GET + GET)

The definitions are

```
TO CALC
SETUP
R. POLISH
```

```
END


TO SETUP
MAKE "SEQ [ ]
END


TO R. POLISH
TYPE ">>\
MAKE "IN READLIST
IF (COUNT :IN) > 1 [PRINT [ALL BUT
        FIRST ITEM IGNORED]]
MAKE "IN FIRST :IN
IF NUMBERP :IN [PUT :IN]
IF :IN = "* [PUT (GET * GET)]
IF :IN = "/ [PUT (GET/GET)]
IF :IN = "− [PUT (GET − GET)]
IF :IN = "+ [PUT (GET + GET)]
IF :IN = "Q [PRINT [QUIT] THROW
     "TOPLEVEL]
IF :IN = "P [PRINT :SEQ] [PRINT
        LAST :SEQ]
R. POLISH
END


TO GET
MAKE "VAL LAST :SEQ
MAKE "SEQ BUTLAST :SEQ
OUTPUT :VAL
END


TO PUT :NUM
MAKE "SEQ LPUT :NUM :SEQ
END
```

Beware of subtraction and division; they are not quite what you
would expect. For example, entering 12, then 24, then / will result in
2 being printed, rather than 0.5. You can add further operations by
adding lines to R.POLISH. One useful addition is an operation
which merely deletes the last number, in case you enter a wrong
number by mistake. Another useful operation is that of swapping
the last two items around.

As it stands above, R.POLISH is not quite satisfactory. It
would be handy if you could enter several numbers and/or operations on one line, rather than ignoring all but the first. Also,
consider what happens if the user just presses ENTER when the

prompt $>>$ appears. READLIST will return an empty list, so FIRST :IN will signal an error. It is straightforward to fix these two problems, by changing R. POLISH and adding an extra procedure:

```
TO R. POLISH
TYPE ">>\
DO. COMMANDS. IN READLIST
R. POLISH
END
```

```
TO DO. COMMANDS. IN :LIST
IF :LIST = [ ] [STOP]
LOCAL "IN
MAKE "IN FIRST :LIST
IF NUMBERP :IN [PUT :IN]
IF :IN = "* [PUT (GET * GET) ]
IF :IN = "/ [PUT (GET/GET) ]
IF :IN = "– [PUT (GET – GET) ]
IF :IN = "+ [PUT (GET + GET) ]
IF :IN = "Q [PRINT [QUIT] THROW
      "TOPLEVEL]
IF :IN = "P [PRINT :SEQ] [PRINT
      LAST :SEQ]
DO. COMMANDS. IN BUTFIRST :LIST
END
```

The extra procedure DO.COMMANDS.IN does all the work. If the list is empty, it just stops, having done nothing, so R. POLISH then invokes itself to get the user's next input. If the list is not empty, then FIRST :IN cannot signal an error. This extra procedure finally invokes itself to handle whatever remains of the user's input beyond the first item — even if that happens to be nothing!

4.7.2 Beautiful printing, Part 2

The set of procedures described below is designed to print the definition of a procedure, on the screen, in a way similar to the one used in this book. In particular, the printout avoids having any words split by overlapping the right-hand edge of the PC's screen. For example, rather than seeing a procedure printed on the 40-character wide screen somewhat like this:

```
TO RUBBISH
PRINT [THIS IS AN EXAMPLE OF A LIST WHI
CH HAS ELEVEN ELEMENTS]
END
```

(the word WHICH looks as thought it has been split into WHI and CH because it overlaps the right-hand edge of the screen), it would be more attractive and less confusing to see

```
THE TEXT OF RUBBISH IS
TO RUBBISH
        PRINT [THIS IS AN EXAMPLE OF A LIST
        WHICH HAS ELEVEN ELEMENTS]
END
```

It is only possible to do this if the definition of a procedure is available in a form that other procedures can use. Fortunately, the definition of the procedure is accessible in the form of a list of lists by using the IBM PC LOGO procedure TEXT. It expects one input, a word naming a procedure. It outputs a list of lists, one list per line. The first list holds the inputs from the title line but with the colons stripped off, or is empty if there are no inputs for the named procedure. An example: if the procedure JUNK is defined as

```
TO JUNK :A :B
REPEAT :A [PRINT :B]
END
```

then TEXT "JUNK will output

```
[[A B] [REPEAT :A [PRINT :B]]]
```

To use the LOGO procedures below, give the command NICE with one input, a word naming the procedure whose definition is to be printed. Treat them as an exercise in trying to read LOGO programs — they are not accompanied by explanations. Note that

```
CHAR 32
```

is really just a synonym for a word consisting of a single space, that is "\ , and that

```
PRINT [ ]
```

is just a convenient way of saying '... and start a new line'. The definitions could be improved a little; try NICE "PLIST to see where.

```
TO NICE :N
PRINT SENTENCE [THE TEXT OF] SENTENCE :N
        "IS
```

```
PRINT. PROC :N
END

TO PRINT. PROC :NAME
LOCAL "PROC. BODY
MAKE "PROC. BODY TEXT :NAME
PRINT. TITLE :NAME FIRST :PROC. BODY
PRINT. BODY BUTFIRST :PROC. BODY
END

TO PRINT. TITLE :NAME :VARLIST
TYPE (SENTENCE "TO CHAR 32 :NAME)
TYPE. VARS :VARLIST
PRINT [ ]
END

TO TYPE. VARS :VL
IF :VL = [ ] [STOP]
TYPE (SENTENCE CHAR 32 ": FIRST :VL)
TYPE. VARS BUTFIRST :VL
END

TO PRINT. BODY :LL
IF :LL = [ ] [PRINT "END PRINT [ ] STOP]
PRINT. LIST FIRST :LL
PRINT. BODY BUTFIRST :LL
END

TO PRINT. LIST :L
LOCAL "COL
MAKE "COL 2
(TYPE CHAR 32 CHAR 32)
PRETTY. PRINT :L
END

TO PRETTY. PRINT :L
IF :L = [ ] [PRINT [ ] STOP]
IF LISTP FIRST :L [PRETTY. PRINT
      (SENTENCE "'[' FIRST :L "']')
      PRETTY. PRINT BUTFIRST :L STOP]
IF COUNT FIRST :L > 37 − :COL [PRINT [ ]
      (TYPE CHAR 32 CHAR 32 CHAR 32 CHAR
      32) MAKE "COL 6]
TYPE FIRST :L
TYPE CHAR 32
MAKE "COL :COL + 1 + COUNT FIRST :L
```

```
PRETTY. PRINT BUTFIRST :L
END
```

If you don't want the square brackets of a list separated from the contents by spaces, then you can amend PRETTY.PRINT to use SHOW. SHOW is a built-in procedure which behaves like PRINT, except that it does print the outermost square brackets of a list.

4.7.3 Beautiful printing on a printer

IBM PC LOGO has a number of commands for working with files, to read and write data. Unfortunately, neither Dr. LOGO nor Waterloo LOGO has similar facilities. This section gives just a brief taste of what is possible.

In IBM PC LOGO, the printer can be treated as a file that it is possible to write to but impossible to read from. If you have an IBM graphic printer or other Epson printer attached to the printer port, then it behaves like a file called LPT1. If you have a printer attached to a serial port, then it will be called COM1 or AUX, but you must initialise the serial port first by using the SETCOM command. This expects five inputs: the number of the serial port, the baud rate, an indicator of the parity (0=none, 1=odd, 2=even), the number of data bits and the number of stop bits. If all that means nothing to you, then consult the manual or a knowledgeable friend or salesman.

Files and devices such as a printer must be opened (that is, deliberately selected as one of the ones to be used in subsequent commands) before writing or reading, and only five can be open at once. Unfortunately it is an error to open something that is already open, so a procedure ALLOPEN is provided which outputs a list of the open files and devices. If nothing has been opened, it outputs the empty list. The procedure OPEN opens a file or device, and CLOSE closes it. It is worth closing files when you no longer want them open, because otherwise you may find yourself trying to open a sixth file at an inopportune moment, which IBM PC LOGO would object to. The procedure SETWRITE selects which of the open files or devices is to be used in subsequent PRINT, TYPE, PO, SHOW and POFILE commands. Correspondingly, SETREAD selects which of the open files or devices is to be used for subsequent READCHAR, READLIST, READWORD or READCHARS procedures.

The 'pretty printing' procedure NICE of the previous section can be used to print out your procedures on the printer in a reasonably attractive way, making use of ALLOPEN and SETWRITE:

```
TO PAPER :PROC
IF NOT MEMBERP "LPT1 ALLOPEN [OPEN "LPT1]
SETWRITE "LPT1
NICE :PROC
SETWRITE "CON
CLOSE "LPT1
END
```

The final SETWRITE "CON instructs LOGO to resume the normal traffic between itself and the screen and keyboard, rather than a file or device. The CON is short for 'console', and is an ersatz device used only in this way. The word CON will never appear in the list output by ALLOPEN.

If an error happens, LOGO does an implicit SETWRITE "CON, to prevent error messages being sent to a file rather than the screen. Thus, if you interrupt PAPER the final SETWRITE and CLOSE may not happen, but you will still see the appropriate message on the screen. That, by the way, is also why the first line is not just OPEN "LPT1. The printer might have been opened but never closed at some earlier moment.

You could modify NICE to cater for the width of the paper in your printer. Just adjust the 37 that figures in the definition of PRETTY. PRINT.

5 | UNDERTAKING A PROJECT

> "I say, look here, you know!" said the Emperor, who was
> getting a little restless. "How many Axioms are you going to
> give us? At this rate, we shan't get to the Experiments till
> tomorrow-week!"
>
> (*Sylvie and Bruno Concluded*, LEWIS CARROLL)

Aims: Being able to define and use new procedures is only one
kind of LOGO skill. There are more general ones which can
only be learnt by undertaking some larger-scale enterprises.
This chapter is mainly devoted to two unretouched project
studies. The aim is to show the bad decisions along the way as
well as the good.

5.1 GENERALITIES

What is needed when you undertake a major project goes beyond
the skills needed to be able to express ideas as procedures. The
work of a project often divides into two parts: the planning, and the
implementation of the plans. Although some planning must be done
first, do not think that all the decision-making must be completed
before starting on the job of implementation. This very rarely works
out, not least because it is almost impossible to forecast all the snags
beforehand. Moreover, few projects are so fully and clearly defined
that it is possible to plan them in complete detail; such projects
usually turn out to be dull, anyway.

Nevertheless, planning and implementation are very different
activities. It is the norm to have many periods of one and many of
the other, interleaved. However, beware of trying to do both at
once. Only a very experienced programmer can appear to do both
at once. Even then it is only appearance, he will still be using his
experience to implement something whose planning side he had
thoroughly explored months or years ago. Unless you have years of
experience to call on, it is better to work somewhat in this fashion:

- Having chosen a project, begin by trying to describe what will
  first give you some real sense of satisfaction. You may well not be
  satisfied with it by the time you achieve it, but it will have been a
  milestone.
- Then plan, in as top-down a fashion as you feel at ease with. That
  is, try to start with general intentions and refine them stage by
  stage into more specific intentions.
- When you feel that some of the ingredients are sufficiently pre-

cisely defined, implement them. You will probably find it necessary to do this before all the planning is complete, in order to reassure yourself that you are still working along reasonable lines. Planning needs confidence; implementation provides it or proves it unjustified.

- Continue with stages of planning and programming until you reach your milestone or find that you cannot. In either case find another milestone and carry on.

Use paper and pencil when planning. You do not have to make elaborate notes, you can probably get away with jotting down terse reminders of important points. Although you may be one of the few who can work reliably by memory alone, it is vastly more annoying to start by supposing this and being proved wrong than it is to work the other way around.

The rest of this chapter is taken up by two sections, each devoted to a project. Each section has various sub-sections. The idea is to show two realistic examples, as might be done by a person with a reasonable amount of experience. Working from the point of view of a novice might exhaust your interest.

5.2 NESTED POLYGONS

This project arose from the kind of doodles I do absent-mindedly, such as when concentrating on speaking on the telephone. Looking at the doodles afterward, a certain conjecture came to mind. The project was an attempt to gather some evidence to see if it was really plausible.

5.2.1 The question

Imagine that you have drawn a somewhat irregular hexagon on your telephone pad. An idle thing to do is to join up the mid-points of the sides. The result is a smaller irregular hexagon. Do it again and again. Figure 5.1 shows the outcome of this after a few minutes. The odd thing is that the innermost hexagon looks much more like a regular hexagon than the original one. Perhaps the more you continue, the more like a regular hexagon it gets. On the other hand it may be only a coincidence, perhaps the initial hexagon was a lucky choice. Maybe some initial hexagons do lead to regular ones and others do not, but if so, why, and what makes the difference? Moreover, what about octagons, heptagons, pentagons? What about quadrilaterals — do you get squares or do you get parallelograms or do you get nothing remarkable at all? [There is a neat mathematical solution to the problem, based on expressing the co-ordinates as trigonometric polynomials. But suppose that is too much like hard work ...]

The initial idea, therefore, is to devise some LOGO procedures to draw the successively smaller hexagons. This will make it possible to check on a variety of initial hexagons with comparative ease. The first hurdle is to figure out how this can be done.

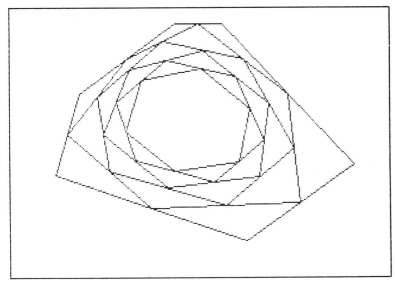

Figure 5.1

5.2.2 Representing the hexagon

Experience will teach you that this is one of the most crucial decisions in almost any project. The right decision can make the whole thing easy; the wrong one can lead to high blood pressure and premature philately.

Two possibilities are apparent. The first is to represent the hexagon as a series of FORWARD and RIGHT pairs, as in the RECORD procedure in Section 4.6.2.

Advantages   It is easy to produce the actual drawing.
Disadvantages It is hard to specify the initial list of lists of pairs of numbers, even if the initial hexagon is nearly regular. Also, it is not immediately clear how to get the representation of the nested hexagon from this one.

The other possibility is to represent the hexagon as a list of six elements each giving the co-ordinates of a corner.

Advantages   It is easy to draw the hexagon, using SETPOS. It is also easy to specify the initial list — use the RECORD system in Chapter 4. It is not too awkward to construct the list that will represent the nested hexagon, either. Given the co-ordinates of two adjacent corners, the co-ordinates of the mid-point can be found by taking the average of the corresponding co-ordinates.

Disadvantages   No major ones (yet).

Therefore, use the second one.

It helps further deliberations if you have a real example to work on. Rather than deal with negative numbers, take a hexagon that lies entirely within the top right quadrant of the screen, say

[[10 30] [30 20] [80 10] [120 80] [50 110] [10 50]]

The procedure PLAYBACK defined in Section 4.6.2 could be used to draw the hexagon represented by this. It is not ideal — try it, e.g.

```
MAKE "HEX [[10 30] [30 20] [80 10] [120
      80] [50 110] [10 50]]
PLAYBACK :HEX
```

draws Figure 5.2. There are two snags. The line from the turtle's starting position to the first corner should not be there. Also, the last side is missing. All would be well if the turtle had started at the last corner. This suggests a simple amendment — make PLAYBACK a sub-procedure of one that puts the turtle at the last corner first, and then invokes it. So,

```
TO PLOT :LL
PENUP
SETPOS LAST :LL
PENDOWN
PLAYBACK :LL
END
```

This works.

5.2.3 Producing the nested hexagon

Given one hexagon, the nested one has its corners at the mid-points of the sides. Suppose a side runs from corner $[x1\ y1]$ to corner $[x2\ y2]$. The mid-point will have X co-ordinate $(x1+x2)/2$ and Y co-ordinate $(y1+y2)/2$. It seems sensible to define a procedure MIDPT which will be given two points (as two-element lists) as inputs, and will output the two-element list for the mid-point:

```
TO MIDPT :PT1 :PT2
```

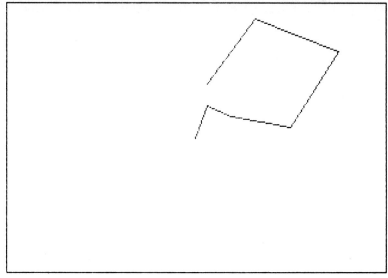

Figure 5.2

```
OUTPUT LIST ( (ITEM 1 :PT1) + (ITEM
        1 :PT2) )/2 ( (ITEM 2 :PT1) + (
        ITEM 2 :PT2) )/2
END
```

Try this to make sure that it does the right thing, before carrying on.

It must now be straightforward to define a procedure that, given the representation of a hexagon, outputs the representation of the nested hexagon. For example:

```
TO NEST :LL
OUTPUT (LIST MIDPT ITEM 1 :LL ITEM 2 :LL
        MIDPT ITEM 2 :LL ITEM 3 :LL
        MIDPT ITEM 3 :LL ITEM 4 :LL
        MIDPT ITEM 4 :LL ITEM 5 :LL
        MIDPT ITEM 5 :LL ITEM 6 :LL
        MIDPT ITEM 6 :LL ITEM 1 :LL)
END
```

This one-line procedure is a big mouthful. If you mistyped it the mistake would be hard to find. Moreover, it is very specifically to do with hexagons. If :LL had only five elements, representing a pentagon instead, then the ITEM 6 :LL would give you an error. However, NEST works: try

```
PRINT NEST :HEX
```

You should be able to predict that it prints

```
[[20 25] [55 15] [100 45] [85 95] [30 80] [10 40]]
```

by looking at the value of HEX, and doing some mental arithmetic.

Principle In general, whenever you create a procedure, try it at once. Don't store up troubles for later.

5.2.4 Trying it out
You now have the ingredients to start experimenting, namely PLOT and NEST. You might be tempted to launch into

```
CS
PLOT :HEX
REPEAT 10 [MAKE "HEX NEST :HEX PLOT
      :HEX]
```

but wait. Doing this, you would lose the original value of HEX. Keep a copy of it first:

```
MAKE "ORIG. HEX :HEX
```

Then the sequence of commands above will produce Figure 5.3. Now you can spend a little time investigating the original conjecture.

5.2.5 Problems and doubts
If you have now tried nesting hexagons several times, starting from various initial hexagons, you might think that the original conjecture is fractionally more plausible than it seemed earlier. However, the innermost hexagon is eventually too small to judge by eye for regularity.

At this point, another doubt might assail you. If you want to move on to looking at heptagons (seven-sided figures) you need a new version of NEST; you need a new one every time you want to move on to another number of sides. This would be nearly acceptable if NEST weren't so easy to mistype.

Principle A warning sign in any project is that one or more of the procedures seems to be getting out of hand.

Perhaps it is possible to define a recursive version of NEST, so that it will work however many sides there are. The algorithm,

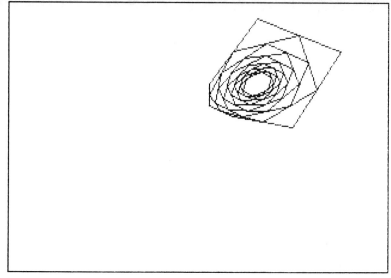

Figure 5.3

relying on past experience, might go like this:

a) If there is only one corner output the empty list.
b) Form the mid-point of the first two corners. Join this onto the list of mid-points formed by starting with the BUTFIRST of the original list, and then output the result.

This is incomplete. If it is applied to a list of six corners it generates a list of five mid-points. The missing mid-point is the one lying between the last corner and the first one.

There are at least two possible cures. One is to keep a note of the first corner, perhaps as the value of some (global) variable or perhaps as a second input to NEST, and then use the value of it in a new step (a):

a) If there is only one corner in the list, output the list whose sole element is the mid-point between it and the corner whose position was noted at the start.

Another solution is to change the representation of the polygon slightly. Instead of having N elements,

    [corner1 corner2 .. cornerN]

let it have N+1:

[corner1 corner2 .. cornerN corner1]

This lets you generate all the N mid-points by a straightforward recursion, as outlined above. To construct the representation of the nested polygon, all that is needed is to glue a copy of the first mid-point onto the end of the list of mid-points.

5.2.6 The new nest procedure

The two solutions are almost equally good. The second one, a changed representation, will be adopted for what follows. It is marginally neater, though neither solution necessitates changes to PLOT.

Principle When in genuine doubt, make a random choice — at least it's progress.

NEST becomes:

```
TO NEST :LL
MAKE "LL MIDPTLIST :LL
OUTPUT LPUT (FIRST :LL) :LL
END
```

```
TO MIDPTLIST :LL
IF (COUNT :LL) = 1 [OUTPUT [ ]]
OUTPUT FPUT (MIDPT ITEM 1 :LL ITEM 2
        :LL) (MIDPTLIST BUTFIRST :LL)
END
```

An interesting detail is the use of LL as though it were a normal variable rather than an input, in the first line of NEST. It was explained in Chapter 3 that inputs are variables; the only point to remember is that LL supersedes any other variable of the same name while NEST is being run — that is, it is a local variable rather than a global one.

Remember to amend both HEX and ORIG. HEX:

```
MAKE "HEX LPUT (FIRST :ORIG. HEX) :ORIG. HEX
MAKE "ORIG. HEX :HEX
```

5.2.7 Fault tracing

It is timely to discuss how to set about tracking down faults in procedures, using a specific example. Suppose that you have just copied MIDPTLIST into your LOGO system, but you carelessly omitted the BUTFIRST in the last line. When you use NEST, nothing happens, not even a prompt to show that it has finished.

The best thing to do is to type CTRL-G to terminate whatever is happening, with extreme prejudice. Thereafter, begin by looking at the definitions of NEST and MIDPTLIST. If the problem doesn't catch your eye, one recourse is to include some extra commands in each definition. You could insert

```
CHECK "LL
```

at the start of each definition; CHECK was defined in Section 4.5.2. Running NEST again, you should see that LL only changed value once, and thereafter never changed. This might alert you to the problem; MIDPTLIST ought to be invoking itself recursively with successively shorter input lists each time.

Another action you can take is to press the F5 key, or to insert the command PAUSE at one or more points in your procedures. Either causes whatever is running to pause, giving you a message like this:

```
PAUSING... IN <procedure name>:
<the line where the pause happened>
<procedure names> ?
```

It then waits for you to do something. You can give whatever commands you like. For instance, you can print the value of any input or other local variable that was in existence at the time you pressed the F5 key. To make LOGO resume give the command

```
CO
```

(a mnemonic for "continue"), or to make LOGO abandon what it was doing give the command

```
THROW "TOPLEVEL
```

You can pause something that you started while something else was paused. CO only resumes the most recently paused activity. A drawback with pausing is that, if you use the command PAUSE, you must have some idea about where to insert it in your procedures; if you cause a pause by using the F5 key, it is difficult to know exactly when to press it.

The final recourse is to use the IBM PC LOGO procedure STEP, which is *not* built-in but is provided within the toolkit that is in a file on the IBM PC LOGO disk. To use it, you must first load it, for example by the commands

```
LOAD "TOOLS "TOOLKIT
```

```
BURY "TOOLKIT
```

It is a good idea to 'bury' the toolkit, since there are a large number of procedures in it. If you didn't, and used POTS to look at your procedure titles, your own procedure titles would be lost in the blizzard of others. The toolkit is big: if your IBM PC has only 128 kb of memory, there won't be much room left after you load it. In that case, it is a good idea to break the toolkit into several smaller files, by loading it all, packaging part under a new name and saving only that package in a new file. For instance, to save the procedure STEP and the related ones in a file called STEPKIT:

```
LOAD "TOOLS
PACKAGE "STEPPKG [STEP UNSTEP STEPPER
      IGNORE SHOWARGS SHOWLINES]
SAVE "STEPKIT "STEPPKG
```

The procedure STEP takes one input: either the name of a procedure you have defined, or a list of such names. It modifies the definition of each of these procedures. When such a modified procedure is run, the value of each input is printed, and then each line is printed followed by a question mark. LOGO will wait for you to press ENTER before obeying the line. Alternatively, of course, you can press CTRL-Break to abandon everything and return to the top level.

The procedure UNSTEP also takes one input, like STEP. It restores the original definitions of the procedures. If you gave the command

```
STEP "NEST
```

then the definition of NEST above would be preserved, for later restoration, as the definition of a procedure called .NEST. The definition of NEST would then become

```
TO NEST :LL
PRINT [ENTERING NEST]
PRINT SENTENCE [LL IS] :LL
TYPE [MAKE "LL MIDPTLIST :LL]
STEPPER
MAKE "LL MIDPTLIST :LL
TYPE [OUTPUT LPUT (FIRST :LL) :LL]
STEPPER
OUTPUT LPUT (FIRST :LL) :LL
END
```

The procedure STEPPER just types a question mark and waits for you to press ENTER — it uses READLIST to detect when you've pressed it.

All these fault-finding aids may help you. It is hard to give more advice; everyone develops their own style of setting about the hunt, and everyone gets plenty of opportunities to develop it! Just bear these points in mind:

- Be patient.
- Be systematic.
- 99% of all faults are simple ones and have a single cause.
- Test each of your procedures in turn, using various test cases for inputs: 'likely' values, 'unlikely' values and special cases such as the empty list or the empty word.
- Work from the bottom up; test those procedures first which depend least on other procedures. This spares you a lot of trouble if it turns out that there is more than one fault to be found.
- KEEP NOTES!

5.2.8 More about nested polygons

Both NEST and PLOT now cope with a polygon of any number of sides. There still remains the problem of what to do when the innermost nested polygon becomes too small to judge properly. One proposal is to switch from drawing the polygon to printing out the lengths of the sides. Presumably more regular polygons have sides which are more nearly equal:

```
TO PRINTSIDES :LL
IF (COUNT :LL) = 1 [STOP]
PRINT PYTHAG (ITEM 1 :LL) (ITEM 2
      :LL)
PRINTSIDES BUTFIRST :LL
END


TO PYTHAG :PT1 :PT2
OUTPUT SQRT (SQR (ITEM 1 : PT1) −
      (ITEM 1 :PT2) ) + (SQR (ITEM
      2 :PT1) − (ITEM 2 :PT2) )
END


TO SQR :N
OUTPUT :N * :N
END
```

It turns out, however, that this idea is not very good. The side lengths get so small that it is tricky to compare them; it is hard to assess whether they are getting 'more equal' with successive nestings.

What is really needed is a new idea — or to give up on the whole problem.

Principle When all else fails, indulge in wishful or fantastic speculations.

If you want to try your hand at thinking of a solution to this problem, then *do not read on yet*. Put the book down and think about it for a little while.

The problem of minute nested polygons would not be so bad if you had a powerful magnifying glass for peering at the screen. This suggests an idea: why not magnify the polygon every so often? How often? Answer: when you feel it necessary. How can you magnify a polygon? Simply multiply every co-ordinate by some chosen scaling-up factor. What factor? Rather than indulging in an orgy of calculation, why not just pick one and see? You can always erase the screen and try another if your choice is bad.

First, consider how to rescale one single point:

```
TO RESCALE :PT : SCALE
OUTPUT LIST :SCALE * (ITEM 1 :PT)
       :SCALE * (ITEM 2 :PT)
END
```

To magnify the whole polygon just RESCALE each corner in turn:

```
TO MAGNIFY :LL :SCALE
IF :LL = [ ] [STOP]
OUTPUT FPUT (RESCALE FIRST :LL :SCALE)
       (MAGNIFY BUTFIRST :LL :SCALE)
END
```

To try this, the first thing is to recover the original hexagon — the test case — and to clear the screen:

```
CS
MAKE "HEX :ORIG.HEX
```

Then do some nesting:

```
REPEAT 10 [MAKE "HEX NEST :HEX PLOT :HEX]
```

Then magnify the final one a bit:

```
MAKE "HEX MAGNIFY :HEX 6
```

Now the magnified hexagon may not fit the screen. You can print it and check that no co-ordinate is outside the area of the screen. On the other hand you could just clear the screen and PLOT it. If it is too small or big, just use MAGNIFY again with a suitable scaling factor.

5.2.9 The next snag

The trick of magnification lets you continue the nesting process for a while. However, you will find that magnification tends to make the polygon drift off to the edge of the screen. (For the technically minded: magnification moves the centre of area of the polygon further from the centre of the screen, so you would expect this.) The remedy is clear: move the magnified polygon across a bit. This means adding a chosen number to every X co-ordinate, and another chosen number to every Y co-ordinate. A tidy way to specify the two numbers is as a list with two elements, e.g. [50 30] meaning 'add 50 to the X co-ordinates, add 30 to the Y co-ordinates'. To adjust one corner is easy:

```
TO ADJUST :PT :AMOUNT
OUTPUT LIST (ITEM 1 :PT) + (ITEM 1
        :AMOUNT) (ITEM 2 :PT) + (ITEM
        2 :AMOUNT)
END
```

Shifting the whole polygon is almost as easy:

```
TO SHIFT :LL :AMOUNT
IF :LL = [ ] [STOP]
OUTPUT FPUT (ADJUST FIRST :LL :AMOUNT)
        (SHIFT BUTFIRST :LL :AMOUNT)
END
```

To use it:

```
MAKE "HEX SHIFT :HEX [−50 −60]
```

You now have a toolkit which allows you to pursue the original conjecture as far as you want.

PLOT	This draws a polygon on the screen.
NEST	This constructs the list of lists representing the next nested polygon.
MAGNIFY	This is used whenever the polygon gets too small.
SHIFT	This is used whenever the polygon drifts too far from the middle of the screen.

EXERCISES

1. Investigate the conjecture. If it's false, can you modify it to fit the facts from the investigation?
2. Would you come to a different conclusion if you formed nested polygons according to a different rule? For instance, instead of mid-points, use one of the points of trisection of each side.
3. A very interesting variation is to form the nested polygon by joining the mid-points of diagonals instead of sides. To start with, use the diagonals which link each corner to the one two round from it.
4. Have you tried using really irregular polygons, such as non-convex ones (that is, having one or more inward bulges)?

5.3 DIFFERENT NUMBER BASES

This project was originally mentioned in a paper[*] describing a study of how LOGO might be used in a school mathematics classroom. The work was funded by the Social Science Research Council of Great Britain.

Numbers are conventionally written 'in base 10'. This means that the group of digits

754

is the conventional way of writing the number

$$7*100 + 5*10 + 4*1$$

The multipliers, from right to left, are 1, 10 and 100: successive powers of 10. If you were told that 754 was really meant to be read 'in base 8' here, the number in question would have been

$$7*64 + 5*8 + 4*1$$

which is 448 + 40 + 4 or 492 in the customary 'base 10' notation. The multipliers here, from right to left, are 1, 8 and 64: successive powers of eight. In base 8 numbers, the digits 8 and 9 are not used. The reason is that if they were, there would be at least two different ways of expressing most numbers, for example, the number written '91' would be

$$9*8 + 1$$

[*]'Teaching Mathematics through Programming in the Classroom', by J.A.M. Howe, P.M. Ross, K. Johnson and R. Inglis, *Computers and Education*, Vol. 6, 1982.

which is the same as

$$(8 + 1)*8 + 1$$

which is

$$1*64 + 1*8 + 1$$

which can be written in base 8 as '111'. Similarly, when numbers are written in base 2 notation, the only digits are 0 and 1. It is important to realise that when dealing with numbers in unconventional bases, it is only the representation of the numbers, as marks on paper or syllables in speech, that is different. The number written as '43' in base 8 is exactly the same number denoted by '35' in base 10, or by '50' in base 7, or by '100011' in base 2.

The aim of this project is to devise a set of LOGO procedures for experimenting with numbers written in unconventional bases. The motive is pure curiosity.

5.3.1 First thoughts

The first need that comes to mind is for a means of converting a number from one base to another. Take an example: how is '91' in base 10 to be written in base 8? It is bigger than 64 and less than 512 (=64*8), so the leftmost digit in the base 8 representation will be standing for the number of 64s involved. Now

$$91 = 1*64 + 27$$

so the leftmost digit will be one. The remainder, 27, is

$$27 = 3*8 + 3$$

so

$$91 = 1*64 + 3*8 + 3*1$$

and therefore '91' is written as '133' in base 8. It should be possible to formalise this somehow, though it may look confusing at the moment.

In fact, the method looks sufficiently confusing to make one think twice. The problem is to determine what the digits are when 91 is rewritten in base 8. Suppose they are A, B and C. Then

$$91 = A*64 + B*8 + C*1$$

The right-hand side of this is C plus some multiple of 8, because

A*64 + B*8 is a sum of multiples of 8. This means that C is just the remainder when 91 is divided by 8 — and there is a LOGO procedure REMAINDER to work this out in any general case. Since 91 = 11*8 + 3, C must be 3. Moreover,

$$11*8 = A*64 + B*8$$

so

$$11 = A*8 + B$$

This means that 'AB' is the representation of 11 in base 8. By the same process, B is 3 and A is 1.

Formalise this. Instead of working with 91, consider how to do it for any number — call the number N. The final digit of the representation of N in base 8 is the remainder when N is divided by 8. Unfortunately this is, literally, the last digit to be written down. As the example above suggests, the digits that come earlier are those which form the representation, in base 8, of the integer quotient of N divided by 8. There is also one easy point to note: it is only when N is more than 7 that you need to consider quotients at all.

A restatement of all this, closer to LOGO, is

a) If N is more than 7, write the base 8 representation of the integer quotient of N divided by 8.
b) Write the remainder of dividing N by 8.

This turns directly into LOGO:

```
TO BASE8 :N
IF :N > 7 [BASE8 INT :N/8]
TYPE REMAINDER :N 8
END
```

TYPE is used, rather than PRINT, so that the digits all appear on the same line. It is also easy to generalise BASE8 so that it works for other bases. Let the base be given as the value of a variable called BASE. A suitable generalisation might be:

```
TO CONVERT :N
IF :N > (:BASE − 1) [CONVERT INT
      :N/:BASE]
TYPE REMAINDER :N :BASE
END
```

Test this.

```
MAKE "BASE 2
CONVERT 30
```

prints 11110. However, there is room for improvement:

```
MAKE "BASE 8
CONVERT 13.216
```

prints 15.216, which is wrong. The part to the left of the (octal) point is correct, but the fractional part is not.

5.3.2 Difficulties

There are faults. In particular,

- It gets negative numbers wrong.
- It would be more useful if it could OUTPUT something instead of PRINTing.
- If the base is larger than 10, the number it prints is very odd because, for instance, it will treat a remainder of 10 as though it were a single digit.
- It only copes correctly with integers. INT disposes of any fractional part, but REMAINDER — used in generating the last digit of the integer part — just leaves the fractional part alone. For instance, REMAINDER 13.216 8 is 5.216.

Each of these is understandable but annoying. The immediate question is the order in which to try tackling them. It is wise to leave the first one till last, for this reason:

Principle When a number of difficulties compete equally for your attention, try the most all-embracing or most elaborate one first. If you solve it, some of the others may disappear. If you cannot (yet) solve it, move on to the next worst.

Applying this is hard: it is only your opinion as to which is the worst. In this case the question of decimals looks very intractable; the earlier discussion never got round to them at all. The best thing to do is to ignore it, by deciding that CONVERT will only be used with integers.

Principle If a problem looks too nasty, change the rules.

It is amazing how few people make conscious use of this, although it is a valuable and much-applied principle in every branch of mathematics. When you have made enough progress with the amended problem, you may begin to see how to tackle the original.

The second and third deficiencies of CONVERT go hand in hand. One answer to the problem of representing outsize digits is commonly used in computer science, namely to use letters as extra digits. The sixteen possible digits in base 16 — a digit being defined as something that is acceptable as a 'place value' in the written form of a number — are conventionally denoted by 0, ..., 9, A, ..., F. But there are only 26 letters (assuming upper and lower case should be treated as equivalent) and so there is still a problem if the base is bigger than 36. The crux of the trouble is that it seems necessary to use a single symbol for a single digit. If you were to use a pair of symbols, it would always be possible for two pairs to appear side by side in the written form, and so cause confusion. To illustrate this: imagine you are a Venusian on the point of inventing written forms of numbers. You ponder using ⌢ for the Earthling 1, and ⌢⌢ for the Earthling 2. It is a bad choice — would the Venusian ⌢⌢⌢ be the Earthling 111, or 12, or 21?

The way forward is to ignore that problem. Now look at the second deficiency, wanting to make CONVERT output instead of print. What sort of thing can any procedure output? A word, number or list. A list looks best: why not make CONVERT output a list of digits, for instance [9 1] to represent 91 in base 10? In fact why not include the base in the list — why not decide that 91 will be represented as [9 1 [10]]? The base is itself within a list, to avoid thinking of it as another digit.

The more you consider this, the better it looks. The list would be easy to read when PRINTed, since PRINT omits the outermost brackets. The number −91 can be represented as [− 9 1 [10]]. Also, the problem of representing outsized digits goes away! Now that there is a space between each digit when a number is printed, it is perfectly satisfactory to use two or more symbols together to represent one single digit. For example the number 22, when represented in base 12, would be the list [1 10 [12]]. This is unambiguous.

This gives you a good example of how the two general principles stated earlier can work out advantageously in practice. The final deficiency of CONVERT has also been resolved by adopting the list notation. To CONVERT a negative number, convert the positive number and glue a minus sign onto the front of the result.

5.3.3 Redesigning the procedure

Things have now moved from planning to implementation. There are three ingredients, not necessarily in this order:

- Constructing the list of digits.
- Attaching the information about the base to the end of the list.
- Worrying about whether the number is negative or positive. This must be the first step.

There ought to be a sub-procedure for generating the unadorned list of digits. This procedure will only ever have a positive input.

If you are doubtful of the translation from algorithm to LOGO, then work through, on paper, what happens during the command

```
PRINT DEC [- 1 3 7 [8]]
```

Now the armoury for investigating numbers in different bases consists of CONVERT and DEC. There are two extensions:

- It would be useful if CONVERT also accepted a list as input, so that it could convert a number not in base 10 to yet another base.
- It would be useful to have procedures to do simple arithmetic using the list forms of numbers.

Both of these are easy.

5.3.5 Improving CONVERT and DEC

The improvement to CONVERT consists of checking whether the input is a list. If it is, just use DEC to turn it into a base 10 number first:

```
TO CONVERT :N
IF LISTP :N [MAKE ''N DEC :N]
etc. etc.
END
```

The improvement to DEC consists of checking whether the input is a number. If it is just output it:

```
TO DEC :L
IF NUMBERP :L [OUTPUT :L]
etc. etc.
END
```

5.3.6 Arithmetic in any base

About the hardest task in devising arithmetic procedures is choosing names for them. Use ADD, SUBTRACT, MULTIPLY and DIVIDE. The procedure ADD is

```
TO ADD :N1 :N2
OUTPUT CONVERT ( (DEC :N1) + (DEC :N2) )
END
```

and the others are similarly defined. Here is a sample session of using the procedures:

```
?MAKE "BASE 8
?MAKE "X CONVERT 15
?MAKE "Y CONVERT 17
?PRINT :X
1 7 [8]
?PRINT :Y
2 1 [8]
?MAKE "BASE 16
?PRINT CONVERT 15*17
15 15 [16]
?PRINT CONVERT (MULTIPLY :X :Y)
15 15 [16]
?PRINT CONVERT :X
15 [16]
?PRINT CONVERT :Y
1 1 [16]
?PRINT DEC MULTIPLY :X :Y
255
?MAKE BASE 2
?PRINT CONVERT 255
1 1 1 1 1 1 1 1 [2]
```

and so on. Observations such as the fact that [15 [16]] multiplied by [1 1 [16]] is [15 15 [16]] will help to give you a feel for simple arithmetic in bases other than 10.

EXERCISES

5. Is it sensible for the base to be negative, using the current procedure definitions? If not, can they be suitably modified? Is the idea of a negative base reasonable?
6. Can you now extend the work to cover numbers with decimal parts? (Hint: 3.74 is 374/100)
7. Is the idea of a non-integer base reasonable? The existing procedures are not adequate for investigating this.

5.4 A FINAL PROJECT

Various general principles were mentioned in this chapter. Keep them in mind when you embark on any of the projects outlined in Chapter 7. Other useful general maxims will strike you as you get more experienced. The only one you ought to stick to without exception is

KEEP NOTES
KEEP NOTES
KEEP NOTES

There is the basis of another project: how was the diagram produced?

6 | IDEAS AND WHERE THEY MIGHT COME FROM

> "Rub it the wrong way" was Bruno's next suggestion. "Which is the wrong way?" Sylvie most reasonably enquired. The obvious plan was to try both ways.
>
> (*Sylvie and Bruno*, LEWIS CARROLL)

> *Aims*: In most projects there comes a point at which you find yourself stuck, if only temporarily. This chapter offers a few thoughts and strategies which may help you when you are in a mess.

6.1 PICKING A PROJECT

"Project?", many people say to themselves, "well ... um ... I can't think of one." There is a widespread fancy that having sufficient originality of mind to think up a worthwhile project and carry it through is (a) rare, (b) a gift rather than an acquisition, (c) a personal characteristic which is somehow independent of experience and knowledge. It is not so. Confidence is a major factor in determining success. While success also creates confidence, there are other sources as well.

The best way to pick a project is to select something which has caught your interest. Your interest gets you started, and keeps you going on those frequent occasions when your expertise temporarily fails you. The object of the interest does not have to be part of the world of LOGO. The initial thought can be very woolly:

- Write procedures to generate chunks of English text.
- Investigate ways of tiling a floor.
- Devise mazes.
- Experiment with abstract patterns.
- Play chess.

and may turn out to be impossible.

The initial idea does not have to be specific, or sharply defined. If it is not, you can take for a project the task of seeing to what extent the initial idea is practicable. Bear in mind that trying but failing to do the project is just as worthwhile as succeeding. In fact, it is usually more worthwhile, since you will probably have done more investigating.

Do not set your sights too low. In particular, do not reject a project idea on the grounds that you cannot immediately see how to turn the details into LOGO. On the other hand, do not set your sights too high. A useful guard against this is to measure how much description the idea needs. Suppose you think, "I'll get LOGO to play me at chess." As you probably know, playing chess in anything other than a mindless way demands some experience and some ability to look forward. Even writing down the fundamental rules takes a while to do. All this would have to be captured somehow within LOGO procedures, not necessarily explicitly but at least in such a manner that a person who knew LOGO but no chess could learn quite a lot about the game by reading the procedure definitions. Looked at this way, the task is too daunting. It would be possible to narrow the scope, of course. You could make your IBM PC into a chessboard, merely recording and displaying the moves of two human players on the screen. Or you could use LOGO as a simple tool to show you how many times each square is attacked; this is useful if you are a devotee of one- and two-move chess problems, or a player of postal chess. Unlike chess, the instructions for tic-tac-toe are very short and a foolproof strategy is easy to explain. A project concerned with playing that game would therefore seem to have a good chance of success, even though you cannot at once envisage the details.

Another fruitful source of project ideas lies in following up possibilities that have occurred to you in earlier work (so keep notes of them). For instance, the IBM PC can be equipped with up to four 'paddles' (via a Game Control Adapter), each having a rotatable knob and a button. IBM PC LOGO provides the means to use them. The procedure PADDLE takes one input, a number between 0 and 3, and outputs a number between roughly 4 and 130 (the actual limits are a characteristic of each paddle) that depends on how far the knob on the relevant paddle has been turned. The procedure BUTTON takes a similar input, and outputs TRUE if the appropriate button is being pressed at the time, or FALSE otherwise. Therefore, you have a means of controlling something. What? With two paddles you can control two quantities (at least). It may have struck you, when working through Chapter 3, that it would be nice to have a simple sketching system that is easier to use than typing in turtle commands. The combination of the ingredients of paddles, the turtle and the thought about sketching suggests an idea, namely using SETPOS to move the turtle around according to the rotation of the two knobs.

6.2 EVALUATING IDEAS

When trying to pick a project, or when tackling some part of one, you are sometimes faced with the job of assessing an idea before launching into it. The assessment is purely to decide whether the idea merits the effort of some exploration.

If you do this, it is likely that you are neutral about the idea in question. If you were emotionally attached to the idea you would just plunge in. If it did not appeal to you, you might reject it out of hand. It is surprising, however, how productive a few moments of consideration can be. There are almost no guidelines for you; this is another of those matters which depend heavily on temperament and experience. About the only reliable rules are to leave questions of programmability until last — LOGO is meant to be very flexible — and to look into the question of what resources are required.

As an illustration, consider this question: can LOGO be used to construct some useful word-processing tools? On the positive side: it is possible to print words almost anywhere on the screen, it is easy to determine the length of words, the technical manual explains how to get things printed on paper, and so on. On the negative side: with LOGO there is not so much free space for the text itself, unless your machine is equipped with lots of memory, and a reasonable quality printer is needed. The balance depends on your priorities. If you spend a lot of time constructing notices using transfer lettering, where the letters are of various widths, then you can make up a LOGO toolkit containing all the relevant details to help you lay out the letters on paper. See Chapter 8 for some suggestions.

6.3 LOOKING FOR IDEAS

There are various useful strategies that help in the hunt for ideas. Generalisation and specialisation are two common ones, and there are various ways they can be applied. The example of simple shape recording, in Section 4.6.2, could be generalised to include the possibility of recording whether the turtle's pen was down or up, and what colour it was, as well as the turtle's position. This would make it possible to record and replay much more sophisticated shapes. The same example could be generalised in another direction entirely, towards simple command recording. A command recording system could be used either to allow you to replay recent commands, or (using DEFINE) to allow you to define a procedure and have the commands obeyed while defining.

Generalisation depends on being able to answer the question "what am I really trying to do here?", in detail. Traditional wisdom says that the thing to do is to write down all your assumptions and aims about the matter in hand, and then pick over the list in a systematic way. If you can do that, you do not need help. The only useful recommendation for you if you cannot specify your assumptions, is to turn over the goals in your mind and pick on the bits that annoy you. Indulge in wishful thinking: ask yourself "wouldn't it be

nice if..." and "what would happen if ...". For instance: wouldn't
it be nice if LOGO did arithmetic to an accuracy of some large
number of significant digits? This is a project discussed further in
Chapter 7.

Specialisation tends to be easier than generalisation, because it
happens more naturally. It arises when you find some goal too hard
and you have to cut down your ambition a bit. There have been
several examples earlier in this book, such as the limitation of the
number bases project to integers only in Section 6.3.2. As another
simple case: think about defining some LOGO procedures that
accept a date as input, and output the day of the week on which it
fell, or will fall. It is messy, especially if you want it to work for
years before 1752 when the calendar was reformed. Start by working
only in the current year. If that is too much, start by working only in
the current month of the current year.

Another useful strategy goes by the quaint name of 'defocuss-
ing'. The idea is to examine something well known and understood,
but consciously to ignore certain aspects of it. It is very much akin
to specialisation, but you start with something familiar. This was
applied in Chapter 2 to the REPEAT command, to see it as a
command that contained another command. As another example,
look at the procedure CHAR mentioned in Section 4.5.4. It is
normally used in conjunction with ASCII; ASCII expects a single
character word as input, and outputs the number associated with it
by international conventions, and CHAR does the reverse. However, CHAR is just a procedure which takes a number as input, and
outputs a word consisting of a single character. CHAR 65 outputs
A, and CHAR 32 outputs a word consisting of a single space, but
there are many more possible numbers to input than there are
characters to output. If you investigate, you will make some useful
discoveries, such as the fact that CHAR 1 outputs a character which
looks like a small smiling face (if you are using the American IBM
PC character set — in other countries it may be different). CHAR
will accept as input any integer from 0 to 255 inclusive. Some more
idea of the usefulness of the character set can be found in Chapter 8.

Perhaps the most useful strategy is analogy. It lets you import
ideas, if not solutions, from other domains familiar to you. There
are dangers, as you can easily stretch an analogy too far, but it is
also the main aid to imagination. Consider the paddles again. The
sketchpad system suggested earlier has a bad drawback; it is hard to
control the paddles accurately in order to draw straight lines or
smooth curves. A better sketchpad system can be conceived by
analogy with a radar screen. Imagine the turtle anchored at a particular spot, moving forward and back a chosen distance along a
chosen heading. The distance and heading can be selected by the
paddle knobs, so that rotating the knob controlling the heading

makes the line repeatedly drawn by the turtle sweep round like a radar beam. If a button is pressed then the turtle leaps to the other end of the beam, and that becomes the new centre of rotation. As a sketchpad system this is much better: all the lines are straight, and it is possible to provide an informative digital readout at the bottom of the screen by using SETCURSOR. Here are the details; the sketcher is started by the command START:

```
TO START
CS MIXEDSCREEN
SETCURSOR [20 6] TYPE "X
SECTCURSOR [20 20] TYPE "DISTANCE
SETCURSOR [21 6] TYPE "Y
SETCURSOR [21 20] TYPE "HEADING
LOCAL "X
LOCAL "Y
LOCAL "D
SKETCH
END

TO SKETCH
MAKE "X XCOR
MAKE "Y YCOR
SETH 360 * ( (PADDLE 0)−4) / 126
MAKE "D PADDLE 1
SETCURSOR [20 8]
(TYPE ROUND :X "\ \ )
SETCURSOR [20 29]
(TYPE ROUND :D "\ \ )
SETCURSOR [21 8]
(TYPE ROUND :X "\ \ )
SETCURSOR [21 29]
(TYPE ROUND HEADING "\ \ )
PX
FD :D
PU SETPOS LIST :X :Y PX
FD :D
PU SETPOS LIST :X :Y PD
IF BUTTON 0 [FD :D]
SKETCH
END
```

Some points: local variables X, Y and D are created in START to avoid corrupting the values of any already existing variables with those names. The beam is drawn by doing FD :D twice, with the reversing pen (selected by PX), rather than FD :D and BK :D because sometimes BK :D does not entirely erase all the dots drawn by the FD :D. The only sure way to erase a line is to retrace it in the same direction in which it was drawn. The reversing pen is used, rather than the background colour, so that the sketcher does not erase previously drawn parts of the sketch. The captions for the digital readout are printed by START because they only need to be printed once. It is a happy accident that SKETCH is not too fast; if it were then it would be difficult to push the paddlebutton and release it fast enough to prevent LOGO obeying BUTTON 0 twice while you still had the button depressed. Try START when the turtle is allowed to wrap.

6.4 WHEN IN A MESS

If you reach the stage of banging your head against the wall, then follow this recipe:

a) Rest for a bit.
b) Try working on something else, unrelated to the source of your frustration.
c) When you are ready, go back and try to crack the nut some other ways.
d) If all fails, give up. There is no shame in it; if you find there is, you are probably taking the enterprise too seriously, and you should do step (a) several times in a row.

Such a recipe is as good as any other. None of them are any use unless you have some reasonably developed self-awareness. Creation, in any area, has several phases: a period of incubation, the 'Eureka' stage when the thoughts hatch, and the stage of thrashing out details. The incubation stage normally takes a while, and proceeds happily while you are doing something else unrelated — so you may as well do something else, such as lie in the bath drinking beer. The 'Eureka' stage is unpredictable, but it need not be sudden or complete. It can equally well appear as a slow increase in certainty that you are on a 'right' track. The thrashing stage is when you actually do the mundane things to make it all work, and is the only phase that an outside observer would recognise as effort.

7 | PROJECTS

Aims: This chapter contains some project suggestions, with
thoughts about each. Some have a mathematical bias, others
don't. They may look ambitious, but they are all possible.

7.1 PROJECTS WITH CLEAR TARGETS

Projects which have clearly defined objectives are not necessarily
any easier than ones with hazy or ridiculously ambitious targets. The
first sub-section consists of four diagrams, suggesting some drawing
projects.

7.1.1 Drawings

Figures 7.1–7.4 should give you some ideas. The face was drawn

Figure 7.1

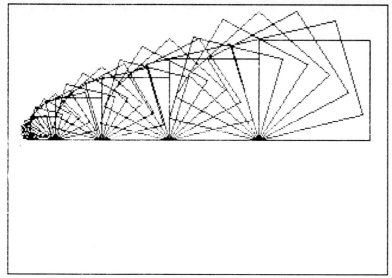

Figure 7.2

using a sketching procedure of the sort hinted at in Chapter 6. The rolling box used nothing more than was in Chapter 2. The set of ellipses is the hardest; devising a procedure to draw one is no easy task. The abstract pattern also used the ideas of Chapter 2, but the fundamental ingredient was an arc rather than a straight line.

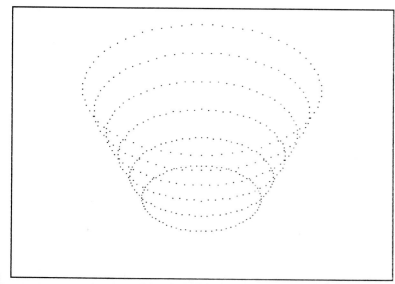

Figure 7.3

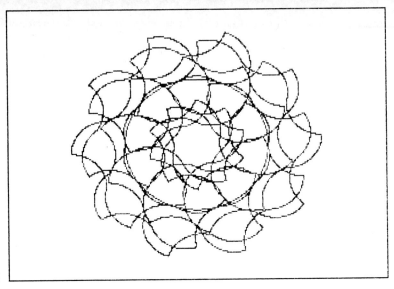

Figure 7.4

7.1.2 Rotation and reflection of shapes

The result of this project might be a useful tool for introducing this topic to someone unfamiliar with it.

The aim is to produce a set of tools for playing about with shapes, reflecting them in specified lines through the origin and rotating them about the origin. There are various ways this might be done, such as the methods outlined in Section 4.6.1. The important feature is that the user of the tools should be able to specify some shape to play with, in a straightforward way. Since it is possible to get hold of the definition of a procedure, using TEXT, it would be possible to devise a system that interpreted the definition, putting LEFT for RIGHT when the reflection of a shape was to be drawn. If you try this, it turns out to be rather cumbersome. The method proposed here, which you need not use, is to require the user to use two new procedures instead of FORWARD and RIGHT, namely AHEAD and TURN:

```
TO AHEAD :DIST
FORWARD :DIST * :SCALE
END

TO TURN :ANGLE
RT :ANGLE * :ASCALE
END
```

As suggested earlier, it would also be possible to redefine FORWARD and RIGHT and BACK and LEFT to look like these. To avoid confusion, however, the names AHEAD and TURN will be used in the description below.

The variables SCALE and ASCALE will initially be 1, so that AHEAD and TURN are synonyms for the traditional FORWARD and RIGHT. The scale of a shape can be changed simply by altering SCALE and rerunning the procedure to draw it. The shape can be drawn as a mirror image, once the turtle is suitably positioned, merely by changing the sign of ASCALE. The value of ASCALE will always be either 1 or −1.

There are two awkward parts to the whole project. One is that shapes defined by the user may not be state-transparent. If they are not, then it will be hard to draw the reflection of a shape in a specified mirror, since the turtle needs to be at the image of the starting place before starting to draw the reflection. A way to get round the problem is to define a procedure SEE, whose input should be the name of a procedure defining the shape:

```
TO SEE :SHAPE
MAKE "OLD.POS POS
MAKE "OLD.H HEADING
REPEAT 1 (LIST :SHAPE)
PU SETPOS :OLD.POS PD
SETH :OLD.H
END
```

This version only works in a state-transparent way if the shape starts and finishes with the pen down, but you can improve it if you want. Incidentally, the command

```
REPEAT 1 [ . . . ]
```

is such a convenient way to have the contents of a list treated as a command that there is a separate but equivalent command:

```
RUN [ . . . ]
```

The other tricky part is to figure out how to reflect the turtle's position and heading in a given mirror. The procedures MIRROR and REFLECT, defined below, draw a dotted line representing the mirror along a specified heading through the origin and reflect the turtle in that mirror:

```
TO MIRROR :A
MAKE "OLD.POS POS
```

```
MAKE "OLD.H HEADING
PU HOME PD
RT :A
REPEAT 30 [FD 1 PU FD 3 PD]
PU HOME PD
RT 180 + :A
REPEAT 30 [FD 1 PU FD 3 PD]
PU SETPOS :OLD.POS PD
SETH :OLD.H
END

TO REFLECT :A
MIRROR :A
MAKE "AA (2 * :A − ATAN YCOR XCOR)
PU
SETPOS LIST R * SIN :AA R * COS :AA
SETH (2 * :A − HEADING)
PD
END

TO R
OUTPUT SQRT (XCOR * XCOR + YCOR * YCOR)
END
```

This is the bare bones of the set of procedures. It would be an improvement if SEE also caused the name of the shape it draws to be preserved as the value of some variable, say LAST. DRAWN, so that REFLECT could also draw the reflection of the shape last SEEn after reversing the sign of ASCALE. Figure 7.5 shows an example of a shape reflected in a 45-degree mirror. A useful extra would be a procedure to rotate the turtle's location about the origin by a given angle, so that the user could play with rotating the reflecting shapes.

7.1.3 Precise arithmetic in any base

IBM PC LOGO can work to 99 significant figures when doing arithmetic. By default it works to 10 significant figures, but you can change that by means of the SETPRECISION command. The aim of this project is to provide high-precision arithmetic to more than 100 significant figures. A drawback to SETPRECISION is that numbers are only stored to an accuracy given by the current precision. With the following commands:

```
SETPRECISION 12
MAKE "X 1/17
```

the variable X will have the *exact* value 0.058823529412, rather than

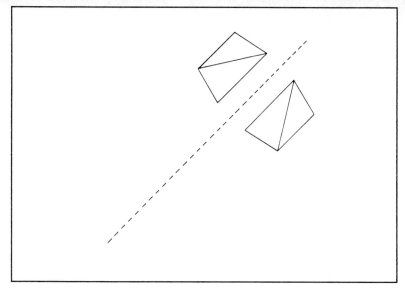

Figure 7.5

0.0588235294117647 (recurring), so that if you increase the precision at a later point then the value of X is no longer the best approximation to 1/17.

While one approach would be to capitalise on the effort in Section 6.3, it is neater and conceptually better to work with lists of digits without the final list indicating the base. For instance, 82371964 could be represented as

[8 2 3 7 1 9 6 4]

If you wanted to work with decimals as well, it would be better to represent a number such as 82371964.003 as

[8 2 3 7 1 9 6 4 0 0 3 [−3]]

So that you continue to work essentially with integers, but can adjust the mutiplying power of ten at the end of a calculation, and you have some record of the precision to which that number is known. You should start by defining a procedure to add two numbers represented in some such way; this is the easiest of arithmetic operations.

It is awkward to have to enter numbers in a list form. You cannot merely enter them as numbers, because LOGO will treat them as such and give them to your procedure as an approximation correct to the current number of significant figures. The solution is to use READCHAR, RC for short, to get hold of the digits and any sign or decimal point one by one. Here is a procedure to get hold of a positive integer. A procedure to read in a positive or negative number, possibly with a decimal part, is rather more complex.

```
TO GETINT :L
MAKE "CHAR RC
TYPE :CHAR
IF AND (:CHAR = "\ ) (:L = [ ] [OUTPUT GETINT :L]
IF MEMBERP :CHAR [0 1 2 3 4 5 6 7 8 9]
    [OUTPUT GETINT LPUT :CHAR :L]
OUTPUT :L
END
```

This is used by giving it the empty list as input; it glues digits onto the end of its input. The TYPE command ensures that the user gets to see the character he typed in that was read by RC. The first IF command ensures that any initial spaces are forgotten. The second IF command glues the latest digit onto the end of the story so far, which is handed on as the input to a recursive use of GETINT. If some digits have been collected and the character read by RC is not a digit, then the last line is obeyed, thus ending the collecting of digits. An interesting thought is that the procedure could also be used for collecting words — just use a different list in the MEMBERP check.

Procedures for multiplication and division can be defined essentially by mimicking the way these are done on paper. You will probably not have enough space or speed to let you define a really high-precision SIN or COS, but you could include the high-precision basic operations with the reverse Polish calculator in Section 4.7.1.

7.1.4 Tangrams

This is an ancient chinese puzzle. It consists of seven pieces, as shown in Figure 7.6. They are used to try to compose a variety of puzzle shapes, from a simple parallelogram and other regular patterns to elaborate outlines of animals and people. It is possible to write LOGO procedures for playing about with them, although if that is all you want to do it is easier to use carboard. With quite a lot of work it is possible to devise procedures for analysing an outline, to see if it can be composed of the seven tangrams. The project acquires more point when you start experimenting with sets of pieces of your own choice, rather than the seven in Figure 7.6. It is much easier to play about with shapes in LOGO than it is to cut up bits of cardboard every time you want to alter one of the basic shapes somewhat.

The key idea is to represent the outline of a basic shape as a list of lists. Each list in the list contains two numbers, the first being the length of a side and the second being the amount by which to turn right at the end of that side. The list describes the shape in a clockwise direction. When you want to stick two shapes together along an edge, the method for constructing the description of the new shape is suggested by Figure 7.7. Copy one shape till you reach the edge where the second is to be attached, then switch to the second shape and copy edges till you meet the edge where the first is to be attached. At the last edge before you switch from first to second shape, you need to adjust the turning angle. A similar adjustment is necessary when stepping from the second to the first.

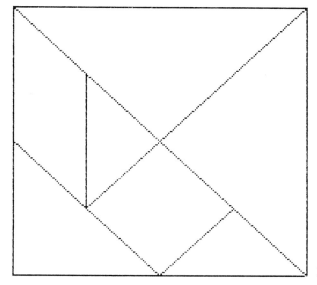

Figure 7.6

A neat trick which greatly simplifies the programming is to describe a shape by going round it twice. This means that the list describing a four-sided shape will have eight lists in it. The virtue of this is that when you are looking for the edge to start from, you will definitely find it in the first half of the description. Copying all but one edge of the figure, from that one on, will not result in you meeting the end of the list and having to jump back to the beginning. Expressing this in a symbolic form, imagine that you have two shapes each with four sides. Their list descriptions can be viewed as

{e1, e2, e3, e4, e1, e2, e3, e4}

and

{E1, E2, E3, E4, E1, E2, E3, E4}

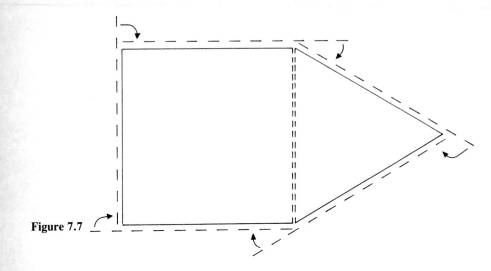

Figure 7.7

where each element is actually a list, with two elements. If edge e3 of the first shape is to be joined to edge E2 of the second shape, and e3 and E2 have the same length, then the result will have edges

{e1, e2(new angle), E3, E4, E1(new angle), e1}

and the list description can be formed by joining the list with these elements to itself, using SENTENCE. The result is not so neat if the edges to be joined have different lengths. In such a case there will be remnants of one or both of the two edges and these will need to be included in the description. You will also need to devise a suitable way of expressing exactly how the two edges are to be joined.

Your procedure for joining two shapes must also take into account two special cases. One is made obvious by the observation that joining two squares of equal size gives you a rectangle with four sides rather than a six-sided shape. The other is when one or both shapes have concave bits. Joining along two of the concave edges may not be possible, but you should be able to convince yourself that if you try to do this, then the turning angle at one of the joining points will be greater than 360 degrees. This needs to be detected by the procedure, and treated as an error.

This project is one of the most elaborate in this chapter. It takes time to do well.

7.2 OPEN-ENDED PROJECTS

The projects outlined here can take you in many different directions. They have no 'ultimate' goal.

7.2.1 Mazes

There are several types of mechanical turtle in the world, and some have touch sensors so that they can be programmed to avoid obstacles and explore their surroundings. This project aims to make similar things happen on the screen. In particular, the aim is to get the turtle to explore a maze drawn by the user.

The principal problem is that there is no way for the turtle to detect lines drawn on the screen. The solution proposed here is to have two representations of the maze, which agree but are independent. The maze will be made out of squares 10 units on a side, as shown in Figure 7.8. There will also be a list showing where the walls of the maze are. The turtle will be able to tell if it has hit a wall on the screen by checking its co-ordinates to see which square it is in, and seeing if that square is in the list. An easy way to identify a square is by the co-ordinates of the bottom left corner, or rather by a relative displacement from the bottom left corner of the whole maze. An example will make this clearer: suppose that the bottom left corner of the maze is at X=−80, Y=−60. If a square of the maze wall has its bottom left corner at X=−20, Y=30, then the X displacement is +60, the Y displacement is +90. The square can therefore be identified by the list [6 9], and the turtle can tell if it is in this square by seeing if the expression

LIST INT (XCOR − (−80))/10 INT (YCOR − (−60))/10

is equal to [6 9]; this works because INT outputs the integer part of

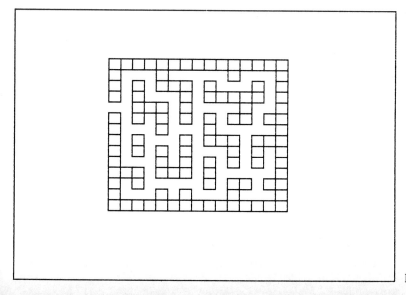

Figure 7.8

the division, so the turtle's X co-ordinate can be anywhere between
−20 and −10, its Y co-ordinate can be anywhere between 30 and 39
and the list output by the expression will be the same.

It seems at first sight as though it will be very tedious to set up
the two representations. The task can be made very easy by defining
a small 'maze editor' which allows the user to draw the maze and
construct the list at the same time. In the following definitions, the
variable WALL is where the list description is kept, and the editor
is the procedure MAKEMAZE. It does some initial setting up and
then invokes MAP to map out the maze according to keys pressed
by the user:

```
key L  = move 1 square left
key R  = move 1 square right
key U  = move 1 square up the screen
key D  = move 1 square down the screen
key S  = include this square in the list, and draw it
key Q  = quit from the editor
```

Here are the procedures. The co-ordinates of the bottom left of the
whole maze are recorded as the values of the variables MX and
MY:

```
TO ADD. SQUARE
SETX XCOR + 10
SETY YCOR + 10
SETX XCOR − 10
SETY YCOR − 10
LOCAL "CELL.ID
MAKE "CELL.ID LIST INT (XCOR − :MX)/10 INT (YCOR − :MY)/10
IF NOT MEMBERP :CELL.ID :WALL [MAKE "WALL LPUT :CELL.ID
        :WALL]
END


TO MAP
MAKE "K READCHAR
IF :K = "L [PU SETX XCOR − 10]
IF :K = "R [PU SETX XCOR + 10]
IF :K = "U [PU SETY YCOR + 10]
IF :K = "D [PU SETY YCOR − 10]
IF :K = "S [PD ADD. SQUARE]
IF :K = "Q [THROW "TOPLEVEL]
MAP
END


TO MAKEMAZE
```

```
MAKE "MX-80
MAKE "MY-60
MAKE "WALL [ ]
PU SETX :MX SETY :MY
SETH 45
MAP
END
```

The SETH 45 near the end of MAKEMAZE ensures that the turtle is pointing into the square whose bottom left corner it is standing on. This helps the user to know where the square will be drawn if he presses S when using the editor. A useful addition might be a key to allow the user to delete a drawn square, and remove the details of it from the list. It is not enough just to erase the square, since any side of it might be part of another square too. A suitable procedure might look like this:

```
TO DEL.SQUARE
LOCAL "CELL.X
LOCAL "CELL.Y
MAKE "CELL.X INT (XCOR − :MX)/10
MAKE "CELL.Y INT (YCOR − :MX)/10
IF NOT MEMBERP (LIST :CELL.X :CELL.Y)
     :WALL [STOP]
MAKE "WALL REMOVE (LIST :CELL.X :CELL.Y)
     :WALL
IF MEMBERP (LIST :CELL.X :CELL.Y−1)
      :WALL [PU] [PE]
SETX XCOR+10
IF MEMBERP (LIST :CELL.X+1 :CELL.Y)
      :WALL [PU] [PE]
SETY YCOR+10
IF MEMBERP (LIST :CELL.X :CELL.Y+1)
     :WALL [PU] [PE]
SETX XCOR−10
IF MEMBERP (LIST :CELL. X−1 :CELL. Y)
      :WALL [PU] [PE]
SETY YCOR−10
END

TO REMOVE :EL :LIST
IF :LIST=[ ] [OUTPUT [ ]]
IF :EL = FIRST :LIST [OUTPUT BF :LIST]
OUTPUT FPUT FIRST :LIST REMOVE :EL BF
      :LIST
END
```

The procedure REMOVE outputs a list formed by removing a given element from a given list. It only removes the first occurrence, which is all that is needed in this case because ADD.SQUARE checks before adding a square to see if it is already part of the wall. Other useful additions to the maze editor might be a single-character command to print a summary of the commands, and a single-character command to jump the turtle to an opening at the outside of the maze in preparation for starting to explore it.

The following procedure shows how the turtle can be made to grope around the maze at random. The turtle starts where it was left by the maze editor. It draws using the reversing pen (selected by PX) so that it can wipe out its own tracks if it needs to retreat and so that it does not irrevocably delete parts of the maze walls. To run it, give the command START:

```
TO START
PU
SETX XCOR + 5
SETY YCOR + 5
PD
PX
GROPE
END

TO GROPE
SETH 90 * RANDOM 4
FD 10
IF MEMBERP LIST INT (XCOR − :MX)/10
        INT (YCOR − :MY)/10 :WALL [BK 10]
IF KEYP [STOP] [GROPE]
END
```

The SETX and SETY in START puts the turtle in the middle of a square. In GROPE, the SETH gives the turtle a heading randomly chosen from 0, 90, 180, 270. The last line checks to see if the user has typed anything — typing any key stops the search.

Although it may seem as though almost all the work has been done for you, this is in fact just the beginning. The main work of the project is to get the turtle to explore the maze in a sensible way. One way to start is to get the turtle to record its path as it explores. This might be as a list of F's, L's and R's representing the FORWARDs, LEFTs and RIGHTs it has taken to get to its current position, or as a list representing the squares it has traversed. If you adopt the FLR form, the thing to do is to update the path list first, then make the move, so that if the move turns out to land the turtle in the wall it has the information about how to get out.

The major hurdle is to cope with mazes that have 'islands', parts which are not connected to the outside walls of the maze. A dumb turtle could happily walk around the outside of an 'island' for ever, nor realising the fact. To overcome this the turtle must have a means of knowing where it has been, so that it can tell whether it has visited the current square some time in the past.

An interesting experiment is to make the turtle explore in a limited way. It can follow alleys for a certain distance, and give up if it has not found turnings by then. If it fails to find the way out, it can then return to explore those alleys further. This is based on the assumption that many mazes have long blind alleys.

It is possible to speed up searching if you let the turtle 'teleport', using SETPOS. This implies that the turtle must record suitable places to leap back to, as it explores. An advantage is that the turtle will not erase its tracks when it teleports, and so there will be a complete record on the screen of where it has searched.

7.2.2 Language programs

There is a wide variety of possibilities for LOGO procedure sets which work with language. This section only hints at the possibilities, the idea being to give you enough to get yourself started.

The first idea is to try playing about with synonyms of words. It is entertaining, and can be instructive, to try recasting sentences using synonyms for various of the words in them and to see if the sense changes. The recasting of a sentence ought to be done under the user's control, by means of a simple sentence editor including commands such as 'replace the fifth word by a synonym if possible', 'replace all adjectives by synonyms' and so on. The LOGO procedure SPIN defined below is not so elaborate; all it does is to replace every word in a given sentence by a synonym if possible. For example,

```
PRINT SPIN [THE BIG BUT DUMB DOG
        WAS BITTEN BY THE SMALL BUT
        CLEVER CAT]
```

might print

```
THE LARGE BUT DOPEY CANINE WAS
    BITTEN BY THE TINY BUT SMART CAT
```

The synonyms are provided as a list of lists:

```
MAKE "SYNL [[BIG LARGE HUGE GIANT VAST]
        [SMALL TINY WEE MINUTE] [INTELLIGENT
        CLEVER BRAINY SMART] [DUMB STUPID
```

THICK DOPEY BRAINLESS] [FAT ADIPOSE
PODGY HEFTY] [DOG CANINE POOCH]]

The definition of SPIN and its sub-procedures are

```
TO SPIN :SENT
IF :SENT=[ ] [OUTPUT [ ]]
OUTPUT FPUT (SYN FIRST :SENT :SYNL)
      (SPIN BUTFIRST :SENT)
END

TO SYN :WORD :SLIST
IF :SLIST=[ ] [OUTPUT :WORD]
IF MEMBERP :WORD FIRST :SLIST [OUTPUT
      RANDLIST FIRST :SLIST]
OUTPUT SYN :WORD BUTFIRST :SLIST
END

TO RANDLIST :L
OUTPUT ITEM 1 + RANDOM COUNT :L :L
END
```

The job of RANDLIST is to output a random element of the list it
receives as input. The procedure SYN takes a word and a list of
synonym lists, and tries to find the word in one of those lists. If
found, it outputs a random element of that list. If no list containing
the word is found, it just outputs the word because it is then the
only available synonym for itself.

Another useful procedure is INSERT, which inserts an element
between two adjacent items in a list. It can be used as the basis of a
simple sentence editor, allowing the user to do such things as insert
extra adjectives and adverbs. Its counterpart, DELETE, can be
defined in a similar way. INSERT expects three inputs: the item to
insert, the list in which it is to be inserted, and the number of the
element after which it is to be inserted. Items are numbered from 1,
so INSERTing after item 0 is equivalent to putting the new item at
the start.

```
TO INSERT :EL :L :NUM
IF :N=0 [OUTPUT FPUT :EL :L]
OUTPUT FPUT FIRST :L INSERT :EL BF :L
      :NUM − 1
END
```

There are many word games which can be turned into LOGO
procedures. The game 'Hangman' requires the user to guess the

letters which spell an unknown word, with only seven mistakes allowed. If a letter is guessed correctly, the player is told all the positions within the word where it appears. A game like 'Hangman' is hard to do well, because it depends on having a reasonably sized dictionary of words from which to choose the mystery word to spell. An arithmetic version is possible, in which the idea is to guess the numbers and operations which make up a specified equation, because it is possible to generate correct equations. An interesting variation is 'Textman', in which the idea is to guess the words which make up a mystery sentence. This depends on some of the grammatical ideas described below. Another entertaining game is 'Aunt Hettie Likes'. The idea is for the user to ask questions of the form

```
DOES SHE LIKE <something>
```

The reply depends on the application of a secret rule: the classic one is that Auntie Hettie likes anything that has a double letter in it. The aim is to guess the secret rule. Two players could take turns to devise a LOGO procedure, with a standard name such as RULE, that takes a word as input and outputs TRUE or FALSE appropriately. There are many variants of this idea, such as guessing the verb in a sentence, cracking a code, or predicting the next item in a linguistic or arithmetic sequence.

It is possible to write LOGO procedures to check whether a given sentence complies with a limited subset of English grammar. One way to specify the grammar is like this:

```
MAKE "SENTENCE.FORM
    [[NOUN.PHRASE VERB NOUN.PHRASE]
    [NOUN.PHRASE INTRANSITIVE.VERB]]

MAKE "NOUN.PHRASE. FORM
    [[DETERMINER NOUN]
    [DETERMINER ADJ NOUN]]

MAKE "DETERMINER. FORM [A THE]
MAKE "NOUN.FORM [DOG ELEPHANT BAKER SAUSAGE]
MAKE "VERB. FORM [ATE LIKED PAINTED]
MAKE "INTRANSITIVE.VERB. FORM [FAINTED]
MAKE "ADJ.FORM [GREEN BIG SWEATY]
```

The way to tell whether an item in a list, such as DOG, is meant to be an ordinary word or the name of a grammatical construction, is to check what

```
NAMEP "DOG   "'.FORM'
```

outputs. If it is TRUE then DOG is the name of a construction; if it is FALSE then it is just a word and nothing more. The task of checking whether the sentence

THE BIG SWEATY DOG ATE THE BAKER

fits the mini-grammar is almost identical in concept to the task of searching a maze.

7.2.3 A database
This project involves some sophisticated points of list programming, and can be taken a very long way. It also introduces some rudimentary ideas of Artificial Intelligence. The aim is to create a database package. The basic definitions below provide four useful procedures:

SETUP   This sets up the system.
FACT   This takes a list as input, recording that as a fact.
FACTS   This takes no input, and prints the list of facts nicely.
QUERY   This takes a list as input, and prints any known fact that matches it. The input can have elements that begin with a question mark, and these are taken to match anything at all.

The sample session using these procedures should give you the idea:

```
?FACT [FRED LIKES HAGGIS]
OK
?FACT [FRED HATES BEANS AND BEER]
OK
?FACT [HAGGIS IS CHEAP]
OK
?FACT [WALTER LIKES HAGGIS]
OK
?FACT [WALTER LIKES WHISKY]
OK
?FACT [WALTER LIKES WALTER]
OK
?FACTS
——— FRED LIKES HAGGIS
——— FRED HATES BEANS AND BEER
——— HAGGIS IS CHEAP
——— WALTER LIKES HAGGIS
——— WALTER LIKES WHISKY
——— WALTER LIKES WALTER
?QUERY [FRED LIKES ?X]
FRED LIKES HAGGIS
```

```
?QUERY [?X LIKES HAGGIS]
FRED LIKES HAGGIS
WALTER LIKES HAGGIS
?QUERY [?THIS LIKES ?THAT]
FRED LIKES HAGGIS
WALTER LIKES HAGGIS
WALTER LIKES WHISKY
WALTER LIKES WALTER
?QUERY [FRED HATES ?X]
... NO MATCH
?QUERY [FRED HATES ?A AND ?B]
FRED HATES BEANS AND BEER
?QUERY [?A LIKES ?A]
WALTER LIKES WALTER
```

In each case, all the facts that precisely match the query are printed. Note the last case, in which the goal is to find something that likes itself; the 'database variable' ?A turns up twice in the query.

The facts are held as a list of lists, the value of a variable called FACTS. LOGO does not object that this is also the name of a procedure. The definitions of SETUP, FACT and FACTS are very simple:

```
TO SETUP
MAKE "FACTS [ ]
END

TO FACT :L
MAKE "FACTS LPUT :L :FACTS
END

TO FACTS
IF :FACTS=[ ] [PRINT [... NO FACTS]]
        [PRINTFACTS :FACTS]
END

TO PRINTFACTS :L
IF :L=[ ] [STOP]
TYPE "————\
PRINT FIRST :L
PRINTFACTS BUTFIRST :L
END
```

The definition of QUERY is fairly short but much more sophisticated. QUERY invokes a procedure called SCAN to look for matches in the list of facts. SCAN works through the list of facts, applying MATCHP to see if the query matches each fact in turn. The procedure MATCHP takes two inputs — the first is the query, the second is one fact from the list of them. It works recursively.

```
TO QUERY :Q
MAKE "NOMATCH "TRUE
SCAN :Q :FACTS
IF :NOMATCH [PRINT [. . . NO MATCH]]
END


TO SCAN :QUERY :FACTS
IF :FACTS=[ ] [STOP]
IF MATCHP :QUERY (FIRST :FACTS) [PRINT
      FIRST :FACTS]
SCAN :QUERY (BUTFIRST :FACTS)
END


TO MATCHP :Q :FACT
IF AND :Q=[ ] :FACT=[ ] [MAKE "NOMATCH
      "FALSE OUTPUT "TRUE]
IF FIRST FIRST :Q = "? [MAKE "Q REPLACE
      FIRST :Q FIRST :FACT :Q]
IF NOT (FIRST :Q) = (FIRST :FACT)
      [OUTPUT "FALSE]
OUTPUT MATCHP BUTFIRST :Q BUTFIRST :FACT
END
```

The REPLACE procedure used in MATCHP is the one defined in Section 4.5.4. The inputs are, in order, the element to be replaced throughout the list, the element to replace it by, and the list itself. If MATCHP finds an element of the query which begins with a question mark, it replaces all occurrences of that element in the rest of the query by the corresponding element from the fact being examined, before proceeding to check the match. If this is confusing, work through some of the examples from the sample session above, on paper.

   There are many ways this embryo package can be extended. One possibility is to alter FACT to allow 'input inferences'. The idea is to define a new procedure, say INFER, that will allow the user to command the package to make certain inferences when FACT is used in future. For example, the command

```
INFER [?X LIKES HAGGIS] [?X IS SCOTTISH]
```

should be taken to mean that, if a fact 'someone likes haggis' is entered, then the fact 'the person is Scottish' should be entered automatically. INFER need only update a list of lists, each of which consists of the two inputs from an INFER command. This list can then be used by FACT, which should check whether the fact matches the first input to any previous INFER. If it does, the corresponding second input should be treated as the input to a new use of FACT, so that after these commands

```
INFER [?X EATS HAGGIS] [?X IS SCOTTISH]
INFER [?A IS SCOTTISH] [?A HAS A KILT]
FACT [DONALD EATS HAGGIS]
```

the facts [DONALD EATS HAGGIS], [DONALD IS SCOTTISH] and [DONALD HAS A KILT] are all included in the FACTS list.

A severe test of your programming skill is to amend QUERY to allow conjunctions of queries, for example

```
QUERY [[?Z LIKES ?Y] [?Y IS CHEAP]]
```

should print (assuming the facts in the sample session)

```
FRED LIKES HAGGIS
HAGGIS IS CHEAP
WALTER LIKES HAGGIS
HAGGIS IS CHEAP
```

and nothing else. The hurdle is producing a new version of MATCHP. It must know the entire query, not just one component of it. To illustrate the problem: suppose the new MATCHP has been trying to match [?Z LIKES ?Y] with [FRED LIKES WHISKY], and has reached the stage of matching [?Y] with [WHISKY] in its recursing. Then it must go on to examine whether there is any match for the fact [WHISKY IS CHEAP], and return to examining the previous part of the query when it finds none. Of course, it should be equally possible to conjoin three or more parts for a single query.

A further refinement is to attach probability values to facts, and have QUERY print a probability value for each answer to a conjunction.

The ideas here are developed somewhat in Section 8.2, as an illustration of a feature of LOGO called 'property lists'.

7.2.4 Simple pattern recognition
Many so-called 'intelligence tests' in books and newspapers ask for the answers to questions such as this:

Give the next term in the sequence —

> A B A B D D C F G . . .

The first step is to recognise that the letters are grouped in threes. To generate the next three, the rule is to update the first of the three by one letter, the second by two and the third by three. If the question were to find the next term in the sequence

> 1 2 1 2 4 4 3 6 7 . . .

it would be much easier to recognise the arithmetic progression 121, 244, 367 . . . in disguise. You can write LOGO procedures to analyse such questions to determine the pattern. The approach is to try values from 1 upward for the length of the group, and see whether there is some arithmetic progression visible. With as letter sequence, the letters can be turned into numbers by using the procedure ASCII: the letter sequence given above would be

> 65 66 65 66 68 68 67 70 71 . . .

Split into lists of length three, this gives three lists representing numbers in base 1000 (say), and the procedures you produced for the project in Section 5.3.6 can be used to check whether this forms an arithmetic progression. Since at least three terms are needed to confirm that the pattern is an arithmetic progression, the LOGO procedure can safely give up if the length of the group reaches one third of the length of the given sequence without finding a progression.

Sometimes letter sequences assume that the alphabet wraps round from Z back to A. In this case you need to be looking for an arithmetic progression using arithmetic modulo 26.

7.2.5 Games
There are vast numbers of games. They fall into three groups:

a) those in which you play the machine
b) those in which you play someone else, and the machine referees,
c) those in which the machine acts as board or dice or rulebook.

Those in category (a) tend to be simple. There are many variants of games such as tic-tac-toe, fox-and-geese and other easy board games for which you can write LOGO procedures to play you. They nearly all suffer from the same fault, which is that you know how the machine plays. Games with an element of chance are more fun — consult a book of games for ideas. The simplest are games such as 'Shoot' where the turtle lies near one corner of the screen, a slowly animated target moves near the other corner and you have to guess a range and heading to get the turtle to hit the target. Variants such as 'turtle golf', with many targets to be hit in sequence, naturally follow from this.

Category (b) offers a very wide scope. Competitive versions of one-person games like 'Shoot' are usually possible. At the other end of the scale of difficulty, there are very elaborate games such as 'Kriegspiel'. This is chess, but neither player can see his opponent's pieces, and has to try moves in the dark. Normally there is a referee, who announces check when it happens, and removes pieces (without naming them to the capturer) as appropriate, and checks on the legality of moves. You may find it possible (but difficult) to write LOGO procedures to act as referee, showing each player his own pieces when it is his turn and erasing them when it is not.

Category (c) is dull. There are few games in which the record-keeping powers of a computer really make a difference. Do not let that stop you trying to invent ones, though.

7.2.6 Three-dimensional graphics

There are many books about the many ways to display three-dimensional shapes on a two-dimensional screen. It takes a great deal of computing power to create images of solid bodies with the surfaces realistically shaded in an acceptably fast way. However, it is much easier to work with what is called 'wire frame' representations, showing just a skeleton made up of straight lines. Figure 7.9 shows the skeleton of a cube. There are two initial problems:

- How does one tell the program where the straight lines are in three dimensions?
- How does the program transform that information into a two-dimensional display?

A simple answer to the first problem is to give the co-ordinates of the end-points, or even just to give the co-ordinates of the other end-point on the assumption that the turtle is at the first end, in the fashion of SETPOS. For example, imagine that there is a procedure 3D.POS which takes three inputs specifying the X, Y and Z co-ordinates of a point. It could output a list giving the two-dimensional equivalent of that point. The following procedure would then be one way of drawing the outline of the cube with a side of 70:

```
TO CUBE
PU SETPOS 3D.POS 0 0 0 PD
SETPOS 3D.POS 70 0 0
SETPOS 3D.POS 70 70 0
SETPOS 3D.POS 0 70 0
```

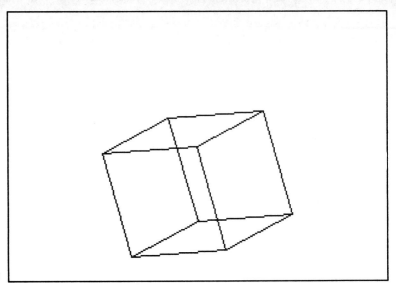

Figure 7.9

```
SETPOS 3D.POS 0 0 0
SETPOS 3D.POS 0 0 70
SETPOS 3D.POS 70 0 70
SETPOS 3D.POS 70 70 70
SETPOS 3D.POS 0 70 70
SETPOS 3D.POS 0 0 70
PU SETPOS 3D.POS 0 70 0 PD
SETPOS 3D.POS 0 70 70
PU SETPOS 3D.POS 70 70 0 PD
SETPOS 3D.POS 70 70 0
SETPOS 3D.POS 70 70 70
PU SETPOS 3D.POS 0 0 0 PD
END
```

The Z axis comes straight out of the screen. If the cube is not rotated at all, its two-dimensional image will just be a square of side 70. How can rotations be specified? The easy thing to do is to imagine that the shape is rotated by some given angle about the X axis, and then by another angle about the Y axis, and then about the Z axis.

Consider what happens when, for instance, everything is just rotated about the Z axis by an angle a, turning from the X axis towards the Y axis. If a point had co-ordinates

$$(x, y, z)$$

before the rotation, then a bit of trigonometry may show you (if you remember much trigonometry) that the co-ordinates after rotation are

$$(x \cos(a) - y \sin(a), x \sin(a) + y \cos(a), z)$$

Rather than work out a complicated formula for the final result after three rotations, it is easier to work out the result step by step. Define two procedures CMS (which stands for 'cos minus sin') and SPC (which stands for 'sin plus cos'):

```
TO CMS :V1 :V2 :COSA :SINA
OUTPUT :V1 * :COSA − :V2 * :SINA
END
```

```
TO SPC :V1 :V2 :COSA :SINA
OUTPUT :V1 * :SINA + :V2 * :COSA
END
```

Since the sines and cosines will be needed more than once, and a short experiment will show you that IBM PC LOGO takes a few moments to work either out, it makes sense to work out the sines and cosines of the rotation angles at the time they are specified, and then store them as values of variables. The procedure EYE, whose three inputs are the X-, Y- and Z-rotation angles, does this:

```
TO EYE :AX :AY :AZ
MAKE "CX COS :AX
MAKE "SX SIN :AX
MAKE "CY COS :AY
MAKE "SY SIN :AY
MAKE "CZ COS :AZ
MAKE "SZ SIN :AZ
END
```

Now the procedure 3D.POS can be defined. It uses six local variables; three to hold the new co-ordinates after the first rotation, and three to hold the co-ordinates after the second rotation. Only the X and Y co-ordinates resulting from the third rotation are needed — you get the two-dimensional image from the three-dimensional co-ordinates just by making the Z co-ordinate be 0. The final X and Y co-ordinates do not need to be stored, just formed into a list and output for use by SETPOS:

```
TO 3D.POS :X :Y :Z
(LOCAL "X1 "Y1 "Z1 "X2 "Y2 "Z2)
```

```
MAKE "X1 :X
MAKE "Y1 CMS :Y :Z :CX :SX
MAKE "Z1 SPC :Y :Z :CX :SX
MAKE "Z2 CMS :Z1 :X1 :CY :SY
MAKE "X2 SPC :Z1 :X1 :CY :SY
MAKE "Y2 :Y1
OUTPUT LIST CMS :X2 :Y2 :CZ :SZ SPC :X2
     :Y2 :CZ: SZ
END
```

Try it, using the procedure CUBE given above. For example,

```
CS
EYE 200 50 30
CUBE
CS
EYE 290 40 30
CUBE
```

The kind of three- to two-dimensional conversion done by 3D.POS is about the simplest possible. You can develop it in many ways from this starting point. One would be to allow translations as well as rotations. Another would be to take account of perspective, by moving the two-dimensional points towards or away from the line of gazing by an amount which depends on the Z co-ordinate and on how far away the eye is supposed to be. This is somewhat trickier than it sounds — for instance, what does a cube look like from inside it? The next level of difficulty beyond that is to tackle some kinds of curved surfaces, and shading of flat and spherical surfaces by using DOT (a built-in procedure whose input is a list — like POS — which puts a single dot at the specified position) to add dots to suggest how much each part of a surface reflects the light from a chosen point source.

7.3 BEYOND LOGO

Now you should know a lot about using LOGO. Nobody can claim to know all there is to know about it, because it is constantly developing as a language. The last project in this chapter is to attempt to invent further features, or even redesign LOGO. The criteria to use in judging changes are their usefulness and comprehensibility.

To get you started, the FOR command is defined below. It is used in the following way. The command

```
FOR "Z IN [10 25 100] [BOX :Z RT 10]
```

is equivalent to

```
BOX 10 RT 10
BOX 25 RT 10
BOX 100 RT 10
```

and the command

```
FOR "Z RANGE [1 4] [BOX :Z JUMP :Z]
```

is equivalent to

```
BOX 1 JUMP 1
BOX 2 JUMP 2
BOX 3 JUMP 3
BOX 4 JUMP 4
```

The definition is

```
TO FOR :QXRY :KEYWORD :L :COMM
IF :L=[ ] [STOP]
IF :IN. VALUE = "OUTPUT.BY.IN [MAKE
        :QXRY FIRST :L REPEAT 1 :COMM
        FOR :QXRY :IN. VALUE BF :L :COMM
        STOP]
IF NOT :KEYWORD = "OUTPUT. BY. RANGE
        [ERR [FOR: NEEDS IN OR RANGE]]
IF NOT NUMBERP FIRST :L [ERR [FOR: RANGE MUST BE NUMERIC]
IF (ITEM 1 :L) > (ITEM 2 :L) [STOP]
MAKE :QRXY FIRST :L
REPEAT 1 :COMM
MAKE "L FPUT 1 + FIRST :L BF :L
FOR :QXRY :KEYWORD :L :COMM
END

TO IN
OUTPUT "OUTPUT.BY.IN
END

TO RANGE
OUTPUT "OUTPUT. BY. RANGE
END
```

The procedures IN and RANGE are included largely to make the
FOR command easier to read when used in procedures. FOR can
be improved in many ways. For example, as it stands, the command

```
FOR "X IN [PRINT FORWARD] [:X 100]
```

will not work. This is because

```
REPEAT 1 [:X 100]
```

will not work, as the elements inside the list are not a legal command. A solution is to use the REPLACE procedure defined in Section 4.5.4 to replace all occurrences of a colon followed by the word given as first input to FOR by the value of the variable named by that word.

Many people also want a means of adding comments in the middle of a line of a procedure. The cheap answer is

```
TO COMMENT :L
END
```

so that comments in procedures will look like this:

```
. . .
FD 100
COMMENT [SENDS THE TURTLE FORWARD]
. . .
```

As well as annotating your procedures in this way, you should also cultivate the habit of writing down your procedures and keeping them with your other LOGO notes — in a loose-leaf binder, say. That way you can also note down such points as why you did something in a particular way, and what the problems and potential improvements are.

8 | MORE ADVANCED FEATURES

"Is that all?" I asked despondingly.
"Not quite all," Sylvie slily replied, "There's a sentence or two
more. Isn't there, Bruno?"
"Yes," with a carelessness that was evidently put on: "just a
sentence or two more."

(*Sylvie and Bruno Concluded*, LEWIS CARROLL)

Aims: This chapter explains some of the more sophisticated
features of LOGO on the IBM PC and gives some further
examples using these features.

8.1 MORE ABOUT THE KEYBOARD

So far, all the examples in IBM PC LOGO have been given exclusively in upper case. It is possible to make use of lower case too. Normally, when you use the alphabetic keys, IBM PC LOGO reads what you type as upper case (Dr. LOGO and Waterloo LOGO read it as lower case). To get lower case instead, you need to use the 'shift' keys. They are not explicitly labelled as such; however, to the left and right of the space bar you should see two keys labelled 'Alt' and 'Caps Lock', and the shift keys are the two immediately above them. They have upward-pointing solid arrows engraved on them. If you hold down one of the shift keys while typing an alphabetic character you will get the lower case version of the character.

If you want to type in a lot of text in lower case, you would find it very tedious to hold down the shift key all the time. You can use the 'Caps Lock' key to avoid this. Normally LOGO ignores that key — if you want to make use of it you must first give the command

    SETCAPS "FALSE

Thereafter, each press of the 'Caps Lock' key swaps over what the alphabetic keys and the shift keys do about case. If you press it once, then the alphabetic keys give lower case and you must use the shift keys to get upper case. Press it again, and then you must use the shift keys to get lower case. If you want to disable the 'Caps Lock' key again, give the command

    SETCAPS "TRUE

You can find out whether the key is usable by looking at what the procedure CAPS outputs — if it is TRUE, then the key is disabled, and if FALSE then it is active.

IBM PC does care about the case of letters in procedure and variable names. For example, initially the command

```
print "HELLO
```

will cause an error. You could define the procedure, of course:

```
TO print :IT
PRINT SENTENCE [Very well:] :IT
PRINT [. . . but you ought to use PRINT]
END
```

This raises a question: how can a LOGO procedure tell whether a word is entirely in upper case or not? Imagine you have written a collection of LOGO procedures to provide help for beginners, and that they read in commands and either run them or comment on them. A beginner might easily hit one of the shift keys at the wrong moment, or might not realise that the case of letters matters. The answer is that LOGO can distinguish between lower and upper case letters by their ASCII codes. The codes of the letters A−Z run from 65 to 90, and the codes of the letters a−z run from 97 to 122. The following procedure will output TRUE if the word input has no lower case letters in it:

```
TO NO.LOWER.P :WORD
IF EMPTYP :WORD [OUTPUT "TRUE]
LOCAL "CODE
MAKE "CODE ASCII FIRST :WORD
TEST AND (:CODE > 96) (:CODE < 122)
IFTRUE [OUTPUT "FALSE]
IFFALSE [OUTPUT NO.LOWER.P BF :WORD]
END
```

If you can type fast, you may find that a LOGO program which reads your typing and takes a little while to process it is unable to keep up with you. To see this happening, define this procedure:

```
TO TRY. IT
TYPE RC
WAIT 18
TRY. IT
END
```

The WAIT 18 causes LOGO to wait for about a second before

carrying on. Run TRY. IT and try typing on the keyboard (if you're really slow, just hold down a key!). You will find that LOGO does not mind you getting a bit ahead of it. If you get too far ahead, it will lose any subsequent characters. However, you'll know when this happens, because you will hear the computer beeping once for each character you type that is too far ahead of it. Unfortunately there is no easy way round this. If you know in advance how many characters are wanted you can use the procedure READCHARS, RCS for short. It takes one input, the number of characters wanted. If necessary, it waits until sufficient have been typed. It outputs a word composed of that many characters, in the order in which they were typed. So, if you give the command

```
PRINT RCS 4
```

and type the first four letters of the alphabet, the word ABCD will be printed. If you want to get hold of the individual characters again, you will need to use a procedure such as this:

```
TO EXPLODE :WORD
IF EMPTYP :WORD [OUTPUT [ ]]
OUTPUT FPUT FIRST :WORD EXPLODE BF
       :WORD
END
```

For example, EXPLODE "BOMB outputs [B O M B].

Certain keys on the IBM PC keyboard output two characters rather than one each time they are pressed — the jargon is that these keys 'generate extended codes' instead of a single ASCII code. By and large, these are keys that do not normally correspond to a printable character, such as the F-keys at the left of the keyboard. The first of the two characters always has ASCII code 0, and the second depends on the key pressed. Useful examples are shown in Table 8.1, though there are many more — consult your reference manual. The F5 key is always interpreted by IBM PC LOGO as a request to pause whatever is happening.

Because a program cannot predict in advance which key the user will press next, it is a good idea to use an algorithm such as this:

a) Use RC to read the next character (not necessarily the next keypress — it might just be half of a keypress). Is its ASCII code 0?
b) If not, a complete keypress has now been read. Do the appropriate action.
c) If so, use RC to read the second character. Use its ASCII code to select the appropriate action.

Table 8.1

Key	ASCII codes
Back tab	0 + 15
F1−F4	0 + 59−62
F6−F10	0 + 64−68
Home	0 + 71
Up arrow	0 + 72
PgUp	0 + 73
Left arrow	0 + 75
Right arrow	0 + 77
End	0 + 79
Down arrow	0 + 80
PgDn	0 + 81
Ins	0 + 82
Del	0 + 83
Shift F1−F10	0 + 84−93
CTRL F1−F10	0 + 94−103
Alt F1−F10	0 + 104−113

8.1.1 A simple text display editor

This section describes a program that makes fairly full use of the keyboard. It is a simple editor that allows you to add or delete characters anywhere on the graphics display, not just in one of the 25 rows and however many columns available, by using SETCURSOR. It will let you insert any of the 256 characters in the character set. You can use it to put captions on pictures, or to create elaborate text displays for use on notices or in making slides. Figure 8.1 shows an example. A limitation is that you can only work with one screenful at once. The simple editor makes use of the arrow keys to move the 'cursor' — which is actually the turtle disguised as the normal cursor — around the screen in character-sized steps. What this means is that up-arrow and down-arrow move the turtle by 10, and left- and right-arrow move it by 8 units. Other keys on the right of the keyboard move the turtle one step at a time:

Home   moves left 1.
PgUp   moves up 1.
PgDn   move down 1.
End   moves right 1.
Ins   makes subsequently inserted characters appear white on black, as normal.
Del   makes subsequently inserted characters appear black on white.

These choices were meant to make it easier to remember which is

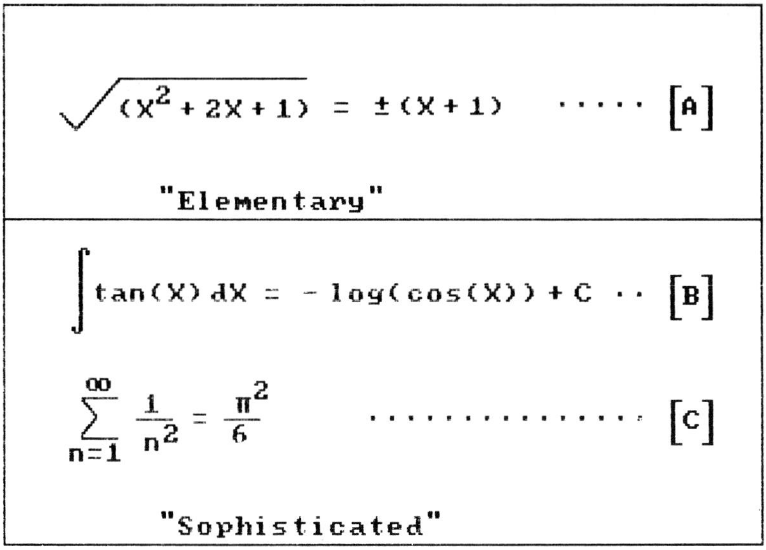

$$\sqrt{(X^2 + 2X + 1)} = \pm(X + 1) \quad \cdots \cdots \quad \boxed{A}$$

"Elementary"

$$\int \tan(X)\,dX = -\log(\cos(X)) + C \quad \cdots \quad \boxed{B}$$

$$\sum_{n=1}^{\infty} \frac{1}{n^2} = \frac{\pi^2}{6} \quad \cdots \cdots \cdots \cdots \quad \boxed{C}$$

"Sophisticated"

Figure 8.1

which: the PgUp and PgDn keys move the turtle up and down, and the End key moves the turtle towards what you naturally think of as the ends of lines on the screen. In addition, various of the F-keys are used:

F6   The turtle vanishes if it was visible, or reappears if it was hidden.

F7   After typing this key, you should type precisely three digits, representing the ASCII code of the character that you want inserted. By this means, you can insert any of the 255 characters.

F8   Inserts the character whose ASCII code is 255. This is normally a blank. However, you can change it to anything else you like, before starting editing, by drawing the desired shape with the turtle, putting the turtle over it, and then giving the commands

```
HT
SNAP 255
```

The HT is needed, otherwise the SNAP will also pick up part of the current turtle shape and store it as shape 255.

F9   clears the display and returns the turtle to the top left corner, for when you want to start again.

F10   exits from the editor.

Otherwise, any character that you type is inserted into the display, and the turtle moves right for the next character. If the next character would overlap the right-hand edge of the screen, a new line is started. The ENTER and RUBOUT (back-arrow) keys work as normal. When you first enter the editor, any drawing is unaffected, so that you can use the editor to add to your pictures, or to erase small parts by using RUBOUT.

The program is not very long. A variable called NORMAL is set to TRUE or FALSE according to whether characters should be appearing white on black or black on white. The top level procedure looks like this:

```
TO EDITSCREEN
IF NOT NAMEP "NORMAL [MAKE "NORMAL "TRUE]
FS
PU SETPOS [−156 120] SETSHAPE 219 PD
FAKE.CHAR
END
```

The first line ensures that if the variable NORMAL doesn't exist — for instance, the first time EDITSCREEN is used — then it is created and given the value TRUE. The procedure FAKE. CHAR is recursive. It processes one keypress, and then calls itself to process the next.

```
TO FAKE.CHAR
LOCAL "KEY
MAKE "KEY RC
IF 0 = ASCII :KEY [EXTRA.KEY ASCII RC]
     [SHOW.CHAR ASCII :KEY]
FAKE. CHAR
END
```

In FAKE. CHAR one character is read, using RC. If it has ASCII code 0, then the user must have pressed one of the special keys, and so EXTRA. KEY is called to take the appropriate action. EXTRA. CHAR has one argument, the ASCII code of the next character.

```
TO EXTRA.CHAR :N
IF :N = 64 [IF SHOWNP [HT] [ST] STOP]
IF :N = 65 [SHOW. ALL. CHAR 1*(WORD RC
     RC RC) STOP]
IF :N = 66 [SHOW.CHAR 255 STOP]
IF :N = 67 [CS PU SETPOS [−156 120] PD
     STOP]
IF :N = 68 [MIXEDSCREEN THROW
     "TOPLEVEL]
```

```
IF :N = 72 [PU SETY YCOR + 10 STOP]
IF :N = 75 [PU SETX XCOR − 8 STOP]
IF :N = 77 [PU SETX XCOR + 8 STOP]
IF :N = 80 [PU SETY YCOR − 10 STOP]
IF :N = 82 [MAKE "NORMAL "TRUE STOP]
IF :N = 83 [MAKE "NORMAL "FALSE STOP]
TONE 440 10
END
```

There are various points to notice about this. If none of the right special keys was pressed, then the last line is obeyed. It causes a short tone from the loudspeaker, to indicate that you have made a mistake. In addition to SHOW.CHAR (below) which inserts a character into the display, a similar procedure SHOW. ALL. CHAR is also used which does not react in a special way to ENTER and RUBOUT.

Here are SHOW.CHAR and SHOW.ALL.CHAR:

```
TO SHOW.CHAR :K
IF :K = 8 [PU SETX XCOR−8 PD SETPC 0
        SETSHAPE 219 STAMP SETPC 3]
IF :K = 13 [NEWLINE]
IF :K < 32 [STOP]
SHOW.ALL.CHAR :K
END


TO SHOW.ALL.CHAR :K
IF NOT :NORMAL [STAMP SETPC 0]
SETSHAPE :K STAMP
SETPC 3
SETSHAPE 219
IF XCOR < 156 [PU SETX XCOR + 8 PD]
        [NEWLINE]
END


TO NEWLINE
PU
IF YCOR > −110 [SETPOS LIST −156
        YCOR−10 PD] [SETPOS [−156 120]]
END
```

The first line of SHOW.CHAR is for when RUBOUT is pressed. In the standard character set of IBM PC LOGO, the ASCII code 219 represents a solid rectangle, which is used as EDITSCREEN's simulation of the cursor. The second line is for when ENTER is pressed — the procedure NEWLINE makes sure that the turtle does not vanish when it is at the bottom of the screen and ENTER is then pressed. The number 32 is the ASCII code for a space; codes less than 32 generally correspond to special characters such as CTRL-A to CTRL-Z. The third line ensures that these characters are ignored.

The procedure SHOW.ALL.CHAR is responsible for inserting any character, inverted or normal according to the value of NORMAL, and moving the turtle right for the next character if there is room for one. If not, it moves the cursor to the start of the next line.

For reference, Figures 8.2, 8.3 and 8.4 show all the ASCII codes and the corresponding characters in the standard character set for IBM PC LOGO.

8.2 PROPERTY LISTS

It was mentioned in Chapter 1 that the language LISP has been used a great deal in research in Artificial Intelligence. A great deal of Artificial Intelligence is concerned with investigating how knowledge is, or can be, represented, either for efficiency's sake or in an attempt to mimic how information might be stored mentally by humans and other intelligent beings. A natural though dangerous starting point for such research is to indulge in introspection. It is natural because it is easy and unusually cheap; it is dangerous because it is idiosyncratic and not amenable to objective scientific experiment — no-one can dispute your observations.

Nevertheless, introspection suggests what conversation with

000		001	☺	002	☻	003	♥	004	♦
005	♣	006	♠	007	•	008	◘	009	○
010	◙	011	♂	012	♀	013	♪	014	♫
015	☼	016	►	017	◄	018	↕	019	‼
020	¶	021	§	022	▬	023	↨	024	↑
025	↓	026	→	027	←	028	∟	029	↔
030	▲	031	▼	032		033	!	034	"
035	#	036	$	037	%	038	&	039	'
040	(	041	)	042	*	043	+	044	,
045	-	046	.	047	/	048	0	049	1
050	2	051	3	052	4	053	5	054	6
055	7	056	8	057	9	058	:	059	;
060	<	061	=	062	>	063	?	064	@
065	A	066	B	067	C	068	D	069	E
070	F	071	G	072	H	073	I	074	J
075	K	076	L	077	M	078	N	079	O
080	P	081	Q	082	R	083	S	084	T
085	U	086	V	087	W	088	X	089	Y
090	Z	091	[	092	\	093	]	094	^
095	_	096	`	097	a	098	b	099	c

Figure 8.2

100	d	101	e	102	f	103	g	104	h
105	i	106	j	107	k	108	l	109	m
110	n	111	o	112	p	113	q	114	r
115	s	116	t	117	u	118	v	119	w
120	x	121	y	122	z	123	{	124	|
125	}	126	~	127	⌂	128	Ç	129	ü
130	é	131	â	132	ä	133	à	134	å
135	ç	136	ê	137	ë	138	è	139	ï
140	î	141	ì	142	Ä	143	Å	144	É
145	æ	146	Æ	147	ô	148	ö	149	ò
150	û	151	ù	152	ÿ	153	Ö	154	Ü
155	¢	156	£	157	¥	158	₧	159	ƒ
160	á	161	í	162	ó	163	ú	164	ñ
165	Ñ	166	ª	167	º	168	¿	169	⌐
170	¬	171	½	172	¼	173	¡	174	«
175	»	176	░	177	▒	178	▓	179	│
180	┤	181	╡	182	╢	183	╖	184	╕
185	╣	186	║	187	╗	188	╝	189	╜
190	╛	191	┐	192	└	193	┴	194	┬
195	├	196	─	197	┼	198	╞	199	╟

Figure 8.3

anyone seems to confirm: that related items of information are somehow stored 'close together' (whatever that means) in a person's head. Talk of a social occasion, mention a suit, and clothing comes to mind; talk of the law, mention a suit, and a legal contest comes to mind. In an attempt to take account of this, AI researchers con-

200	╚	201	╔	202	╩	203	╦	204	╠
205	═	206	╬	207	╧	208	╨	209	╤
210	╥	211	╙	212	╘	213	╒	214	╓
215	╫	216	╪	217	┘	218	┌	219	█
220	▄	221	▌	222	▐	223	▀	224	α
225	ß	226	Γ	227	π	228	Σ	229	σ
230	µ	231	τ	232	Φ	233	Θ	234	Ω
235	δ	236	∞	237	φ	238	ε	239	∩
240	≡	241	±	242	≥	243	≤	244	⌠
245	⌡	246	÷	247	≈	248	°	249	·
250	·	251	√	252	ⁿ	253	²	254	■
255									

Figure 8.4

structed simple tools in LISP for grouping items of information, with each group having a heading. For example,

```
LOGO Programming Book:
    Title:      "LOGO Programming"
    Author:     Peter Ross
    Language:   English
    Publisher:  Addison-Wesley
    Date:       1985
    . . .


Peter Ross:
    Born:       Edinburgh Scotland
    Birthday:   19 November
    . . .
```

The practicalities of running large AI programs even on large computers required that the operations of consulting and modifying such information be done very fast. For this reason, a feature called 'property lists' was added to LISP, and is now included in LOGO too.

In LOGO, any word or number can have a property list. A property list consists of a collection of pairs. The first item of the pair is the name of some entry (or 'attribute' or 'property') associated with that word. The second item is the associated value. Various procedures exist to add, modify, obtain or remove properties associated with any chosen word or number. In IBM PC LOGO the possibilities are:

PPROP   This expects three inputs. The first is the word or number used as the heading. The second is the word or number used as the name of the property. The third is the word, number or list giving the value of that property, which is then stored. If there was already a value associated with the given property name under the given heading, that old value is lost.

GPROP   This expects two inputs, the name of a heading and the name of the property. It outputs the associated value, or the empty list if there is no such property name.

REMPROP   This also expects two inputs, like GPROP. It deletes the property name (and associated value) for that heading.

PLIST   This expects one input, the name of a heading. It outputs a list of the property name and property value pairs. It is not a list of lists, just a list with an even number of elements. Every odd-numbered element is a property name and the following element is the associated value. It is unwise to make any assumptions about the order in which the pairs appear.

Here are some examples of using these, to give you the idea:

```
?PPROP "ROSS "FIRST.NAME "PETER
?PRINT GPROP "ROSS "FIRST.NAME
```

prints PETER.

```
?PPROP "ROSS "BORN "EDINBURGH
?PRINT PLIST "ROSS
```

now prints the list [BORN EDINBURGH FIRST.NAME PETER].

```
?REMPROP "ROSS "FIRST.NAME
?PRINT GPROP "ROSS "FIRST.NAME
```

now prints the empty list, and

```
?PRINT PLIST "ROSS
```

prints the list [BORN EDINBURGH]. Sometimes it is convenient to have a procedure which behaves like PPROP, but does not destroy the old property value when a new one is added. The idea is to use a list of values rather than a single one. A suitable procedure might be:

```
TO ADD.TO.PROP :HEADING :NAME :VALUE
PPROP :HEADING :NAME (FPUT :VALUE (GPROP
     :HEADING :NAME))
END
```

and, to remove one of the values.

```
TO DEL.FROM.PROP :HEADING :NAME :VALUE
PPROP :HEADING :NAME (REMOVE :VALUE
     (GPROP :HEADING :NAME))
END

TO REMOVE :EL :LIST
IF :LIST=[ ] [OUTPUT [ ]]
IF :EL = FIRST :LIST [OUTPUT BF :LIST]
```

```
OUTPUT FPUT FIRST :LIST REMOVE :EL BF
        :LIST
END
```

The REMOVE procedure is the same as that given in Chapter 7.

In some applications, it is useful to have several ways of getting at the information. For example, rather than just doing

```
PPROP "ROSS "FIRST. NAME "PETER
```

it can be useful to do the following at the same time:

```
ADD.TO.PROP "FIRST. NAME "ROSS "PETER
PPROP "ROSS "PETER "FIRST. NAME
```

In other applications it makes sense to create tools which, in general, do a similar job to PPROP and GPROP, but take special action when certain values are encountered. The most obvious case is when there is no value:

```
TO GET.PROP :HEADING :NAME
LOCAL "VAL
MAKE "VAL GPROP :HEADING :NAME
TEST :VAL = [ ]
IFFALSE [OUTPUT :VAL]
PRINT (SENTENCE [There is no value for]
        :NAME [under] :HEADING)
PRINT [Give one, or just press ENTER:]
MAKE "VAL READLIST
PPROP :HEADING :NAME :VAL
OUTPUT :VAL
END
```

Property lists are saved by the SAVE command and reloaded by LOAD. This means that you can keep a database in the form of property lists in a file on disk, and update it from time to time.

8.2.1 An example: a conversational database
This section describes the rudiments of a friendly database program. One of the ingredients is a more sophisticated matching procedure than that described in Section 7.2.3. The aim is to allow the user to enter commands that look like bits of English, such as

```
THE <name> OF <heading> IS <value>
TELL <whoever> THE <name> OF <heading>
TELL <whoever> ABOUT <name>
```

The matching procedure needs to be able to do more than confirm that a list matches a pattern like one of these, and print out successful matches in the way that the earlier one did. It must be able to get hold of the fragments that match the general parts, in such a way that other procedures can make use of those fragments. The matcher whose definition is given below does the following:

```
PRINT MATCH [THE ?PERSON IS ?SOMETHING
        AT ?TIME] [THE OLD KING IS VERY
        HUNGRY AT NIGHT TIME]
```

prints TRUE, and gives a variable called PERSON the value [OLD KING], a variable called SOMETHING the value [VERY HUNGRY] and a variable called TIME the value [NIGHT TIME]. The command

```
PRINT MATCH [HELLO ?NAME] [HELLO]
```

will print FALSE, and will not affect the variable NAME, if it exists at all. The command

```
PRINT MATCH [THE ?SUBJECT ?VERB. PHRASE]
        [THE YOUNG DOG IS MAD]
```

will print TRUE. However, SUBJECT will have value [YOUNG] and VERB.PHRASE will have value [DOG IS MAD]. The general rules are:

- The first input is the pattern, the second is the target such as a sentence typed in by the user.
- In the pattern, any word beginning with a question mark can stand for any non-zero number of elements at that point in the target. A variable whose name is found by removing the initial question mark is given as its value a list of the matching elements of the target, provided that the whole match succeeds.
- In the pattern, any word beginning with a sharp sign (#) can stand for exactly one element at that point in the target. A variable whose name is found by removing the initial sharp sign is given as its value a list containing just that one element, provided that the whole match succeeds.
- In cases of ambiguous match, such as the last example above, the rule is that matching proceeds left to right and each question-mark-element matches as little as it can of the remainder of the target in order to make the match succeed.

An algorithm to achieve this is not quite straightforward. The idea is to start looking at both pattern and target, left to right, matching on the way along and using recursion to handle the matching of remnants. So, to start with:

a) If both pattern and target are empty, the match has succeeded.
b) If just one is empty, not both, then the match has failed.

Therefore, at this point we can assume that neither is empty. So:

c) If the first element of the pattern is the same as the first element of the target, then all depends on matching the rest of them. This is so even if the element starts with a question mark or a sharp sign — we shall just stipulate that normally, there shouldn't be such an element in the target and if there is, then the appropriate variable is not affected.
d) If the two first elements are not equal, and the first element of the pattern does not begin with a question mark or sharp sign or is not a word, then the match fails.

At this point, we know that both lists are non-empty and that the first element of the pattern begins with a sharp sign or a question mark. So:

e) If the first element does begin with a question mark or sharp sign, and the remainder of the pattern matches the remainder of the target, then give the appropriate variable a value of a list containing just the first element of the target, and output TRUE to show that the match succeeds. Note that the variable doesn't get the value until the rest of the match succeeds — that is, until the whole match is guaranteed to succeed.
f) If the remainders didn't match in step (d), then if the first element of the pattern begins with a sharp sign the whole match fails.
g) (the ingenious bit) At this point the match can only succeed if the first element of the pattern matches more than one element of the target. The way to test this is to see if the whole of the pattern matches the rest of the target. For example, to match [?X IS BIG] with [NEW YORK CITY IS BIG], try matching [?X IS BIG] against [YORK CITY IS BIG]. If that succeeds, X will have the value [YORK CITY] — so the match is definitely going to succeed, just change the value of X to [NEW YORK CITY] by using FPUT, and output TRUE.

If you are unsure, try a few examples on paper. The full definition of this new MATCH is significantly shorter but harder to understand than the English description:

```
TO MATCH :PAT :TGT
IF AND :PAT = [ ] :TGT = [ ] [OP "TRUE]
IF OR :PAT = [ ] :TGT = [ ] [OP "FALSE]
```

```
IF FIRST :PAT = FIRST :TGT [OP MATCH BF
      :PAT BF :TGT]
IF NOT WORDP FIRST :PAT [OP "FALSE]
IF NOT OR ("? = FIRST FIRST :PAT) ("#
      = FIRST FIRST :PAT) [OP "FALSE]
IF MATCH BF :PAT BF :TGT [MAKE BF FIRST
      :PAT (LIST FIRST :TGT) OP "TRUE]
IF "# = FIRST FIRST :PAT [OP "FALSE]
IF MATCH :PAT BF :TGT [MAKE BF FIRST
      :PAT FPUT FIRST :TGT THING BF FIRST
      :PAT OP "TRUE]
OP "FALSE
END
```

The matcher is the most difficult part of the conversational database system. It is used to try to match sentences typed in by the user against various standard patterns, such as

```
THE <property> OF <name> IS <value>
```

To be useful to PPROP, <name> and <property> must not be lists. This means that the user must type single words only at these points. What, for example, should be done about the sentence

```
THE PRICE OF THE ALLIGATOR IS HUGE
```

There are two simple ways out. One is to use

```
[THE ?PROP OF ?NAME IS ?VALUE]
```

and, if the value of NAME has more than one element, match it against subsidiary patterns such as [THE ?OBJECT] or, for economy, just [THE ?NAME]. The other is to match the whole sentence against another pattern:

```
[THE ?PROP OF THE ?NAME IS ?VALUE]
```

but this offers less flexibility. It means that a precise pattern is needed for every possible acceptable input. In the first method, at least the general form of the input is recognised. If any specific part is not recognised, then if all else fails the user can be asked for clarification.

Here are the rudiments of the system:

```
TO DATABASE
PROCESS READLIST
```

```
DATABASE
END

TO PROCESS :L
IF ". = LAST LAST :L [MAKE "L LPUT
        BUTLAST LAST :L BUTLAST :L]
(LOCAL "PROP "NAME "VALUE)
IF MATCH [THE ?PROP OF THE ?NAME IS
        ?VALUE] :L [TRY.TO.ADD :PROP :NAME
        :VALUE STOP]
IF MATCH [WHAT IS THE ?PROP OF ?NAME]
        [TRY.TO.FIND :PROP :NAME STOP]
IF MATCH [WHAT IS KNOWN ABOUT ?NAME]
        [TRY.TO.TELL.OF :NAME STOP]
PRINT [Eh? Try rephrasing that, please]
END

TO TRY.TO.ADD :PROP :NAME :VALUE
(LOCAL "P "N)
MAKE "P TRY.TO.TIDY :PROP
IF :P=[ ] [OBJECT.TO :PROP STOP]
MAKE "N TRY.TO.TIDY :NAME
IF :N = [ ] [OBJECT.TO :NAME STOP]
PPROP :N :P :VALUE
END

TO TRY.TO.FIND :PROP :NAME
(LOCAL "P "N)
MAKE "P TRY.TO.TIDY :PROP
IF :P=[ ] [OBJECT. TO :PROP STOP]
MAKE "N TRY.TO.TIDY :NAME
IF :N = [ ] [OBJECT.TO :NAME STOP]
PRINT GPROP :N :P
END

TO TRY.TO.TELL. OF :NAME
LOCAL "N
MAKE "N TRY.TO.TIDY :NAME
IF :N = [ ] [OBJECT.TO :NAME STOP]
PRINT PLIST :N
END

TO TRY.TO.TIDY :L
IF 1 = COUNT :L [OUTPUT FIRST :L]
LOCAL "W
IF MATCH [THE #W] :L [OUTPUT FIRST :W]
```

```
IF MATCH [THE ?W] :L [IF 2 = COUNT :W
       [OUTPUT (WORD FIRST :W ". LAST :W]]
OUTPUT [ ]
END

TO OBJECT.TO :IT
PRINT SENTENCE [I don't understand] :IT
END
```

The first line of PROCESS strips a full stop off the last word of the user's input if he has added one. TRY.TO.TIDY tries to output a single word. If its input is [THE PRICE] it outputs the word PRICE. If its input is the phrase [THE GREY RABBIT] it outputs the word GREY.RABBIT.

This is still not very sophisticated. For example, it does accept the input

```
THE THE DOG OF THE MOON IS
```

and meekly does the command PPROP "MOON "DOG ". rather than objecting. You can extend this simple system in a variety of ways, perhaps the most profitable of which is to build a better matcher that allows more general forms of pattern. Here are two suggestions:

- Allow pattern elements that cause matching against sub-patterns. For example, a pattern element of ??WHAT might be taken to mean that what matches it cannot just be a list, it must be a list that matches the pattern specified as the value of the variable called WHAT.
- Allow pattern elements with associated conditions. This might mean that such elements should be lists rather than words beginning with a special symbol. For instance,

```
[THE [W [IF :V=[ARE] PLURAL] [IF
       :V=[IS] SINGULAR]] #V #ADVERB]
```

might be a match for

```
THE HOUSE IS DUSTY
THE BOXES ARE STACKED
```

but not for

```
THE HILLS IS BLOOMING
```

As a further refinement, this simple database system can be extended to handle elliptical references, such as

WHAT IS THE HEIGHT OF THE BOX
WHAT IS THE WIDTH OF IT

8.2.2 Another example: simple reasoning

It is possible to use similar ideas to create a simple automated reasoning system. The key ideas are these:

- keep a list of known facts, and a list of rule names;
- give each rule name two properties called, say, PREMISES and CONCLUSION. The value of PREMISES will be a list of patterns, each of which may or may not match a known fact. The value of premise will be a template for a fact to be added to the known facts if all of the components of PREMISES are found to hold.

For instance, the notion of being a grandparent could be expressed as 'rule 39: if X has parent Y and Y has parent Z then X has grandparent Z'. This could be represented by giving RULE39 a PREMISE property of

[[?X HAS PARENT ?Y] [?Y HAS PARENT ?Z]]

and a CONCLUSION property of

[?X HAS GRANDPARENT ?Z]

An important point here is that the ?Y in the two PREMISES patterns must stand for the same thing. It is therefore not good enough just to use the MATCH procedure of the previous section to look for facts which match the first pattern and then for facts which match the second. However, that matcher can be modified to output a list of names paired with associated values, for use in subsequent processing. It could be given an extra input, a list of the 'match variables' of interest, so that, for example, the procedure

ASSOC. MATCH [?X IS ?Y IN ?Z] [THE NEW
        POPE IS LIVING IN ROME] [X Z]

outputs the list [[X [NEW POPE]] [Z ROME]]. Lists of this form appear so often in Artificial Intelligence programs that they merit a special name — they are called 'association lists'. It is an easy task to extend MATCH so as to output an association list by adding a few lines at the end to collect up the values of the appropriate variables. This is not wholly satisfactory in practice, since it means that (as with MATCH) the names of the 'match variables' must not be the names of any variables whose values you want left alone. The cure for this slight drawback is simple: replace the MAKE and THING procedures in the definition of MATCH above by procedures which use property lists instead. These procedures would do:

```
TO M.MAKE :NAME :VALUE
PPROP :NAME "MATCH.VALUE :VALUE
END

TO M.THING :NAME
OUTPUT GPROP :NAME "MATCH.VALUE
END
```

so that a command such as

```
M.MAKE "X FPUT "POPE M.THING "X
```

will leave the value of the variable named X undisturbed. A useful advantage of M.THING is that it will always output something if its input is a word or number, whereas THING will give an error if its input has no value. Provided MATCH is modified, by replacing MAKE with M.MAKE and THING with M.THING, then ASSOC. MATCH can be defined like this:

```
TO ASSOC. MATCH :PAT :TGT :VARS
TEST MATCH :PAT :TGT
OUTPUT ASSOCIATIONS :VARS
END

TO ASSOCIATIONS :VARLIST
IF EMPTYP :VARLIST [OUTPUT [ ] ]
OUTPUT FPUT LIST FIRST :VARLIST M. THING
      FIRST :VARLIST ASSOCIATIONS
      BUTFIRST :VARLIST
END
```

The only point of the TEST in ASSOC.MATCH is to consume the output of MATCH. Of course, MATCH could be modified further so that it didn't output, but it is frequently useful to have both MATCH and ASSOC.MATCH available at the same time.

ASSOC.MATCH is the key to solving the problem of handling multi-part premises such as the premise of RULE39 above. For a given premise

```
[pattern1 pattern2 ...]
```

one algorithm is

- Scan 'pattern1' to create a list of the 'match variables'.
- Look for matches for 'pattern1'. For each, create a modified 'pattern2' by replacing any match variables shared with 'pattern1' by their found values. Look for matches for this pattern. Do this recursively, to generate a cumulative association list that makes the whole premise true.
- For each such cumulative association list, turn the general template of the conclusion into a specific fact.
- Add each fact to the database.

This approach is fairly simplistic — there is no provision for logical negation, for example. A full treatment deserves a book to itself — but it is an impressively large topic to explore.

8.3 THROW AND CATCH

Normally, when an error happens in IBM PC LOGO, an error message is printed and control returns to the command interpreter, which prints the prompt and waits for your next command. It is sometimes useful to be able to change this behaviour. If you are trying to find the faults in a set of your LOGO procedures that take quite a while to run, it is extremely annoying to have to return to the start every time an error happens.

There are two ways in which you can affect LOGO's behaviour when an error happens. The first is simple. There is a variable called ERRACT (a contraction of 'error action') which normally has the value FALSE. If you set it TRUE, then LOGO will pause whenever an error happens, printing the name of the procedure in which it happened followed by the prompt. You can then give whatever commands you like. The command CO means 'continue' — LOGO will carry on from a point just after the error. To illustrate this, imagine that you have defined these two silly procedures, whose only function is to allow you a lot of possibilities of errors!

```
TO TRY :N
FD :N PRINT [DOES THIS GET PRINTED?]
PRINT [HOW ABOUT THIS?]
END

TO REALLY.TRY :N
TRY LPUT "A :N
END
```

Here is a sample of misusing them — there being no way that you can use them correctly:

```
?MAKE "ERRACT "TRUE
?TRY "Z
```

LOGO prints an error message, including the line of the procedure where it happened if it's not the last line to be run in that procedure, followed by a pause:

LOGO prints:	FORWARD DOESN'T LIKE Z AS INPUT IN TRY:
LOGO prints:	FD :N PRINT [DOES THIS GET PRINTED?]
LOGO types:	TRY ?
You enter:	CO
LOGO prints:	DOES THIS GET PRINTED?
LOGO prints:	HOW ABOUT THIS?
LOGO types:	?

Now, try harder to make mistakes:

You enter:	REALLY.TRY 3
LOGO prints:	LPUT DOESN'T LIKE 3 AS INPUT:
LOGO prints:	JUST BEFORE LEAVING REALLY.TRY
LOGO types:	REALLY.TRY?
You enter:	CO
LOGO prints:	CO DIDN'T OUTPUT TO TRY:
LOGO prints:	JUST BEFORE LEAVING REALLY.TRY
LOGO types:	REALLY.TRY?

When paused, you can use OUTPUT to provide a missing value. LOGO will continue as though the LPUT had just been done, so that the TRY <whatever> will be done next:

You enter:	OUTPUT "AH
LOGO prints:	FORWARD DOESN'T LIKE AH AS INPUT IN TRY:
LOGO prints:	FD :N PRINT [DOES THIS GET PRINTED?]
LOGO types:	TRY ?
You enter:	OUTPUT 100

which is a mistake! LOGO will attempt to continue immediately after the FD :N and immediately encounter your 100:

LOGO prints:	I DON'T KNOW WHAT TO DO WITH 100 IN TRY:
LOGO prints:	FD :N PRINT [DOES THIS GET PRINTED?]
LOGO types:	TRY ?
Your enter:	CO
LOGO prints:	DOES THIS GET PRINTED?
LOGO prints:	HOW ABOUT THIS?

LOGO types: ?

All this is very useful for tracking down mistakes in your procedures. It does, however, require a lot of decision-making on your part. It is possible to get your procedures to make the decisions by using the built-in procedures THROW and CATCH. THROW takes one input, a word. CATCH takes two inputs, a word and a list. They work together and are best explained by means of an example. The command

CATCH "CASE13 [...commands...]

will run the commands, just like RUN [...commands...] or REPEAT 1 [... commands ...], up to the point (if any) where the command

THROW "CASE13

is obeyed. The effect is that whatever remains to be done of the commands is skipped — the next command obeyed is the one that follows the CATCH.

The only point of the word input to CATCH and THROW is to act as a tag to identify which CATCH goes with which THROW — or THROWs. If there is more than one CATCH with the same tag word then it is the most recent CATCH that counts.

There are three special tag words, TRUE, ERROR and TOPLEVEL (in Waterloo LOGO they must be in upper case; in Dr. LOGO they should be in lower case). CATCH "TRUE catches any THROW, no matter what the tag. THROW "TOPLEVEL returns control to the top level, the command interpreter, unless of course there is a CATCH "TOPLEVEL [...] in the way. Whenever an error occurs or you press CTRL-Break, LOGO implicitly does a THROW "ERROR. The command interpreter also catches it and reports on the error, unless there is a CATCH "ERROR in the way or (in IBM PC LOGO) you have set ERRACT to TRUE.

Information about the last error is available in a list output by the procedure ERROR, described in the example below. ERROR is peculiar: it outputs the information the first time it is called after the error. Thereafter, it outputs only the empty list, until the next error.

8.3.1 An example: a LOGO interpreter
This IBM PC LOGO interpreter beeps once whenever an error occurs. It outputs more distinctive error messages, in a different colour so that they stand out from your commands. To remind you that you are using it, it prints a double question mark and space as

the prompt, instead of the normal single question mark.

```
TO LOGO
MAKE "HAD.ERROR "TRUE
TYPE "??
CATCH "ERROR [CATCH "TOPLEVEL [RUN
     READLIST] MAKE "HAD.ERROR "FALSE]
IF :HAD.ERROR [EXPLAIN.ERROR]
LOGO
END
```

If an error happens during the RUN READLIST, the next command obeyed is the IF :HAD.ERROR ... — the MAKE "HAD.ERROR "FALSE is skipped. If there is no error, then HAD.ERROR is set to FALSE and so EXPLAIN.ERROR is not run.

The procedure EXPLAIN.ERROR uses ERROR to get the details. The first time that ERROR is run after an error, it outputs a six-element list consisting of (in order):

1. A number identifying the general form of the error message. You can use it to identify the types of error made.
2. A list containing the specific message.
3. The name of the procedure within which the error occurred, or the empty list if it happened at the (genuine) top level.
4. A list containing the prcedure line in which it occurred, or the empty list.
5. The name of the built-in procedure that actually signalled the error.
6. In cases where the problem was an inappropriate input to the procedure named in 5, the input; otherwise the empty list.

A useful definition of EXPLAIN.ERROR is given below. It assumes that changing the foreground colour to 2 and the background colour to 0 is adequately distinctive. This works if you haven't changed the text colour from the default values and you have a screen capable of displaying colours. It uses TC to get details of the current text colour, and SETTC to change it:

```
TO EXPLAIN.ERROR
TONE 400 5
(LOCAL "ERR "MESS "PROC "LN "PRIM "OB
     "OLD.TC)
MAKE "ERR ERROR
MAKE "MESS ITEM 2 :ERR
MAKE "PROC ITEM 3 :ERR
```

```
MAKE "LN ITEM 4 :ERR
MAKE "PRIM ITEM 5 :ERR
MAKE "OB ITEM 6 :ERR
MAKE "OLD.TC TC
SETTC [2 0]
PRINT :MESS
IF OR :MESS = [STOPPED!] :PROC = "LOGO
      [SETTC :OLD.TC STOP]
PRINT SE [It happened in] :PROC
IF NOT :LN [ ] [PRINT SE [The line was] :LN]
PRINT SE [The primitive was] :PRIM
PRINT SE [The culprit was] :OB
SETTC :OLD.TC
END
```

TONE 400 5 causes a short 400 Hz beep. The message STOPPED! normally results from pressing CTRL-Break. If the user enters faulty commands, such as FORWARD "TURTLE, then the procedure name in the output of ERROR will be LOGO.EXPLAIN. ERROR suppresses some information in these special cases, to avoid confusion.

How do you stop the interpreter? CTRL-Break will not do, since LOGO treats it as though it were an error and catches it. There is only one way, short of reloading your computer. It is, naturally, to give the command STOP.

A change that has sometimes been proposed for LOGO is to get rid of the colon. This would mean that instead of a command such as

```
MAKE "X BUTFIRST :Y
```

you would have to use the command

```
MAKE "X BUTFIRST Y
```

Provided there was no doubt about whether Y was the name of a variable or the name of procedure, this would be unambiguous. The commands

```
MAKE "Y [WHAT DO YOU THINK?]
MAKE "X BUTFIRST Y
PRINT Y
```

would print DO YOU THINK?

The LOGO interpreter can easily be modified to let you experiment with colon-less commands and procedures. All that is needed is a procedure which will translate the user's colon-less commands back into commands that do use the colon, so that RUN will work on them. Replace RUN READLIST by

```
RUN TRANSLATE.LINE READLIST
```

TRANSLATE.LINE can be defined like this:

```
TO TRANSLATE.LINE :L
IF EMPTYP :L [OUTPUT [ ]]
OUTPUT FPUT TR. ITEM FIRST :L
        TRANSLATE.LINE BUTFIRST :L
END
```

```
TO TR.ITEM :X
IF OR NUMBERP :X LISTP :X [OUTPUT :X]
IF PRIMITIVEP :X [OUTPUT :X]
IF NAMEP :X [OUTPUT WORD ": :X]
IF NOT MEMBERP :X :TRANSLATED.PROC.LIST
        [DEFINE WORD "TR. :X TR.PROC :X]
OUTPUT WORD "TR. :X
END
```

The input to TR.ITEM is a word, number or list. If the input is a number or list, it is output unmodified. The IBM PC LOGO procedure PRIMITIVEP will determine whether it is the name of a built-in procedure; if so, it is output unmodified. (Note: PRIMITIVEP treats the parentheses as built-in procedures.) If it is the name of a variable, it is modified by putting a colon at the front of it. The only possibility remaining is that the input is the name of a user-defined procedure (fortunately there are no keywords such as 'then' and 'else' to cope with). Such a procedure is translated the first time it is run, and that fact is recorded by adding its name to a list called TRANSLATED.PROC.LIST. The translated version has TR. at the front of its name. The built-in procedure DEFINE defines procedures in a non-interactive way. The inputs it requires are a word naming a procedure and a list of lists giving the lines of the definition. The built-in procedure TEXT, used below, outputs such a list of lists defining the procedure named by the input.

```
TO TR.PROC :P
MAKE "TRANSLATED.PROC.LIST FPUT :P
        :TRANSLATED.PROC.LIST
OUTPUT TR.PROC.BODY TEXT :P
END
```

```
TO TR.PROC.BODY :L
IF EMPTYP :L [OUTPUT [ ]]
OUTPUT FPUT TRANSLATE.LINE FIRST :L
        TR.PROC.BODY BUTFIRST :L
END
```

In TR.PROC, the name is added to the list of translated procedures just before translation, lest the procedure is a recursive one. Otherwise, a recursive procedure would lead to a recursive attempt to translate it.

These procedures do not cope with commands such as REPEAT, IF, IFTRUE and IFFALSE which treat a list as a command. You will need to redefine them, by preserving the original definition:

```
MAKE "REDEFP "TRUE
COPYDEF "OLD.REPEAT "REPEAT
```

and then defining a new version:

```
TO REPEAT :N :L
OLD.REPEAT :N TRANSLATE.LINE :L
END
```

The procedure IF poses a small problem. Normally it takes who or three inputs — the word TRUE or FALSE and one or two lists. When you redefine it, it will have to take three. This, however, is only a slight inconvenience. You could just use TEST/IFTRUE/IFFALSE instead.

A sample of a session using this modified LOGO is given below:

```
?LOGO
?? MAKE "X 34
?? MAKE "Y X+6
?? PRINT Y
40
?? PRINT X * Y
1360
?? MAKE "IT "X
?? PRINT THING X
34
?? MAKE "Z [HELLO]
HELLO
HELLO
HELLO
```

```
?? REPEAT 3 [PRINT Z]
?? EDIT "RECURSE
        IBM PC LOGO doesn't mind if you leave
        the colons out of the title line:
    TO RECURSE L
    TEST L > 100
    IFTRUE [STOP]
    IFFALSE [RECURSE L+1]
    END
?? RECURSE X
34
35
36
... etc.
??
```

8.4 IN CONCLUSION

Try to develop the ideas in this book in your own way, and to create
new paths of your own. Not all the facilities of IBM PC LOGO, Dr.
LOGO and Waterloo LOGO have been mentioned (though the
appendixes describe them) — investigating the remainder will give
you a starting point if you need one. But remember, computing can
be and should be a social activity. The best way to find new ideas
and new projects is to discuss them with other people, in competition or in co-operation. Try brainstorming sessions, to explore a
project or devise a method of representation. Form groups and get
them into friendly competition. Don't restrict yourself to LOGO;
look at other people's programs in other languages for their ideas,
and give them some of your own. If you create something you're
really proud of, then tell others about it or send it to one of the
many magazines.

Enjoy it!

Appendix A
IBM PC LOGO

A.1 IBM PC LOGO
This appendix describes the IBM PC LOGO language, created by
LOGO Computer Systems Inc. and distributed by IBM.

A.2 Conventions
The description uses the following notation:

FORWARD (FD)	n
BUTFIRST (BF)	nwl $\Rightarrow$ nwl
PRINT	nwl...
LIST	nwl nw1... $\Rightarrow$ 1
SETWIDTH	n (n)

meaning

a) FORWARD can be abbreviated to FD, and it expects a number as input.
b) BUTFIRST can be abbreviated to BF, it expects a number, word or list as input and it outputs a number, word or list.
c) PRINT expects a number, word or list as input, and it can be greedy.
d) LIST normally expects two inputs, each a number, word or list, and outputs a list, but it can be greedy.
e) SETWIDTH normally expects one input, a number. It accepts an optional second input, also a number.

The abbreviations used are

n	number
w	word
l	list
t	truth value, the word TRUE or the word FALSE
p	word naming a package
nw	number or word
nwl	number, word or list
...	and so on ...

A.3 Naming conventions
In general, the more commonly used commands have abbreviations
of two or three letters. If the command name is a portmanteau
word, such as CLEARSCREEN, then the abbreviation is usually

the first letter of the component words. Otherwise, it is usually the first and the last letter of the name. There are exceptions — for example, PALETTE is shortened to PAL rather than PE because PENERASE was judged the more frequently used and so is what PE stands for.

A number of commands are named SETsomething, which set some parameter. In general, provided the 'something' is more than one letter long, there is a corresponding command whose name omits the 'SET', which outputs the current value of the parameter. Examples are SETBG and BG, SETSHAPE and SHAPE; SETX has counterpart XCOR because X is too short.

A.4 Turtle graphics

The screen is 320 turtle units wide and 250 turtle units high, although the height can be changed by the .SETSCRUNCH command. The origin of co-ordinates is at the middle of the screen. When the turtle has a heading of 0 degrees it is pointing straight up the screen. The heading increases as the turtle turns clockwise.

FORWARD (FD)	n
BACK (BK)	n
LEFT (LT)	n
	In degrees.
RIGHT (RT)	n
	In degrees.
HOME	
CLEAN	Clears the drawing, does not affect the turtle.
CLEARSCREEN (CS)	
	Different from earlier LOGOs; equivalent to DRAW.
WRAP	After this command, if the turtle leaves one edge of the screen it reappears at the other.
FENCE	After this command, the turtle is not allowed to cross the edges of the screen.
WINDOW	Makes the display behave like a window onto the centre of a large drawing area. Co-ordinates up to 9999 allowed; wraps if larger.
SETX	n
XCOR	$\Rightarrow n$
SETY	n
YCOR	$\Rightarrow n$
SETHEADING (SETH)	n
	Sets the heading to be in the range $0-360$ degrees.
HEADING	$\Rightarrow n$
TOWARDS	$l \Rightarrow n$
	The input is a position of a point on the screen. The output is a heading towards that point, in degrees.

SETPOS   l
       Takes a list of two numbers, an X and a Y.
POS   ⇒ n
PENDOWN (PD)
PENUP (PU)
PENREVERSE (PX)
       Sets the pen to the reversing colour.
PENERASE (PE)
       Sets the pen to the background colour.
SETPC   n
       Sets the pen colour (0−3). To get the reversing colour use PENREVERSE.
PENCOLOR (PC)   ⇒ n
SETPAL   n
       Sets the colour palette (0 or 1).
PALETTE (PAL)   n
       Outputs the palette.
SETPEN   l
       Sets the pen state, a list of three elements. The first is one of PENDOWN, PENUP, PENERASE or PEN-REVERSE, the second is the pen colour (an integer), the third is the palette (an integer).
PEN   ⇒ l
SETBG   n
       Sets the background colour (0−15).
BACKGROUND (BG)   ⇒ n
SHOWTURTLE (ST)
HIDETURTLE (HT)
SHOWNP   ⇒ t
       Outputs TRUE if the turtle is being shown, FALSE if hidden.
FULLSCREEN (FS)
MIXEDSCREEN (MS)
TEXTSCREEN (TS)
SETSHAPE   nw
       Changes the turtle's shape to the character whose ASCII code is given. The input TURTLE resets it.
SHAPE   ⇒ nw
SNAP   n
       Copies the part of the drawing under the turtle. Stores it as the character whose ASCII code (only 128−255) is given.
STAMP   Inserts the turtle's shape into the drawing.
SAVEPIC   w
       The input will be trimmed to eight characters, for use as a file name.

LOADPIC   w
DOT   l
            Puts a dot at that position. The turtle does not move.
FILL   Fills the closed shape inside which the turtle is standing
            with the current colour.
.SETSCRUNCH   n
            Sets the ratio of size of a vertical turtle step to size of a
            horizontal vertical step.
SCRUNCH $\Rightarrow$ n

A.5 Variables

MAKE   w nwl
THING (:)   w $\Rightarrow$ nwl
            The colon is not a true abbreviation — see the comments
            in Chapter 2.
NAME   nwl w
            MAKE with the inputs swapped.
LOCAL   w
            Creates a variable having the given name, which tem-
            porarily supersedes any other of the same name. The
            variable ceases to exist when the procedure in which it
            was created by LOCAL comes to an end.
ERN   wl
            Makes LOGO forget about the named variable(s).
ERNS   (pl)
            Erases all (unburied) variables. Can also take a package
            name, or a list of them, when it confines the effect to
            those packages.
EDNS   (pl)
            Starts the editor to edit variables. Can also take a pack-
            age name, or a list of them, when it confines the effect to
            those packages.

A.6 Arithmetic
Numbers can be given in various forms, such as:

35
3.6
$-3.7E2$ meaning -370
3.8E+2   meaning 380
3.9E-2 meaning 0.039

The integer after the E can have up to four digits. If there is an E,
there must be a digit rather than the decimal point just before it.
    All the trigonometric functions deal with angles measured in

degrees rather than in radians or grads.

+, −, *, /	n n $\Rightarrow$ n

These four are used in a conventional way: 3 + 4, not + 3 4. Use parentheses to avoid ambiguity. The minus sign should have space on both sides of it, or on neither side, to avoid confusion about negative numbers.

PI	$\Rightarrow$ n

Outputs the well known constant.

SIN	n $\Rightarrow$ n
COS	n $\Rightarrow$ n
ARCTAN	n (n) $\Rightarrow$ n

Outputs the angle, in degrees between 0 and 360, whose arctangent is the first input divided by the second. If the second input is missing it is assumed to be 1.

SQRT	n $\Rightarrow$ n
INT	n $\Rightarrow$ n

Removes any fractional part.

ROUND	n $\Rightarrow$ n

Rounds the input to the nearest integer.

REMAINDER	n n $\Rightarrow$ n

Outputs the remainder on dividing first input by second.

EXP	n $\Rightarrow$ n

Outputs e to the given power.

LN	n $\Rightarrow$ 0
POWER	n n $\Rightarrow$ n

Outputs first input raised to the power given by the second.

SETPRECISION	n

Sets the number of significant digits to be used. Can be between 5 and 1000, but some procedures work to a maximum of 100.

PRECISION	$\Rightarrow$ n
EFORM	n n $\Rightarrow$ n

Outputs the first number in E-form notation. The second input is the number of digits before the E; there is always just one before the decimal point.

FORM	n n (n) $\Rightarrow$ n

Outputs the first number in a chosen form. The second gives the number of digits before the decimal point; the third, if given, the number after the point. If the third number is not given it is taken to be 0. Superfluous leading zeros are replaced by spaces.

SUM	n n... $\Rightarrow$ n
DIFFERENCE	n n... $\Rightarrow$ n
PRODUCT	n n... $\Rightarrow$ n

QUOTIENT	n n $\Rightarrow$ n
RANDOM	n $\Rightarrow$ n

Rounds its input, then outputs a random integer in the range 0 to one less than the input.

RERANDOM

Resets the random number generator to a known state.

A.7 Procedures

TO	w
EDIT	wl
DEFINE	w l

The first input is a name, the second is a list of lists defining a procedure to be known by that name.

TEXT   w $\Rightarrow$ l

Input is a name. Output is a list of lists, giving the definition of the procedure named.

ERASE (ER)   wl

Makes LOGO forget about the named procedure(s).

ERPS   (pl)

Erases all procedures not buried. Can also take a package name or a list of them as input, in which case the effect is confined to those packages.

ERALL   (pl)

Like ERPS, but erases names too.

COPYDEF   w w

Copies the procedure named by the second input. The first input is the name of the copy.

A.8 Words and lists

FIRST	nwl $\Rightarrow$ nwl
LAST	nwl $\Rightarrow$ nwl
BUTFIRST (BF)	nwl $\Rightarrow$ nwl
BUTLAST (BL)	nwl $\Rightarrow$ nwl
LIST	nwl nwl... $\Rightarrow$ l
SENTENCE (SE)	nwl nwl... $\Rightarrow$ l

Like LIST, but input lists get broken into the collection of separate elements first.

FPUT   nwl l $\Rightarrow$ l

Puts the first input onto the front of the list.

LPUT   nwl l $\Rightarrow$ l

Puts the first input onto the end of the list.

WORD   nw nw... $\Rightarrow$ nw

Concatenates its inputs.

COUNT $l \Rightarrow n$
Outputs the number of elements of the list. Does not accept a word as input.

ITEM $n \; nwl \Rightarrow nwl$
Outputs the chosen element from the list, or chosen character from the number or word.

A.9 Condition procedures

IBM PC LOGO uses a final P in naming the various condition testing procedures.

IF t l (l)   The one or two lists contain commands. If the condition is TRUE, the first is obeyed. The second list is only obeyed if the condition is FALSE.

TEST t

IFTRUE ... (IFT)   l

IFFALSE ... (IFF)   l

$>, <$ $n \; n \Rightarrow t$
Used in the customary way: $2 > 1$, not $> 2\,1$.

$=$ $nwl \; nwl \Rightarrow t$
Used in the customary way: $2 = 2$, not $= 2\,2$.

LISTP $nwl \Rightarrow t$

WORDP $nwl \Rightarrow t$

NUMBERP $nwl \Rightarrow t$

EQUALP $nwl \; nwl \Rightarrow t$

EMPTYP $wl \Rightarrow t$
Outputs TRUE if the input is the empty word or list.

MEMBERP $nwl \; l \Rightarrow t$
Outputs TRUE if the first input is a member of the list.

NAMEP $nwl \Rightarrow t$
Outputs TRUE if the input is the name of an existing variable.

DEFINEDP $w \Rightarrow t$
Outputs TRUE if the input is the name of an existing procedure.

PRIMITIVEP $w \Rightarrow t$
Outputs TRUE if the input is the name of a built-in procedure.

KEYP $\Rightarrow t$
Outputs TRUE if there are characters that have been typed but not read.

BUTTONP $n \Rightarrow t$
The input must be in the range $0-3$, specifying a paddle. The output is TRUE if the button on that paddle is being pressed.

FILEP $w \Rightarrow t$
Outputs TRUE if the named file exists.

AND	t t ... $\Rightarrow$ t
OR	t t ... $\Rightarrow$ t
NOT	t $\Rightarrow$ t

A.10 Control

STOP	
OUTPUT (OP)	nwl
REPEAT	n l
RUN	l

      Like REPEAT 1 ...

GO	w

      Transfers control to the matching LABEL in the same procedure.

LABEL	w
CATCH	w l
THROW	w
ERROR	Outputs information about the most recent error — see the technical manual for details.

A.11 Text display

FULLSCREEN, MIXEDSCREEN and TEXTSCREEN affect how much of the screen can be used for displaying text. There are at most 25 lines of text. The number of columns depends on SET-WIDTH; the default is 40.

SETTC	l

      It expects a list of two numbers specifying foreground and background colours for text.

TEXTCOLOR (TC)	$\Rightarrow$ l
SETWIDTH	n (n)

      Sets the width of lines of text. The input must be between 2 and 80 inclusive. The optional second input moves the whole screen that many columns right, or left if negative.

WIDTH	$\Rightarrow$ n
SETTEXT	n

      Selects how many lines of text are to be used when graphics are also displayed.

SETCAPS	t

      Disables the Caps Lock key if TRUE.

CAPS	$\Rightarrow$ t
SETSCREEN	n

      Informs LOGO of the number of screens you have (1 or 2).

SCREEN	$\Rightarrow$ n

A.12 Screen input/output

CLEARTEXT

PRINT (PR)   nwl. . .

TYPE   nwl. . .

SHOW   nwl

> Like PRINT, but also prints the outermost brackets of lists.

READLIST (RL)   ⇒ l

READWORD (RW)   ⇒ w

READCHAR (RC)   ⇒ w

> Outputs a single-character word consisting of the least recent character typed but not yet read.

READCHARS (RCS)   n ⇒ w

> Gathers up the given number of characters and outputs them as a word.

SETCURSOR   l

> The input is a list of two numbers. First is the row (0−24), second is the column (which depends on the selectable width). Top left is 0,0.

CURSOR   ⇒ l

ASCII   nw ⇒ n

> The input must be one character (perhaps a single-digit number). Outputs the ASCII code of that character.

CHAR   n ⇒ nw

> The reverse of ASCII.

TONE   n n

> The first input specifies a frequency, the second a duration measured in eighteenths of a second.

A.13 Packages

In LOGO, variables and procedures can be put into 'packages', and specified packages can be saved on disk or erased from memory.

PACKAGE   p wl

> The first input is the name of a package (if it is unknown this will make it known). The second input is a word, or a list of words, naming variables and procedures to be included in the package.

PKGALL   p

> Packages everything not yet packaged.

BURY   p

> Marks the contents of the package, so that they cannot be affected by POALL, ERALL, ERNS, ERPS, PONS, POPS, POTS or SAVE.

UNBURY   p

> Undoes the effect of BURY.

A.14 Workspace information

PO   w1
                    Prints out definitions of the named procedure(s).
PONS   (pl)
                    Prints out the values of all (unburied) variables. Can take
                    a package name or list as input, to confine printing to
                    those packages.
POPS   (pl)
                    Prints out all (unburied) procedure definitions. Can take
                    a package name or list as input, to confine printing to
                    those packages.
POALL   (pl)
                    Combines PONS and POPS.
POTS   (pl)
                    Prints out the titles of all (unburied) procedures. Can
                    take a package name or list as input, to confine printing
                    to those packages.
CONTENTS $\Rightarrow$ l
                    Outputs a list of all known words.
RECYCLE   Salvages bits of memory that had been needed while
                    previous commands were running, but are not currently
                    needed. This is called 'garbage collection', and causes a
                    perceptible delay.
NODES $\Rightarrow$ l
                    Outputs the number of nodes available. This is a maxi-
                    mum immediately after a RECYCLE. The information is
                    useful if you want to call RECYCLE at a moment when
                    the delay of garbage collection is acceptable rather than
                    at a critical moment.
REPARSE   Any new procedure, or procedure with a changed num-
                    ber of inputs, is reparsed by this. Normally the reparsing
                    happens when the procedure is first run, and causes a
                    perceptible delay. If the delay would be unacceptable
                    then, use REPARSE sometime beforehand.

A.15 Files

The printer is regarded as just another file, although you cannot
read from it. If your printer is connected to a parallel interface it
will be called LPT1. If it is connected to a serial interface it will be
called COM1 or AUX. The command .SETCOM must be used at
some point before writing to COM1 or AUX.

DIR   (w)
                    Displays the names of all files on the current disk, or
                    those matching the given specification.

SAVE	w (pl)

Saves everything (unburied) except the drawing in the named file. Can take a second input — a package name or a list of them — to confine saving to those packages.

LOAD	w (p)

Reads in the contents of the named file. Can also take a package name as a second input, and the file contents will then be loaded into that package.

ERASEFILE	w
EDITFILE	w (w)

Starts the editor to edit the named file. If the second input is given, saves the result in that file.

POFILE	w

Prints out a file.

FILELEN	w ⇒ n

Outputs the length of the file in bytes.

OPEN	w

Opens the named file, for reading or writing. At most five can be open at once.

CLOSE	w

Closes the named file.

CLOSEALL	

Closes all open files.

ALLOPEN	⇒ l

Outputs a list of names of all open files.

SETREAD	w

Selects the file to read from (for RC, RCS, RL, RW). The file must be open.

READER	⇒ w

Outputs the name of the open file being read from, or the empty word.

SETWRITE	w

Selects the file to write to (for PRINT, TYPE, SHOW, PO, POFILE). The file must be open.

WRITER	⇒ w

Outputs the name of the open file last written to, or the empty word.

SETREADPOS	n

Sets the position in the file for reading. The start is 0.

READPOS	⇒ n
READEOFP	⇒ t

Outputs TRUE if reading has reached the end of the file.

SETWRITEPOS	n

Sets the position in the file for writing. The start is 0.

WRITEPOS	⇒ n
WRITEOFP	⇒ t

Outputs TRUE if writing is at the end of the file.

SETDISK   w
                Sets the default disk.
DISK   ⇒ w
DRIBBLE   w
                Starts LOGO keeping a copy of all screen text in the
                named file.
NODRIBBLE
.SETCOM   n n n n n
                The inputs are: serial interface number, baud rate (one
                of the standard ones), parity (0=none, 1=odd, 2=even),
                databits (7 or 8), stopbits (1 or 2).
.DOS   Ends LOGO.

A.16 Tracing

PAUSE   Causes a pause, during which any commands can be
           given.
CO   (nwl)
                Resumes activity, ends a pause. Outputs its input, if
                there is one.

A.17 Editing keys

Any normal text you type is inserted, without overwriting any existing text. The following keys are used for editing. Most can be used
outside the editor too.

Del   Rubs out the character on which the cursor is standing.
Back-arrow
           Rubs out the character to the left of the cursor.
Arrow keys
           Move the cursor in the appropriate direction. The up-
           arrow and down-arrow only work inside the editor.
Tab   Moves the cursor to the end of the current line of LOGO
           (maybe not the current screen line).
Back-tab   Moves the cursor to the start of the current line of
           LOGO (maybe not the current screen line).
CTRL-right-arrow
           Deletes all characters to the right of the cursor on the
           current line of LOGO.
CTRL-left-arrow
           Inserts the last line deleted.
Ins   (Editor only) Splices in a blank line.
PgUp   (Editor only) Moves up by a screenful.
PgDn   (Editor only) Moves down by a screenful.

CTRL-PgUp

(Editor only) Moves the cursor to the start of the edit buffer.

CTRL-PgDn

(Editor only) Moves the cursor to the end of the edit buffer.

Home   (Editor only) Moves the cursor to the top of the screen.

End   (Editor only) Moves the cursor to the bottom of the screen.

Esc   (Editor only) Ends the editing.

CTRL-Break

(Editor) Aborts the editing. (Normal) Aborts the command.

F3   Inserts the last line typed in.

A.18 Other special keys

CTRL-Break

Aborts the command.

CTRL-NumLock

Suspends LOGO command and output. Typing anything causes the command and outputting to resume.

F3   Behaves like PAUSE.

F4   Full graphics screen, no text displayed.

F2   Mixed text and graphics. Six lines (or as set by SETTEXT) of text displayed.

F1   No graphics displayed. Twenty five lines of text displayed.
           Allows you to remove any special significance, as far as LOGO is concerned, from the next character typed in.

Shift-PrtScr

Prints the screen on the graphics printer.

A.19 Properties

PPROP   nw nw nwl

The first input is a name, the second is a property name for that name, the third is the value of the named property.

GPROP   nw nw $\Rightarrow$ nwl

The first input is a name, the second a property name. Outputs the value of the property.

PLIST   nw $\Rightarrow$ l

Takes a name as input. Outputs a list of property names and values.

REMPROP   nw nw

Takes a name and a property name, and erases that property of the name.

PPS   (pl)

With no input, prints the properties of everything. Can take a package name or a list of packages, then confines its effect to those packages.

A.20 Special commands

For these you need some technical knowledge of the machine and of assembly language.

.BLOAD   w (n) (n)

Loads an assembly language file into memory. The optional inputs specify a base and an offset. See the documentation that came with your disk for suitable values.

.BSAVE   w n n n

Saves an area of memory in a named file. The other inputs are a base, offset and length.

.CALL   n n

Calls the sub-routine located at the given base and offset.

.DEPOSIT   n n

The first input is an address in memory, the second is a value. Like BASIC's POKE.

.EXAMINE   n $\Rightarrow$ n

Outputs the value at the given memory address. Like BASIC's PEEK.

A.21 Special words

EDITOR   Recognised by EDITFILE. The command EDITFILE "EDITOR resumes editing what you last edited.

END   Marks the end of a procedure.

ERRACT   A variable, normally FALSE. If TRUE, LOGO pauses when an error happens.

TOPLEVEL

The command THROW "TOPLEVEL returns to the top level, if not caught.

ERROR   Any error causes an implicit THROW "ERROR, unless ERRACT is TRUE.

REDEFP   A variable, normally FALSE. If TRUE, you can redefine the built-in procedures.

VALPKG   A property name of any variable. The value is the name of a package to which the variable belongs.

PROCPKG

Like VALPKG, but for procedures.

Appendix B
Dr. LOGO

B.1 Dr. LOGO for the IBM PC

This appendix describes Dr. LOGO for the IBM PC, created by Digital Research Inc. of Pacific Grove, California. Apart from some standard property names, everything is in lower case rather than upper case as in IBM PC LOGO. Since most procedures are identical to those in IBM PC LOGO, only those that differ will be described.

B.2 Conventions

The descriptions use the conventions described in Appendix A.

B.3 Summary of differences

Various procedures and names differ or have no counterpart. In the following list, items in upper case (except .PAK) are IBM PC LOGO and items in lower case are Dr. LOGO. Those marked ++++ are Dr. LOGO procedures that have no direct equivalent in IBM PC LOGO. Those marked −−−− are IBM PC LOGO procedures with no direct equivalent in Dr. LOGO. In many cases it is possible to construct an adequate replacement.

;	++++
^	<<−− POWER (prefix)
.BLOAD	−−−−
.BSAVE	−−−−
.CALL	−−−−
.DOS	−−>> bye
.PAK (Dr. LOGO)	<<−− VALPKG, PROCPKG
.SCREEN	−−−−
.SCRUNCH	−−−−
.SETCOM	−−−−
.SETSCREEN	−−>> See twoscreen
.SETSCRUNCH	−−−−
.SYSTEM	−−−−
ALLOPEN	−−−−
abs	++++
bye	<<−− DOS
CAPS	−−−−
changef	++++
CLOSE	−−−−
CLOSEALL	−−−−

copyd	$++++$
copyf	$++++$
copyoff	$<<--$ NODRIBBLE
copyon	$<<--$ DRIBBLE "LPT1
debug	$++++$
degrees	$++++$
DIFFERENCE	$----$
DIR	$----$
DISK	$----$
DRIBBLE	$-->>$ See 'copyon'
edall	$++++$
EDITFILE	$----$
edps	$++++$
EFORM	$----$
ERASEFILE	$-->>$ erf
erf	$<<--$ ERASEFILE
ERRACT	$----$
FILELEN	$-->>$ sizef
FILEP	$----$
FILL	$----$
fkey	$++++$
follow	$++++$
FORM	$----$
getfs	$<<--$ DIR
glist	$++++$
initd	$++++$
LN	$-->>$ log
LOADPIC	$----$
log	$<<--$ LN
log10	$++++$
lowercase	$++++$
lpen	$++++$
lpenp	$++++$
MIXEDSCREEN	$-->>$ splitscreen
nodebug	$++++$
NODRIBBLE	$-->>$ copyoff
noformat	$++++$
noprim	$++++$
notrace	$++++$
nowatch	$++++$
OPEN	$----$
PALETTE	$----$
piece	$++++$
pocall	$++++$
POFILE	$----$
popkg	$++++$

poprim	+ + + +
poref	+ + + +
potl	+ + + +
POWER	– – >> ^ (infix)
pps	+ + + +
PRECISION	– – – –
printscreen	+ + + +
PROCPKG	– – >> .PAK
proclist	+ + + +
quote	+ + + +
radians	+ + + +
READCHARS	– – – –
READEOFP	– – – –
READER	– – – –
READPOS	– – – –
readquote	+ + + +
READWORD	– – – –
REDEFP	– – – –
REPARSE	– – – –
resetd	+ + + +
SAVEPIC	– – – –
SETCAPS	– – – –
setd	<< – – SETDISK
SETDISK	– – >> setd
SETPAL	– – – –
SETPRECISION	– – – –
SETREAD	– – – –
SETREADPOS	– – – –
SETSHAPE	– – – –
setsplit	<< – – SETTEXT
SETTC	– – >> See textbg, textfg
SETTEXT	– – >> setsplit
SETWIDTH	– – – –
SETWRITE	– – – –
SETWRITEPOS	– – – –
SHAPE	– – – –
shuffle	+ + + +
sizef	<< – – FILELEN
SNAP	– – – –
spaced	+ + + +
splitscreen	<< – – MIXEDSCREEN
STAMP	– – – –
STARTUP	– – – –
tan	+ + + +
textbg	<< – – See SETTC
TEXTCOLOR	– – – –

textfs	<<−− See SETTC
TONE	−−>> See tones
tones	<<−− See TONE
trace	++++
turtletext	++++
twoscreen	<<−− .SETSCREEN 2
uppercase	++++
VALPKG	−−>> .PAK
watch	++++
where	++++
WIDTH	−−−−
WRITEOFP	−−−−
WRITEPOS	−−−−
WRITER	−−−−

B.4 Turtle graphics

The screen is approximately 320 wide by 200 high. Pen colours are also in the range 0 to 3, but are affected by the background colour, which lies in the range 0 to 63 rather than 0 to 15. This corresponds to palettes 0 and 1 in two intensities in IBM PC LOGO. There is no SETPALETTE or PALETTE. Thus SETPEN and PEN use a two-element list rather than a three-element one.

splitscreen Like IBM PC LOGO's MIXEDSCREEN. The number of lines of text is controlled by 'setsplit'.

twoscreen Informs LOGO that you have a two-screen system — one for graphics, one for text.

turtletext (tt)   nwl
Prints the input at the turtle's current position, adjusted slightly if necessary to line up with the normal text row and columns.

B.5 Variables

quote   whatever
Makes sure that its input is treated as a word, even if it is not preceded by a quote mark. For example, 'print quote this' will print 'this'. Mainly for use inside constructed lists that are to be run.

B.6 Arithmetic

The trigonometric functions use angles measured in degrees. Calculations are done to 14 significant figures.

tan $n \Rightarrow n$
Outputs the tangent of the given angle in degrees.

degrees	$n \Rightarrow n$

Changes radians to degrees.

radians	$n \Rightarrow n$

Changes degrees to radians.

⌃	$n\,n \Rightarrow n$

Infix form of IBM PC LOGO's POWER. For example, 2⌃3 is 8 and 1+3⌃4 is 82.

log	$n \Rightarrow n$

Like IBM PC LOGO's LN. Logarithm to base e.

log10	$n \Rightarrow n$

Logarithm to base 10.

abs	$n \Rightarrow n$

Outputs the absolute value of its input (that is, changes negative numbers to positive).

B.7 Procedures

You can include comments in procedures. Dr. LOGO ignores everything between a semicolon and the end of a line.

edall	(pl)

Edits everything, or just those procedures and variables in the specified package or packages.

edps	(pl)

Edits all the procedures, or just those in the specified package or packages.

B.8 Words and lists

lowercase (lc)	$w \Rightarrow w$

Outputs the word with any upper case letter switched to lower case.

uppercase (uc)	$w \Rightarrow w$

Outputs the word with any lower case letter switched to upper case.

shuffle	$l \Rightarrow l$

Outputs a list with the elements in a random order.

piece	$n\,n\,nwl \Rightarrow nwl$

The first two inputs specify a first and a last item or character of the third input. It outputs a number, word or list formed from the items or characters from the first to the last.

where	$\Rightarrow n$

Outputs the position in some list of the element last sought by a use of 'memberp'.

B.9 Condition procedures

lpenp   ⇒ t

        Outputs TRUE if there is light pen input waiting to be read by 'lpen'.

B.10 Control

B.11 Text display

textfs   n

        Sets the text foreground colour $(0-15)$.

textbg   n

        Sets the text background colour $(0-15)$. Inputs in the range $8-15$ make the characters blink.

setsplit   n

        Sets the number of lines of text to be used when text and graphics are both in use on the one screen.

B.12 Screen input/output

lpen   ⇒ l

        For use with a light pen. Outputs a list containing the column and row closest to the light pen. The column is in the range 0 to 39 and the row is in the range 0 to 24.

fkey   n w

        Assigns a command to be obeyed when the appropriate F-key is pressed. The command must be a word, though perhaps with spaces embedded in it, because any inputs cannot be provided when the key is pressed, but must be provided when the 'fkey' command is run. For example, 'fkey 2 "fd\ 100' will cause key F2 to run the command 'fd 100'.

readquote (rq)   ⇒ w

        Outputs an entire line of input as a single word.

tones   l

        Expects a list of two elements, giving frequency and duration in tenths of a second.

B.13 Packages

popkg   Print the names and contents of each package.

B.14 Workspace information

proclist $\Rightarrow 1$
Outputs a list of the names of all user-defined procedures.

pocall w
Prints the names of procedures that the named one calls.

poref wl
Prints the names of procedures that call the named ones.

potl Prints the names of procedures that are not called by any other.

poprim Prints the names of all the built-in procedures.

noprim Frees a little more space by discarding the records needed for 'poprim'.

follow w w
Reorganises the work space so that the first-named procedure is followed by the second. This is useful if you prefer some order in the information printed out by procedures such as 'pots'.

noformat Frees some space by removing all comments.

B.15 Files

Only the first eight characters of a file name are significant. Longer names are truncated.

getfs $(w) \Rightarrow 1$
IBM PC LOGO's DIR is 'print getfs'. Outputs a list of files on the specified disk, or on the default disk.

copyf w w
Copies the second-named file to the first-named.

copyd w w
Copies the second-named disk to the first-named (but you cannot copy the system disk).

changef w w
Renames the first-named file to be the second-named.

erf w
Erases a file. Like IBM PC LOGO's ERASEFILE.

sizef $w \Rightarrow n$
Like IBM PC LOGO's FILELEN. Outputs the length of the file in bytes.

sized $w \Rightarrow n$
Outputs the number of free bytes on the disk in the named drive.

setd w
Makes the named drive the default one. Outputs the name of the default drive.

resetd	w

Must be used when a disk is swapped for another in the named drive.

initd	w

Formats the disk in the named drive for use as a data disk.

copyon	Causes text to appear on the printer as well as the screen.
copyoff	Stops text appearing on the printer as well as the screen.
printscreen	

Prints everything on your screen on the graphic printer.

bye	Ends LOGO.

B.16 Tracing

Dr. LOGO provides several facilities for watching your procedures running and for tracking down mistakes.

trace	wl

Marks the named procedures for tracing. When they are run their inputs are printed, together with the level number.

notrace	wl
watch	(wl)

Marks the named procedures, or everything if you give no input, for more watching. As each watched procedure is run, each expression is printed and Dr. LOGO pauses. You can give commands at each pause, for instance to inspect the values of variables. Pressing ENTER by itself causes that expression to be evaluated. If the debugging windows are in use the watching information appears in the debugging window rather than the normal window.

nowatch	(wl)
debug	Draws two windows on the screen (and 'splitscreen' is disabled). Any output from 'watch' or 'trace' appears in the upper window, and normal output and your typed-in commands appear in the lower window. This helps you to follow which lines on the screen are debugging messages and which are normal lines.
nodebug	

B.17 Editing keys

The editing keys are different from those used in IBM PC LOGO. For convenience all are described here, not just the differences. Any normal text you type is inserted, without overwriting any existing text. Most can be used outside the editor too.

Del	Rubs out the character on which the cursor is standing.

Back-arrow	Rubs out the character to the left of the cursor.
Arrow keys	Move the cursor in the appropriate direction. The up-arrow and down-arrow only work inside the editor.
Tab	Inserts three spaces.
F10	Moves the cursor to the end of the current line of LOGO (maybe not the current screen line).
F9	Moves the cursor to the start of the current line of LOGO (maybe not the current screen line).
F5	Deletes all characters to the right of the cursor on the current line of LOGO.
F6	Inserts the last line deleted.
Ins	(Editor only) Splices in a blank line.
PgUp	(Editor only) Moves up by a screenful.
PgDn	(Editor only) Moves down by a screenful.
Home	(Editor only) Moves the cursor to the start of the edit buffer.
End	(Editor only) Moves the cursor to the end of the edit buffer.
F1	(Editor only) Ends the editing.
F2	(Editor) Aborts the editing. (Normal) Aborts the command.

B.18 Other special keys

F2	Aborts the command.
F3	Suspends LOGO command and output. Typing anything causes the command and outputting to resume.
F4	Behaves like PAUSE.
F7	Full graphics screen, no text displayed.
CTRL-S	Mixed text and graphics. Six lines (or as set by 'setsplit') of text displayed.
CTRL-T	No graphics displayed. Twenty five lines of text displayed. Allows you to remove any special significance, as far as LOGO is concerned, from the next character typed in.

B.19 Properties

pps	(pl)
	Prints the property lists of everything in the named packages, or of everything if no input is given. Special system properties are omitted, however.
glist	nw (pl) $\Rightarrow$ l
	Outputs a list of all names in the named packages that have the named property.

B.20 Special commands

.getcs $\Rightarrow$ n
        Outputs the current code segment.
.getds $\Rightarrow$ n
        Outputs the current data segment.
.setseg   n
        Sets the segment to be used by subsequent .deposit and .examine commands.
.in   n $\Rightarrow$ n
        Outputs the value of the selected port (ports are numbered 0–255).
.out   n n
        The first input is a port number. The second input is a value to be written to that port.

B.21 Special words

.APV   Property name of the value of a global variable.
.BUR   Property name: when TRUE the object is buried.
.CAT   Property name: a catch tag.
.DEF   Property name: value is a procedure definition.
.ENL   Property name: end of a procedure line that spans more than one screen line.
.FMT   Property name: beginning of a procedure line that was continued from the line before.
.FUN   Property name: a currently running procedure.
.PAK   Property name: name of a package to which the object belongs.
.PAR   Property name: a parameter of a running procedure.
.PKG   Property name: when TRUE, the object is a package name.
.PRM   Property name: when TRUE the object is the name of a built-in procedure.
.REM   Property name: identifies a comment.

Appendix C
Waterloo LOGO

C.1 Waterloo LOGO
This appendix describes the Waterloo LOGO language, created by Waterloo Microsystems Inc. at the University of Waterloo, Ontario, Canada. It uses lower case rather than upper case, except for TRUE, FALSE, ERROR, PACKAGE, TOPLEVEL and BURY. Rather than describe the whole of Waterloo LOGO, this appendix describes only the differences from IBM PC LOGO. Waterloo LOGO makes extensive use of the F-keys, and the meaning of the keys depends on the context of their use. Information about what the keys do is displayed on the screen.

C.2 Conventions
The description uses the conventions described in Appendix A.

C.3 Summary of differences
The following list summarises the main differences. ++++ indicates something in Waterloo LOGO that is not in IBM PC LOGO. ---- indicates something that is in IBM PC LOGO but not in Waterloo LOGO. It is possible to compensate for many of the differences by creating suitable procedures. The main feature which Waterloo LOGO does not have is the set of procedures for reading data from files and writing data to files.

#	++++
%	<<-- REMAINDER (prefix)
&	<<-- AND (prefix)
|	<<-- OR (prefix)
~	<<-- unary minus sign
;	++++
abs	++++
ALLOPEN	----
AND	-->> & (infix)
arcleft	++++
arcright	++++
BUTTONP	----
CAPS	----
catalog	<<-- DIR
catalogue	<<-- DIR
circlel	++++
circler	++++

CLEARTEXT	$----$
CLOSE	$----$
CLOSEALL	$----$
CO	$-->>$ continue
continue	$<<--$ CO
COPYDEF	$----$
CURSOR	$----$
differentp	$++++$
DIR	$-->>$ catalog, catalogue
DISK	$----$
dotcolor	$++++$
dotcolour	$++++$
DRIBBLE	$----$
EDITFILE	$----$
EDNS	$----$
EFORM	$----$
ERN	$----$
ERNS	$----$
ERPS	$----$
ERRACT	$----$
EXP	$----$
FILELEN	$----$
FILEP	$----$
FILL	$-->>$ paint
FORM	$----$
getprop	$<<--$ GPROP
GO	$----$
GPROP	$-->>$ getprop
greaterp	$<<-->$ (infix)
LABEL	$----$
lessp	$<<--<$ (infix)
LN	$----$
LOADPIC	$-->>$ loadpicture
loadpicture	$<<--$ LOADPIC
MIXEDSCREEN	$-->>$ splitscreen
NODES	$----$
NODRIBBLE	$----$
noredef	$<<--$ MAKE "REDEFP "FALSE
OPEN	$----$
OR	$-->>$: (infix)
PADDLE	$----$
page	$++++$
pagep	$++++$
paint	$<<--$ FILL
PALETTE	$----$
PENREVERSE	$----$

PI	– – – –
PLIST	– –>> proplist
PROFILE	– – – –
POWER	– – – –
PPROP	– –>> putprop
PRECISION	– – – –
predicatep	+ + + +
PROCPKG	– – – –
proplist	<<– – PLIST
putprop	<<– – PPROP
READCHARS	– – – –
READEOFP	– – – –
READER	– – – –
READPOS	– – – –
READWORD	– – – –
RECYCLE	– – – –
redef	<<– – MAKE "REDEFP "TRUE
REDEFP	– –>> See redef, noredef
REMAINDER	– –>> % (infix)
REPARSE	– – – –
SAVEPIC	– –>> savepicture
savepicture	<<– – SAVEPIC
scroll	+ + + +
scrunch	<<– – .SCRUNCH
SETCAPS	– – – –
SETCURSOR	– – – –
SETDISK	– – – –
SETPAL	– –>> setpalette
setpalette	<<– – SETPAL
SETPRECISION	– – – –
SETREAD	– – – –
SETREADPOS	– – – –
setscrunch	<<– – .SETSCRUNCH
SETSHAPE	– – – –
SETTC	– – – –
SETTEXT	– – – –
SETWIDTH	– – – –
SETWRITE	– – – –
SETWRITEPOS	– – – –
SHAPE	– – – –
SNAP	– – – –
sound	<<– – TONE
splitscreen	<<– – MIXEDSCREEN
STAMP	– – – –
STARTUP	– – – –
TEXTCOLOR	– – – –

TONE	$-->>$ sould
VALPKG	$----$
WIDTH	$----$
WRAP	$----$
WRITEOFP	$----$
WRITEPOS	$----$
WRITER	$----$

C.4 Turtle graphics

The screen is 267.5 wide by 200 high. Though Waterloo LOGO does use two palettes of colour like IBM PC LOGO, the procedures 'setpen' and 'pen' deal with two-element lists rather than three-element ones. Background colours can lie only in the range 0 to 14.

arcleft (arcl)   n n
> Draws a leftward-turning arc. The first input is its radius, the second the number of degrees subtended at the centre.

arcright (arcr)   n n

circlel   n
> Draws a leftward-turning circle. The input is its radius.

circler   n

dotcolor $\Rightarrow$ n
> Outputs the colour of the dot on which the turtle is standing. Can be spelled 'dotcolour'.

setpalette (setp)   n
> IBM PC LOGO's SETPAL.

splitscreen IBM PC LOGO's MIXEDSCREEN.

setscrunch   n
> IBM PC LOGO's .SETSCRUNCH. The initial value is 1.

scrunch $\Rightarrow$ n
> IBM PC LOGO's .SCRUNCH.

paint   IBM PC LOGO's FILL.

savepicture   w
> IBM PC LOGO's SAVEPIC.

loadpicture   w
> IBM PC LOGO's LOADPIC.

C.5 Variables

C.6 Arithmetic

Calculations are done to 12 significant figures. Waterloo LOGO does not use the minus sign to denote negative numbers; it uses the tilde ($\sim$) instead, to avoid confusion.

%	$n\ n \Rightarrow n$
	An infix form of IBM PC LOGO's REMAINDER.
abs	$n \Rightarrow n$
	Outputs the absolute value of its input (that is, turns negative numbers into positive ones).

C.7 Procedures

Waterloo LOGO allows you to include comments in procedures. It ignores anything lying between a semicolon and the end of the line.

redef	Allows redefinition of built-in procedures.
noredef	Forbids redefinition of built-in procedures.

C.8 Words and lists

C.9 Condition procedures

differentp	$nwl\ nwl \Rightarrow t$
	Outputs TRUE if the inputs are different.
#	$nwl\ nwl \Rightarrow t$
	Infix form of 'differentp'.
|	$t\ t \Rightarrow t$
	Infix form of IBM PC LOGO's OR.
&	$t\ t \Rightarrow t$
	Infix form of IBM PC LOGO's AND.
greaterp	$n\ n \Rightarrow t$
	Infix form of '>'.
lessp	$n\ n \Rightarrow t$
	Infix form of '<'.
predicatep	$w \Rightarrow t$
	Outputs TRUE if the input is the name of a built-in procedure.
primitivep	$w \Rightarrow t$
	Outputs TRUE if the input is TRUE or FALSE.
pagep	$\Rightarrow t$
	Outputs TRUE if the screen is in page mode rather than in scroll mode.

C.10 Control

C.11 Text display

page	Sets the screen to page mode. Rather than scrolling the screen automatically, Waterloo LOGO waits for you to press a key before scrolling the screen. This allows you to read the screen at your leisure.
scroll	Sets the screen to scroll mode.

C.12 Screen input/output

sound   n n
> IBM PC LOGO's TONE. The second input is the duration measured in tenths of a second.

C.13 Packages

C.14 Workspace information

C.15 Files

catalog   Prints the names of files on the disk. Can also be spelled 'catalogue'.

C.16 Tracing

continue (co)
> IBM PC LOGO's CO.

C.17 Editing keys

The Waterloo LOGO editor is not at all like the IBM PC LOGO editor or the Dr. LOGO editor. The image to bear in mind is that of a piece of paper, which you are typing on with a clever typewriter. You can position the cursor anywhere, not just within the text. The arrow keys move the cursor about, and the back-arrow key erases characters, as you would expect. The tab key works as on a normal typewriter, moving the cursor across to the next tab stop. The 'End' key performs a selection function for the subsequent operations of moving or deleting text. Whatever is selected is highlighted in the display. The options are:

- Press it once to select a character.
- Selecting the same character twice selects the whole line.
- If you select two characters on the same line, all characters between them are selected.
- If you select two characters on different lines, then they are regarded as the corners of a rectangular region and the whole region is selected.
- Selecting two lines selects all lines between them.

The F2 key picks up (and deletes from the screen) whatever is currently selected. The F3 key puts down, at the current cursor position, whatever was last picked up. The F4 key inserts a blank line. The 'PgDn' key pulls a previously selected character across to the current cursor position, thus scrolling the display leftward or rightward, and this is the only way of entering long lines. The new character at the position of the previously selected character is automatically selected by this, so that just by pressing 'PgDn' repeatedly the screen can rapidly be scrolled sideways. The F1 key is the way to exit from the editor. You are presented with various options on the screen: exit saving the editing, abort the editing, or don't quit.

C.18 Other special keys

F1   Does a 'pause'.
F2   Does a 'continue'.
F3   Aborts whatever is running, by a 'throw "TOPLEVEL'.

C.19 Properties

putprop (pprop)   nw nw nwl
      IBM PC LOGO's PPROP.
getprop (gprop)   nw nw $\Rightarrow$ nwl
      IBM PC LOGO's GPROP.
proplist (plist)   nw $\Rightarrow$ l
      IBM PC LOGO's PLIST.

C.20 Special commands

C.21 Special words
TOPLEVEL, ERROR, TRUE and FALSE should be in upper case.

BURY   Property name: if the value is TRUE the object is the name of a package.
PACKAGE Property name: the name of a package that includes this object.

ANSWERS TO EXERCISES

Chapter 2

1. It depends. Normally the turtle just reappears at the opposite edge. You can change this by the IBM PC LOGO command FENCE; thereafter, attempting to cross the edge will produce the error message

   TURTLE OUT OF BOUNDS

   To revert to normal, use the command WRAP. You can also use WINDOW, which allows the turtle to wander off the screen but doesn't make it reappear at the opposite edge. Instead, it makes the screen into a window onto the centre of a huge flat drawing area, in which the X and Y co-ordinates are allowed to be anywhere in the range −9999 to 9999. Other LOGOs have other possibilities.

2. In IBM PC LOGO the screen is 320 wide and 250 high. You can change the height by using the command .SETSCRUNCH, whose input is a number representing the ratio of a vertical turtle unit to a horizontal turtle unit. The procedure .SCRUNCH outputs the current ratio; initially it is 0.8. If you set it to 1.6, then the screen will only be 125 high. From the home position of the turtle, it is initially 125 to either the top or to the bottom edge, and 160 to the left edge or to the right edge.

3. To be dreadfully precise:

   52.001 degrees for the top right corner,
   127.999 degrees for the bottom right corner,
   232.001 degrees for the bottom left corner,
   307.999 degrees for the top left corner.

   For nearly all purposes, the answers 52, 128, 232 and 308 are good enough.

4. Yes. FD−100 is BK 100, LT−53 is RT 53 and so on.

5. Yes, they do. Try the command FD 0.3 ten times, and you will get a line 3 units long. The command FD 0.03 one hundred times will do the same thing. However, there is a limit to how many decimal places the turtle will pay attention to. The way to test this without old age catching up on you is in Chapter 2 — the REPEAT command. LT and RT also happily work with numbers with decimal parts.

6. a) For a pentagon the angle is 72 degrees. For a hexagon the angle is 60 degrees. For a 7-sided polygon the angle is 51.429 degrees.

   b) This is up to you.

7. The rules about layout of commands are a mess. There are two worth remembering explicitly: if one space is necessary at some point, then it is acceptable to have more, and it is wise to put a space on either side of a minus sign in IBM PC LOGO, unless you want to indicate a negative number rather than a subtraction.

8. This is up to you.

9. As you might hope, they work. For example, $3 - -4$ is 7.

10. Dividing by zero produces the message

    CAN'T DIVIDE BY ZERO

    Too large a result is signalled by

    NUMBER TOO BIG

    Too minute a number is taken to be zero.

11. Let the increment be N. If N is a multiple of 8 there will be infinitely many blobs. Otherwise there will be

    1 + N/(highest common factor of 360 and N)

    Why is there an exception when N is a multiple of 8, you may ask? Because that is the only time when the highest common factor of N and 180 is not the same as the highest common factor of N and 360. If N is not a multiple of 8, the turtle will at some point reach an effective heading of 180 degrees, and start retracing its steps, BEFORE it reaches an exact multiple of 360 degrees and starts to repeat the figure from its new position.

12. You can get some fancy spirals, at the very least.

13. If 'two-dimensional random walk' means that at each step there are just four choices of direction (up, down, left, right) then the answer is yes, it definitely returns to the start eventually. If there are more choices, the situation is much more complicated, but the short answer is 'probably'.

14. It all depends. Have a look at *An Introduction to Probability Theory* by William Feller, 2 vols, published by Random House, if you really want to get into this and you are good at mathematics.

15. In a one-dimensional walk the turtle definitely returns to the start. Try making the step size depend on direction.

Chapter 3

1. Yes. Change the inputs to ANIMATE a little each time —
    make the last line of the definition something like this:

    ```
    ANIMATE :X * 1.1 :Y * 1.2
    ```

2. Yes. Give SQUARE an input, to be the side of the square, like
    this:

    ```
    TO SQUARE :S
    SETX XCOR + :S
    SETY YCOR + :S
    SETX XCOR − :S
    SETY YCOR − :S
    END

    TO ANIMATE :X :Y :S
    SETPC 3 SQUARE :S
    SETPC 0 SQUARE :S
    PU SETPOS LIST XCOR + :X YCOR + :Y PD
    ANIMATE :X :Y :S + 0.5
    END
    ```

    The effect gets less realistic as the side of the square gets
    bigger.
3. Not really. You can have LOGO do the necessary trigonometric
    calculations, or revert to drawing a square by using FD and RT,
    but either way is significantly slower than the square used in the
    chapter.
4. It doesn't, though you may think otherwise.
5. Basic method A is very poor, because CS takes a fairly long
    time to finish. It makes the gap between each 'frame' much too
    long to give the illusion of animation.
6. Yes. Instead of REPEAT 61000 [], make the last line of TICK

    ```
    PX REPEAT 60 [SEC]
    ```

    where SEC is defined as

    ```
    TO SEC
    SETH :SECOND FD 30
    REPEAT 750 [ ]
    BK 30
    MAKE "SECOND :SECOND + 6
    END
    ```

You will need to initialise SECOND to be 0 before starting the clock. The delay of REPEAT 750 [] may need to be tuned somewhat. The reversing pen, selected by the PX command, is used because you cannot really afford to have a hiccup once a minute to redraw the hour and minute hands if the seconds hand erases them. This is acceptable when there is no seconds hand, because both hands get redrawn every minute; with a seconds hand it would mean redrawing all three once a second, or a much fancier version of TICK.

7. This is left for you.
8. The procedure definition is up to you. It is surprising how hard it is to get used to a backward-running clock at first, and how natural it eventually becomes.
9. It does nothing. The condition is FALSE.
10. It prints OK, because $-12 < 5$.
11. It prints FALSE.
12. It prints FALSE. The condition is $-11.3333 = 7$.
13. It is a trick question. You would get the error message

    -12 IS NOT TRUE OR FALSE

14. You get the message

    OUT OF SPACE:
    JUST BEFORE LEAVING FACTORIAL

    because the stopping condition never holds and recursion continues till there is no more space left for LOGO to keep track of what's happening. Once the message appears, LOGO reclaims a lot of temporarily used space, so don't panic, nothing awful has happened.
15. It can be used, for numbers larger than 1, but it is not particularly sensible, because there is a much more convenient answer. Use SQRT SQRT :N instead!
16. For numbers between 0 and 1, you need to reverse the test

    :AV * :AV * :AV > :N

    You can change CUBE.ROOT so that it checks whether :N lies between 0 and 1, and does the appropriate test. For negative numbers, change CU.RT:

    ```
    TO CU.RT :N
    IF :N<0 [OUTPUT −CUBE.ROOT −:N 1 −:N]
           [OUTPUT CUBE.ROOT :N 1 :N]
    END
    ```

17. There is a problem caused by the limited accuracy of numbers. Suppose :LOW is 1.70994, and :HIGH is 1.70995 and the precision has been set to 5 by SETPRECISION 5. Then LOGO will calculate the value of AV as 1.70994. However, if it is the cube root of 5 that is being sought, the cube of 1.70994 is only 4.99986, so CUBE.ROOT will recurse. The new inputs will be 5, 1.70994 and 1.70995 — which are the same as before. The recursion will not stop until the available space for keeping track of recursion gets used up.

18. It is very like the cube root example:

```
TO ARCSIN :VAL
OUTPUT ASIN :VAL (−90) 90
END

TO ASIN :V :L :H
MAKE "AV (:L + :H) / 2
IF OR :AV = :L :AV = :H [OUTPUT :AV]
IF :V > SIN :AV [OUTPUT ASIN :V :AV :H]
        [OUTPUT ASIN :V :L :AV]
END
```

Chapter 4

1. One of many answers:

```
TO REVERSE :L
IF :L = [ ] [OUTPUT [ ]]
OUTPUT LPUT FIRST :L REVERSE BF :L
END
```

2. One of many answers:

```
TO REVWORD :W
IF EMPTYP :W [OUTPUT " ]
OUTPUT WORD REVWORD BF :W FIRST :W
END
```

3. One of many answers:

```
TO PALINDROME :X
IF COUNT :X < 2 [OUTPUT "TRUE]
IF (FIRST :X) = (LAST :X) [OUTPUT
        PALINDROME BF BL :X] [OUTPUT "FALSE]
END
```

4. A procedure that prints out a list in the way suggested in the exercise would be

```
TO LIST.PRINT :L
LPRINT :L 0
END


TO LPRINT :L :INDENT
IF :L = [ ] [STOP]
IF LISTP FIRST :L [LPRINT FIRST :L
        :INDENT + 4] [REPEAT :INDENT
        [TYPE CHAR 32] PRINT FIRST :L]
LPRINT BF :L :INDENT
END
```

Chapter 5

1. Sorry — it IS false. The truth is that the nested polygons do get somwhat 'more regular', but they also tend to get more like the second one back in the sequence; there are really two inter-leaved sequences of hexagons. Within either sequence, opposite sides tend to become parallel, and to lie parallel to the corre-sponding diagonals. An interesting detail is that the two se-quences both 'converge' on the same point, and that point is the 'centre of mass' of every one of the hexagons.

2. The main difference, if you use points of trisection, is that you get three interleaved sequences of hexagons rather than two. Again, in each sequence, the opposite sides of a hexagon tend to become parallel. Although, within each sequence, the hexa-gons get more like each other, there is not really a 'limiting hexagon'. You will have to take this on trust. [Or, if you are proficient in trigonometry, read the article by J.H. Cadwell, 'A property of linear cyclic transformations', in *Mathematical Gazette*, Vol. 37, No. 320, p. 85 (1953).]

3. With a hexagon, you eventually get a line, which does not shrink to a point. If you start with an irregular pentagon, you eventually get a pentagram. From a regular pentagon, you get a regular pentagon. Experiment with other initial figures, and with different rules for forming the nested polygon.

4. It turns out that the answer to (1) does hold for non-convex polygons. The general theory is elaborate; see the reference given in answer 2 above if you want a full and technical answer.

5. The current definitions are not adequate — for example, the first line of DIGIT.LIST will give a test outcome of TRUE for every non-negative number if the base is negative. In parti-cular, if the input is zero, DIGIT.LIST will recurse until the space for keeping track of recursion is exhausted. While it is

possible to make some changes so that DIGIT.LIST always gives some answer, the idea of a negative base is not really sensible. The main snag is, what are digits? Can they be negative? Consider the number -16 in base -8. Is it represented as $[-\ -2\ 0\ [-8]]$ or as $[2\ 0\ [-8]]$? The number 16 would be either $[-2\ 0\ [-8]]$ or $[-\ 2\ 0\ [-8]]$. This means that either negative digits must be allowed, or that some apparently negative numbers are larger than some apparently positive ones. If you can live with these, fine...

6. Follow up the hint. To convert 3.74 to a base 8 form, keep multiplying by 8 until you get an integer, or you have multiplied by 8 four times. Convert the integer. Then move the decimal (or rather, octal) point leftward in the list the appropriate number of digits. Consider an example. The decimal number 3.74, would be written in base 8 as

    3.572702443650507534I2....

In decimal form, 3.74*8*8*8*8 is 15319.04...; rounding this to an integer gives 15319. Converting this to base 8 using CONVERT gives the list $[3\ 5\ 7\ 2\ 7\ [8]]$. Shifting the point leftward four places gives a list $[3\ .\ 5\ 7\ 2\ 7\ [8]]$. Defining LOGO procedures to do all this is not too hard.

7. The snag, again, is deciding what is a digit or not. What is 2.6 in base 2.5? Obviously, it is just over $[1\ [2.5]]$, but how much over? You could apply the answer to Exercise 6 here. There is a more serious snag. What is 100 in base 0.5? Think about this, and you will see the snag about digits much more clearly. In base 0.5, or any other base between 0 and 1, there is no such thing as a 'biggest digit'. Suppose there were, and that it was N. Then in base 0.5 the number NNN...NNN (however many times the digit N occurs) would be no bigger than

    N * (1 + 0.5 + 0.25 + 0.125 + ...)

which is no bigger than

    N / (1 − 0.5)

which is 2 * N. This means that you could not represent numbers bigger than this!

INDEX TO LOGO PROCEDURES

The index tells you where to find examples of LOGO procedures found in this book. Where several versions of a procedure are defined, a page is mentioned for each of them.

SUBJECT INDEX

This index is only intended to cover the main body of the book, not the various appendixes. Where an item is the main topic of several pages, only the first page is mentioned. There is a separate index to the LOGO procedures defined in the text.